LUCRETIUS

ON THE NATURE OF THINGS

Translated, with Introduction and Notes,
by MARTIN FERGUSON SMITH

Hackett Publishing Company, Inc.
Indianapolis/Cambridge

34 22 21 20 19   5 6 7 8

For further information, please address:
  Hackett Publishing Company, Inc.
  P.O. Box 44937
  Indianapolis, IN 46244-0937
  www.hackettpublishing.com

Cover design by Listenberger & Associates

Library of Congress Cataloging-in-Publication Data
Lucretius Carus, Titus.
  [De rerum natura. English]
  On the nature of things / Lucretius ; translated, with introduction
and notes, by Martin Ferguson Smith.
       p. cm.
  Includes bibliographical references and index.
  ISBN 0-87220-588-6 (cloth) — ISBN 0-87220-587-8 (paper)
  1. Didactic poetry, Latin—Translations into English. 2. Philosophy,
Ancient—Poetry. I. Smith, Martin Ferguson. II. Title.
PA6483.E5 S6   2001
187—dc21   2001026403

ISBN-13: 978-0-87220-588-8 (cloth)
ISBN-13: 978-0-87220-587-1 (pbk.)

ON THE NATURE OF THINGS

For my daughter, Lucinda, with love

carmina sublimis tunc sunt peritura Lucreti
  exitio terras cum dabit una dies.

The verses of sublime Lucretius are destined to perish only
when a single day will consign the world to destruction.

Ovid *Amores* 1.15.23–24

CONTENTS

PREFACE

This translation, a product of my mid-twenties, was first published by Sphere in 1969, but has been out of print since 1972. I am grateful to Hackett for reissuing it in the autumn of my life.

The bulk of the translation has been left unchanged, but many minor alterations—improvements, I hope—have been made. The opportunity has been taken not only to remove misprints, mistakes, and infelicities, but also to take account of advances in Lucretian scholarship over the past thirty years or so; and whereas the original version was based on the Latin text in Cyril Bailey's three-volume edition of Lucretius (Oxford University Press, 1947), the present version follows, except in a few places indicated in the footnotes, my own text in the latest printing of the Loeb Classical Library edition (Harvard University Press, 1992). American English spellings have been substituted for British English ones.

The Introduction has been considerably extended and, where not rewritten, thoroughly revised. The same applies to the footnotes. The Suggestions for Further Reading and Index are new.

It is not only Lucretian scholarship that has moved on since the late 1960s. So has Western society, and I believe that mine is the first English translation of Lucretius to have consistently avoided the most obvious manifestations of sexist language: "man" and "he" are never used unless the reference is to a male.

I gratefully acknowledge my debts to the following: to D. S. Hutchinson of the University of Toronto for helpful comments on a draft of the Introduction; to Maggi Reyner, Foula's school teacher, for expert word processing; to Meera Dash for her careful management of the book's production; above all to Deborah Wilkes, whose constant enthusiasm and warm encouragement spurred me on as I battled, sometimes by the light of a gas lamp or candles, to accomplish my task in the depths of a dark Shetland winter.

M.F.S.
Isle of Foula, Shetland Islands
February 2001

"The autumn of my life" has turned to winter, but it warms my heart to know that this translation continues to be useful to its readers. In his award-winning book *The Swerve: How the Renaissance Began* (Norton: New York, 2011) Stephen Greenblatt describes how the access this translation gave him to Lucretius opened up a whole new world for him. Of course all the credit for changing Greenblatt's life belongs to Lucretius, but I am pleased that it was my translation that introduced him to *On the Nature of Things*, a philosophical and scientific poem of unsurpassed brilliance, whose message is as profoundly relevant and important today as it was two thousand years ago.

M.F.S.
Foula
March 2012

INTRODUCTION[1]

(Numerical references are always, unless otherwise indicated, to the text of Lucretius.)

1. Lucretius

Of all the great Latin writers, we know least about Titus Lucretius Carus, author of the philosophical poem *On the Nature of Things* (*De Rerum Natura*). He does not talk about himself in the way that his contemporary Catullus does, and information from other sources is meager and unreliable. St. Jerome, writing more than four hundred years after Lucretius' death, makes the sensational statement that the poet went mad in consequence of drinking a love potion, wrote in the intervals of his insanity, and committed suicide. Since earlier writers show no knowledge of this story,[2] it can confidently be dismissed as a fabrication, probably designed to undermine the credibility of the materialistic philosophy that Lucretius expounds. The story is used by Tennyson in his poem *Lucretius* and by the contemporary novelist Luca Canali,[3] which is fine; unfortunately, however, it is not always confined to the realm of fiction: under its influence some critics have detected in Lucretius' work signs of morbid pessimism and even mental unbalance and then have used their "discoveries" as confirmation of what St. Jerome says—a circular procedure that is completely out of order. The correct approach is to consign Jerome's statement to the wastepaper basket and to approach *On the Nature of Things* with an unprejudiced mind.

Lucretius was born at the beginning of the first century B.C., perhaps in 99 B.C., and it is most probable that he died in 55 B.C.[4] If we assume that the dates 99–55 are correct, he was born when Cicero was aged seven and Julius Caesar was a toddler; and when he died, Virgil and Horace

---

1. On Lucretius' life, personality, philosophy, mission, and poetry, see also my Introduction to the Loeb edition (pp. ix–liv).

2. For Virgil's ignorance of it, see below n. 18.

3. *Nei pleniluni sereni: autobiografia immaginaria di Tito Lucrezio Caro* (Longanesi: Milan, 1995). French translation by Daniel Colomar, *Aux pleines lunes tranquilles: autobiographie imaginaire de Lucrèce* (Aubier: Paris, 1997).

4. Since *On the Nature of Things* is unfinished, it cannot have been published in the author's lifetime. The Cicero brothers had read Lucretius' poetry by February 54 B.C. So, unless he showed them his incomplete poem, the assumption that he was dead by the beginning of 54 seems certain.

were aged fifteen and nine or ten respectively. Catullus probably died in 54 B.C.

We know nothing of Lucretius' family, but, whether he was highborn or of humbler origin, it is evident that he received an excellent education: a master not only of Latin, but also of Greek, he possessed a wide knowledge of the literature of both languages; and his partiality for legal and political metaphors suggests that he may have been prepared for a forensic or political career.

He was familiar with the city and may have spent much of his life in Rome. He appears to have witnessed military exercises on the Campus Martius (2.40–43, 323–332); he had attended horse races (2.263–265; 4.990) and theatrical performances (2.416–417; 4.75–83, 978–983; 6.109–110). His vivid description of the man who leaves his fine mansion in the city out of boredom, jumps into the ancient equivalent of a fast car, dashes out to his country villa as though on his way to save a house on fire and, as soon as he has arrived, yawns and either goes to sleep or returns to the city (3.1060–1067), must be based on his own experience of the restless and unsatisfactory life led by some wealthy Romans.

It is clear, however, that not all his time was spent in the city. Numerous passages in his poem show his familiarity with the countryside, woods and forests, mountains, rivers, and streams. He has an extraordinary sympathy with nature and possesses the keen powers of observation of an artist. Witness his vivid picture in the opening lines of the poem (1.1–20) of the effect of spring on climate, flowers, pastures, sea, sky, winds, birds, wild animals, and cattle. Witness too his descriptions of animals in the fields: the cow searching vainly for her lost calf (2.352–366); the flock of sheep and lambs moving on the green hillside, but appearing only as a motionless white blur when viewed from the distance (2.317–322); and the newborn calves and lambs, "intoxicated" with milk, frisking on unsteady legs in the tender grass (1.259–261). The probability is that he owned a villa in the country and spent as much time as possible there.

A line in Book 4 (1277) has been taken, perhaps rightly, to imply that he was a married man. Several passages in the poem suggest that he was fond of children, but of course do not prove that he had any of his own. The celebrated attack on sexual love (4.1058–1191), which has sometimes been thought to reflect his own unhappy experience of the opposite sex (compare the story of the love potion), is in line with the Epicurean view that while it is all right to satisfy sexual desire, provided that this does not cause one physical or mental disturbance, the passion of love is disturbing and destructive and therefore to be avoided.

The times through which Lucretius lived were dominated by intense social and political unrest and punctuated with outbreaks of revolution and war. The second decade of the first century B.C. was a period of civil war and bloodshed; and if one takes 99 as the year of his birth, he would have been seventeen when thousands of Samnites were butchered at the Colline Gate near the Quirinal Hill; twenty-six when Spartacus led the great revolt of slaves, six thousand of whom were to be crucified along the Appian Way; and thirty-six at the time of Catiline's conspiracy. It is hardly surprising that one who, as his poem shows, was so sensitive to human suffering, should have become an Epicurean, a follower of a philosopher who taught that one should take no part in the struggle for wealth and power, who attached the greatest importance to friendship, and who offered his adherents tranquillity of mind.

The only friend or acquaintance whom Lucretius mentions is the addressee of his poem, Memmius (see section 2, below). But it is fair to assume that he also knew Catullus and Catullus' poet-friend Helvius Cinna, whom Memmius patronized. There are verbal parallelisms between Lucretius' poem and Catullus 64 (*Peleus and Thetis*), which seem too numerous to be accidental, but we cannot be sure who was the imitator and who the imitated. If Lucretius knew Catullus, he may also have encountered some of those with whom Catullus associated, including Clodia, whose stormy affair with Catullus (exactly the sort of relationship against which Lucretius warns his readers in Book 4) is revealed in Catullus' poetry, where she is called Lesbia.

Jerome states that after Lucretius' death Cicero "emended" (*emendavit*) his work. The Latin verb probably refers here, as elsewhere, to the making of essential corrections to a work in readiness for publication— the sort of corrections that nowadays a proofreader is expected to make. Jerome's statement is less likely to be of trustworthy origin than to be a guess based on the information, given to us by Cicero himself (see section 2, below), that he had read *On the Nature of Things*. Although Cicero thought well of Lucretius' poetry, as we shall see, and wrote poetry himself, his dislike of Epicureanism makes it seem improbable that he would have prepared *On the Nature of Things* for publication. Someone who is more likely, one would suppose, to have helped Lucretius' work reach the public is Cicero's closest friend Atticus, who not only was an Epicurean, albeit a less than fully committed one, but also owned a well-organized publishing business. Perhaps it was his copyists who made the first copies of *On the Nature of Things*.

One naturally wonders whether Lucretius knew other famous contemporaries. Did he meet the Epicurean teachers Siro and Philodemus, the

former of whom is reported to have taught Virgil, the latter of whom, a
writer of poems as well as of philosophical treatises, made Virgil the co-
addressee of one of his books?[5] Was he acquainted with Amafinius,[6]
Catius, and Rabirius, who wrote in Latin (unlike Philodemus, who used
Greek) and did much to popularize Epicurean ideas in Italy with their
prose works? Did he know Julius Caesar, who seems to have had some
sympathy with Epicureanism, or Caesar's destined assassin Cassius, who
certainly counted himself an adherent of the school, though, like many
Roman Epicureans, he was not obedient to Epicurus' advice to keep out
of politics and public life? We can only guess.

2. *On the Nature of Things*

On the Nature of Things is Lucretius' only extant work; and, so far as we
know, it is the only work that he produced, though it is inconceivable that
he had not tried his hand at poetry before he embarked on the composition of his masterpiece, a poem divided into six books and containing
about seven thousand five hundred lines.[7]

The meter of the poem is the dactylic hexameter. This is the meter
used by Greek epic and didactic poets, including Homer and Hesiod, the
philosophers Parmenides and Empedocles, and the Hellenistic poets
Apollonius of Rhodes, Aratus, and Nicander. The first to employ the
meter in Latin was Ennius (239–169 B.C.), author of the epic *Annals,* and
he was followed by later writers of Latin epic and didactic.

Although *On the Nature of Things* has a didactic character and purpose, it is also an epic—an epic whose theme is the universe, the world,
nature, human beings, the soul, death, and the gods. It is to be noted that
it is the Muse of epic poetry, Calliope, whom Lucretius invokes at 6.92–
95. Because the poem is both epic and didactic, its language ranges from
the lofty to the conversational: often, particularly when Lucretius is
introducing a new topic, he addresses Memmius much as a teacher
addresses a pupil, sometimes calling quite sharply for his attention.

The brilliant poetical qualities of Lucretius' work result partly from
his own imagination, observation, experience, reflection, and peculiar
genius, partly from his knowledge and subtle exploitation of a wide

---

5. See M. Gigante and M. Capasso, "Il ritorno di Virgilio a Ercolano," *Studi
Italiani di Filologia Classica* 3rd series 7 (1989) 3–6.

6. Amafinius' dates are uncertain. Modern scholars usually place him in the
late second century or early first century B.C., but he may have been a contemporary of Lucretius.

7. On the structure of the poem, see section 4, below.

range of Greek and Latin literary sources and from his mastery of rhetorical technique. Not all the influences on Lucretius' poetry can be mentioned here. They include the only three poets[8] named by him—Homer, Empedocles, and Ennius, all of whom he deeply admired (see 1.117–119, 124, 716–737; 3.1037–1038). His debt to Ennius and other early Latin poets is significant: he employs archaic words and forms, and he is fond of compound adjectives, assonance, and alliteration—all prominent features of the work of Ennius and company. But, while his poetry retains the vigor of theirs, it is far more polished, and it is only within the last few decades that scholars have properly noticed and explored his not inconsiderable debt to Hellenistic poetry—poetry characterized by, among other things, learning and refinement.[9] One of the prominent manifestations of his poetic art is the extraordinary richness and subtlety of the imagery that he employs.[10] Another remarkable feature of his writing is the way in which, instead of banishing mythology from his work, as one might expect an Epicurean poet to have done, he skillfully exploits it for his poetical and philosophical purposes:[11] see, for example, the opening passage of the poem (1.1–43).

Lucretius probably embarked on the composition of *On the Nature of Things* in or about 59: lines in the opening passage (1.41–43) seemingly allude to Memmius' praetorship of 58. When he died, probably in 55, his work, though almost finished, still lacked final revision. Some of the chief indications of lack of revision may be mentioned: there are alternative introductory passages in Book 4 (see note on 4.45–53); at 5.155 there is a promise of a proof that is not provided; and there are places where the transition from one passage to another is very abrupt: see, for example, 5.235, where the argument of 5.91–109 is resumed as if the intervening refutation of belief in the divine origin and character of the world in 5.110–234 were not there. Repetitions of passages, which are not uncommon in the poem, have sometimes been regarded as another sign of lack of revision, but probably Lucretius intended to retain most, if not all, of the repeated passages: repetition is an effective way of getting important facts to stick in the reader's mind; and a certain amount of repetition is almost inevitable in a scientific work in which the author cannot refer the reader to earlier passages by means of footnotes.

---

8. I do not count Memmius, who wrote some poetry that does not survive.

9. See especially E. J. Kenney, "Doctus Lucretius," *Mnemosyne* 23 (1970) 366–392.

10. See especially D. A.West, *The Imagery and Poetry of Lucretius*.

11. For detailed treatment of this feature, see M. R. Gale, *Myth and Poetry in Lucretius*.

Whether the actual ending of *On the Nature of Things* is (as I believe) the intended ending, or whether Lucretius did not live to add the concluding passage that he had planned, is not agreed, but we can at least be sure that he had no intention of writing more than six books: he makes clear at 6.93–94 that he is working on the last book.

The philosophy that Lucretius expounds in *On the Nature of Things* is not his own, though he believes in it as passionately as if it were. He faithfully reproduces the doctrines of Epicurus. He has sometimes been criticized for making an unfortunate choice of subject. After all, as he himself was well aware (1.136–139), the presentation of Greek philosophy and science in Latin poetry was no easy task. But he did not *choose* his theme. It was not a case of wanting to write a poem, looking about for a suitable subject, and eventually deciding upon Epicureanism. Epicureanism had to be his theme. That this is so becomes obvious if we consider his relation to Epicurus, about which he tells us much. He devotes four magnificent passages, full of emotion, to heartfelt praise of his master (1.62–79; 3.1–30; 5.1–54; 6.1–42).[12] He regards Epicurus as the spiritual and moral savior of himself and of humanity. Epicurus is to him as Jesus is to a Christian. He has complete faith in him and regards his sayings as infallible. He claims to follow him not in rivalry, but out of love for him. He calls him "father"; he even hails him as a god, not because he really believes him to be divine, but because it is the only description that is appropriate to one who possessed seemingly superhuman qualities and who enabled human beings to create a heaven on earth through the attainment of the perfect peace of mind in which perfect happiness consists. Epicurus had discovered the truth and the whole truth, and Lucretius endeavors to communicate that truth as accurately, attractively, and persuasively as he can.

The Epicurean school was very much a "society of friends." Epicurus thought that "of all the contributions that wisdom makes to the blessedness of the complete life, much the most important is the possession of friendship" (*Principal Doctrines* 27) and that "the chief concerns of the right-minded person are wisdom and friendship, of which the former is a mortal benefit, the latter an immortal one" (*Vatican Sayings* 78). In these pronouncements he is referring to something more than ordinary friendship: he means the friendship, fellowship, and love of persons who share the same ideals and the same philosophy—Epicureanism, of course. An

---

12. See also 3.1042–1044, where Epicurus is described as having "outshone the human race in genius and obscured the luster of all as the rising of the ethereal sun extinguishes the stars."

Epicurean could find philosophical friends both by joining a circle of adherents and by making new converts. The making of converts was encouraged, and the recommended method of conversion was by personal contact: just as a doctor treats individual patients, so the philosopher treats individually, if that is possible, those who are morally sick.[13] Obviously the situation is different when Epicureans, wanting to make their master's efficacious remedies available to those not known to them, including those not yet born, communicate them in writing, but it is noticeable that even Epicurean writers, though they want to reach as many readers as possible, frequently address the public through the medium of an address to an individual or to a small group of persons. Epicurus himself does this, and so does Lucretius.

Whether Memmius, to whom *On the Nature of Things* is addressed, was Lucretius' patron or not (I doubt if he was), he is not a mere dedicatee, for Lucretius informs him that the inspiration of the poem is "the hope of gaining the pleasure of your delightful friendship" (1.140–145)—in other words, the hope of converting him to Epicureanism. There can be no doubt that he wants his message to benefit anyone who would read his work, but he speaks to this wider audience through the medium of his address to Memmius.

Gaius Memmius, a member of a senatorial family and the husband of Sulla's daughter Fausta until he divorced her in 55, had been tribune, perhaps in 62;[14] he became praetor in 58 and governor of the province of Bithynia in northwest Asia Minor in 57; in 54 he stood for the consulship but was unsuccessful, and in 52, after being found guilty of using bribery in the elections of 54, went into exile in Greece, where, as we shall see shortly, he showed himself to be no friend of the Epicureans. He is said by Cicero, who was on friendly terms with him, to have been accomplished in Greek literature, but scornful of Latin, and to have been a talented orator, but lazy (*Brutus* 247). He may have been a lazy orator, but he was more energetic in another direction: his adultery with the wives of two of his political enemies, the brothers Marcus and Lucius Lucullus, is reported by Cicero in a letter dated 20 January 60 (*Letters to Atticus* 1.18.3). The erotic poetry that he wrote does not survive: accord-

---

13. The idea that the unenlightened are sick, and that the Epicurean philosopher is a moral healer, is found in Lucretius (1.936–950 [repeated at 4.11–25]; 3.1070), Philodemus, Cicero, and Diogenes of Oinoanda, as well as in Epicurus himself.

14. The date usually given by modern scholars is 66, but see F. X. Ryan, "The Tribunate of C. Memmius L. F.," *Hermes* 123 (1995) 293–302.

ing to Ovid, its language left little to the imagination (*Tristia* 2.433–434), but this does not mean that it was without literary merit, and he showed good taste by patronizing Catullus and Helvius Cinna.

Scholars have often expressed surprise that Lucretius chose to address his Epicurean poem to a man of such imperfect character and un-Epicurean behavior, and some have even doubted the identification of Lucretius' Memmius with Gaius Memmius. But there is no need for either surprise or doubt. Given that Lucretius' purpose is to enlighten the unenlightened, it would have been very odd if he had not chosen to address someone who was in need of enlightenment and reform. Although he tactfully describes Memmius as a man of good character and good reputation (1.26–27, 140; 3.420; 5.8), he was no doubt well aware of his weaknesses and hoped that he would heed his warnings against the dangers of, for example, ambition and sexual passion. The fact is that Memmius' imperfections, together with his prominent position in public life, well qualified him to be the addressee of *On the Nature of Things*. There was also something else, something very important, that so qualified him—his interest in poetry.

When Lucretius decided to expound the Epicurean system in a poem, he was taking a bold, indeed unprecedented, step: no one had done it before in Greek or Latin. In the fifth century B.C. Parmenides and Empedocles had written philosophical poems, and Lucretius, who, despite his disagreement with Empedocles' views, warmly praises him, undoubtedly regarded him as his chief model as a philosopher-poet.[15] Epicurus, however, had discouraged the writing of poetry and, though he could write elegant prose if he wished, usually adopted an arid style, apparently regarding literary adornment as an obstacle, rather than as an aid, to clear understanding. Lucretius is well aware that he is a pioneer, and is extremely proud of the fact (1.921–934; 4.1–9; 5.336–337). He is also fully conscious of the formidable nature of his task: he refers to the difficulty of "illuminating the obscure discoveries of the Greeks in Latin verse" (1.136–137); and he draws attention to the inadequacy of his native language (1.139, 832; 3.260), which means that he has to invent many new terms (1.138).[16] It is evident that he overcame these diffi-

---

15. On Lucretius' debt to Empedocles, see especially D. Sedley, *Lucretius and the Transformation of Greek Wisdom* 1–34. The debt is a considerable one and would almost certainly be seen to be even greater if Empedocles' *On Nature* survived in its entirety instead of in fragments that comprise only a fraction of the work.

16. Actually, Lucretius usually prefers to use an existing Latin word in a new sense rather than introduce a coinage.

culties not only by his genius, but also by sheer hard work: he describes his verses as "the product of long research and the fruit of joyful labor" (3.419), and confesses that he spends "the still calm of the night" working on his poem (1.142–145), reminding one of Robert Bridges's would-be poet "o'er his lamp-lit desk in solitude."

Why did he choose to expound his philosophy in verse rather than in prose? The obvious answer is that he was a natural poet who knew that he could put across his message more effectively in verse. But it is clear too that he believed that a poetic exposition of Epicureanism was more likely to attract and persuade Memmius and no doubt other cultured Romans. In a famous and important passage (1.936–950, repeated at 4.11–25) he explains that, just as doctors trick children into drinking unpleasant-tasting, but beneficial, medicine by first coating the rim of the cup with honey, so he has chosen to coat Epicurean philosophy with the sweet honey of the Muses in the hope of holding Memmius' attention and enabling him to learn the truth about nature. To what extent it was a question of his instinctively knowing that he must write a poem because his own genius demanded it, and to what extent he deliberately chose verse to suit Memmius and others who had found Epicureanism, as usually presented, off-putting, we cannot be sure. What is certain is that the situation in which he found himself was a fortunate one, because the need to write in verse in order to be most effective as an exponent of philosophy enabled him at the same time to satisfy his poetic aspirations. His philosophical purpose, the enlightenment of Memmius, is both the inspiration and the justification of the poem.

Does the fact that Lucretius, on his own admission, uses his poetic art to sugar the somewhat bitter pill of his philosophy mean that he is a great poet in spite of his Epicureanism rather than because of it? Does it mean that, from a poetic point of view, it would have been better if he had not been an Epicurean and thus had been free to compose a poem on a theme that lent itself more readily to poetic treatment than an abstruse philosophical system? The Romantics answered yes to these questions: Shelley complains that "Lucretius had limed the wings of his swift spirit in the dregs of the sensible world"; and Byron comments: "If Lucretius had not been spoiled by the Epicurean system, we should have had a far superior poem to any now in existence." But these criticisms are misguided. As I have written elsewhere: "Certainly it must be admitted that [Lucretius] was a natural poet, and that, if he had taken a more traditional theme, the result would have been an artistic poem. But [*On the Nature of Things*] is one of the world's greatest poems not because it is merely artistic, but because it is also full of passion, fervour, and emotion: the poet is inspired with a deep sense of missionary purpose and puts all his heart and soul, as well as all his intellectual power, into his writing, and that is largely why his work still grips our attention, still throbs with life and excitement. If he had not been an Epicurean, this inspiration would have been lacking."[17] As I have pointed out above, *On the Nature of Things,* though often labeled a didactic poem, is also an epic of the universe and of everything in it, including human beings. Even the ultimate particles of matter, the imperceptible atoms, inspire fine poetry, since Lucretius demonstrates their existence and illustrates their properties and movements by introducing many superbly conceived and brilliantly described analogies from the perceptible world. Coleridge's remark to Wordsworth that "whatever in Lucretius is poetry is not philosophical, whatever is philosophical is not poetry," though valued by teachers as a convenient topic for essays and tutorials, could not be more wrong: in *On the Nature of Things* philosophy and poetry are inextricably intertwined.

The merits of Lucretius' poetry were acknowledged at once, and he exercised a considerable influence on his immediate successors. Cicero, writing to his brother (*Letters to Quintus* 2.9) on 10 or 11 February 54 B.C., comments: "The poetry of Lucretius is, as you say in your letter, rich in brilliant genius, yet highly artistic." Virgil owed a vast poetic debt to Lucretius not only in his pastoral *Eclogues* and didactic *Georgics,* but also in his epic *Aeneid,* and it is undoubtedly Lucretius who is at the front of his mind when he writes: "Blessed is he who has succeeded in finding out the causes of things and has trampled underfoot all fears and inexorable fate and the roar of greedy Acheron"[18] (*Georgics* 2.490–492). Horace, who toyed with Epicureanism, was influenced by Lucretius, though much less deeply than Virgil was, in early life. Ovid admired *On the Nature of Things,* prophesying that "the verses of sublime Lucretius are destined to perish only when a single day will consign the world to destruction" (*Amores* 1.15.23–24). The Stoic Manilius, who wrote an astrological poem early in the first century A.D., though he disagreed strongly with Lucretius' Epicurean views, was influenced by him.

So the influence of Lucretius' poetry is not in doubt. But what of his

---

17. Loeb edition xliv–xlv.

18. Acheron, strictly a river of the underworld, is often used by Lucretius, Virgil, and others, to mean the underworld itself. As I point out in the Loeb edition xx–xxi, it is inconceivable that Virgil could have written the lines quoted, if he had known that Lucretius had gone mad and committed suicide, for "it would have been a sarcastic and cruel comment on a man whose tragic end showed that he was anything but *felix* [blessed], and had anything but conquered all fears and fate and death."

philosophy? Did he succeed in making any converts to Epicureanism? Certainly he failed to convert Memmius. He must have hoped to rescue him from the stormy seas of political life, and he had warned him about the harmful consequences of ambition (see especially 3.59–78, 995–1002; 5.1120–1135); and yet Memmius not only stood for the consulship of 54, but showed himself to be so unscrupulously ambitious that, as we have seen, he used bribery. Moreover, as an exile in Athens, he obtained permission from the city's authorities to build on the remains of Epicurus' house, and thus distressed and angered the Epicureans; he appears to have gone out of his way to annoy them. There is a simple explanation for his behavior. If one assumes, as one reasonably may, that *On the Nature of Things* had been recently published when the Cicero brothers exchanged opinions on Lucretius' poetry early in 54, its publication can be placed late in 55. Soon afterward Memmius was exiled in consequence of a vice against which Lucretius had warned him. If Lucretius had lived to witness Memmius' disgrace, he might well have remarked, "Well, what did I tell you?" Memmius naturally felt that he had been made to look foolish in the eyes of the public and took his revenge on the Epicureans in a rather childish way. I am speculating of course, but such an act of vindictiveness would not have been out of character for a man who was probably motivated partly, if not mainly, by spite against his political opponents when he bedded their wives. Although Lucretius did not succeed in converting Memmius, it is rash to assume, as some have done, that his missionary effort was a total failure. There is evidence that he was not only admired as a poet, but also taken seriously as an exponent of Epicureanism.[19] Virgil was influenced by his thought as well as by his poetry, and it is tempting to suppose that it was a reading of *On the Nature of Things* that persuaded him to study under the Epicurean philosopher Siro in Naples. It would be surprising if many did not derive comfort from Lucretius' philosophy in the dark days of the civil wars (49–31 B.C.) and under Nero (A.D. 54–68) and Domitian (A.D. 81–96), who, after beginning their reigns in good style, dealt ruthlessly with their opponents or presumed opponents. Even when Lucretius' poem did not convince its readers, it must have contributed greatly to their understanding of Epicurean philosophy. The Christian writer Arnobius, writing about A.D. 300, seems to have derived much of his information about Epicureanism from *On the Nature of Things,* and the strong attacks that his pupil Lactantius makes on Lucretius suggest that he regarded him as philosophically significant.

---

19. See, for example, the remarks of Vitruvius 9, *Preface* 17, written within three decades of Lucretius' death.

Although Lucretius is not an original philosopher, he deserves to be reckoned a philosopher in that, as Cyril Bailey observes, he has "a firm and clear grasp of a great world-system, which he expounds with a marvellous vividness and completeness." Whether he relied on a single work of Epicurus, as has recently been argued (see section 3, below), or used several of his master's works, his presentation of Epicureanism is, to a significant degree, his own, and not only because it is in brilliant Latin poetry rather than in dull Greek prose: it is evident that it results from the extraction, condensation or expansion, adaptation and rearrangement of material that he found in Epicurus' work, with the addition of material drawn from non-Epicurean sources and from his own experience. All the material is carefully chosen and organized to suit his missionary purpose. He follows Epicurus faithfully, but not blindly: because he lived more than two centuries after his master and was not a Greek, but a Roman, he takes good care to ensure that what is, after all, not a dead philosophical system, but a living faith, is fully relevant to the needs of Memmius and his contemporaries. He puts Epicureanism into an unmistakably Roman setting.

3. Epicurus and Epicureanism

Epicurus was born on the island of Samos, just off the west coast of Asia Minor, in 341 B.C. His parents were Athenians. His early education was presumably provided by his father, who was a schoolmaster. He is said to have first become interested in philosophy at the age of fourteen. After military service in Athens (323–321), he rejoined his family in the Ionian city of Colophon, near Ephesus, where they had resettled. In nearby Teos he studied under Nausiphanes, a follower of the philosopher Democritus (c.460–c.370), who had developed the atomic theory invented by Leucippus about 440. Epicurus adopted and modified the atomic theory, and it is natural to assume that it was Nausiphanes who introduced him to it.

In 311 Epicurus moved north to Mytilene on the island of Lesbos and began to teach in public. But he was apparently regarded as a subversive influence and had to leave in a hurry. It may have been this experience that persuaded him of the wisdom of "living unnoticed"; at any rate his first attempt to teach in public seems also to have been his last. He made some converts in Mytilene, including Hermarchus, who was to succeed him as head of the Epicurean school, and he made more converts in Lampsacus, a city on the Asiatic shore of the Hellespont, where he sought refuge. One of his converts in Lampsacus was Metrodorus, the most important member of the school after himself, who predeceased him. Another was Colotes, who, on hearing him speak, fell down before him and hailed him as a god. Colotes' reaction is indicative of Epicurus' charisma. Indeed, if he had not been capable of exerting a powerful influence on the minds of others, he would not have succeeded in founding a school that was to be an important presence in the ancient world for six centuries—for three centuries before Christ and for three after him. His followers were noted for their loyalty and devotion to him, and he was revered and loved not only during his lifetime, but also long after his death. We have already seen how Lucretius regarded him. Epicurus encouraged this reverence for himself, because "the veneration of the wise man is a great benefit to those who venerate him" (*Vatican Sayings* 32).

In 307/306 B.C. Epicurus moved to Athens and purchased a house with a small garden. His school was often to be called the Garden, while the school founded in Athens at about the same time by Zeno of Citium was called the school of the Porch—the Stoic school.[20] Epicurus taught in Athens for thirty-six years until his death in 270. During this period he seems never to have taught in public, and he left the city only occasionally to visit friends in Asia Minor.[21] He lived a life of great simplicity with his pupils, who included women and slaves. In his last years he was afflicted with strangury (difficult and painful passage of urine), probably caused by enlargement of the prostate. He bore his illness with the utmost cheerfulness and, when on the verge of death and in great physical pain, wrote a letter in which he refers to his great happiness and joy.

Epicurus was a voluminous writer, but only a small percentage of what he wrote has survived. Thanks to the third-century A.D. writer Diogenes Laertius, who quotes them, we have three letters that Epicurus wrote to pupils—*Letter to Herodotus* (on physics), *Letter to Pythocles*[22] (on as-

---

20. The Stoic school, which was to be the main rival of the Epicurean school under the late Republic and early Empire, derived its name from the Painted Stoa, a colonnaded building in the Athenian Agora where Zeno taught. We do not hear of any hostility between Epicurus and Zeno, but it is difficult to imagine that they approved of one another's views. Although Lucretius never mentions the Stoics by name, those scholars who have recently argued that he never has them in mind are almost certainly mistaken. See notes on 1.638; 4.823–857; 5.22, 110–234, 156–173, 200–203.

21. Once (we do not know when) he was shipwrecked when sailing to Lampsacus and barely escaped with his life. See Plutarch *Moralia* 1090e and especially Diogenes of Oinoanda *fr.* 72. The incident may partly explain his reluctance to travel.

22. *Letter to Pythocles* may be the compilation of a pupil, but there is no doubt about the authenticity of its content.

tronomy and meteorology), *Letter to Menoeceus* (on ethics)—and a collection of forty moral sayings known as the *Principal Doctrines* (*Kyriai Doxai*). We also have eighty maxims (not all of them new and not all of them written by Epicurus himself), which, because they were discovered (in 1888) in a manuscript in the Vatican Library, are known as the *Vatican Sayings.* Epicurus' other writings either are lost or survive only in fragments. The most abundant source of fragments has been the volcanic ash of Herculaneum near Naples. Herculaneum, like Pompeii, was overwhelmed by the eruption of Vesuvius in A.D. 79, and in the middle of the eighteenth century excavation of a fine villa, the so-called Villa of the Papyri, brought to light the charred remains of an Epicurean library. The villa is undoubtedly that occupied by the first-century B.C. Epicurean teacher and writer Philodemus. Some of the papyrus texts are so seriously carbonized that little or nothing can be read, but others are legible or partly legible. They include not only works by Philodemus himself and several other followers of Epicurus,[23] but also significant fragments of Epicurus' own chief work, *On Nature* (*Peri Physeōs*), which was in thirty-seven books, each book representing an installment of a lecture course.

Our most important sources for Epicureanism, in addition to those just mentioned, are Lucretius, Cicero, Plutarch, and Diogenes of Oinoanda. Lucretius gives us our fullest account of Epicurean physics. Cicero and Plutarch, though hostile to Epicureanism, provide much information, especially on ethics and, in the case of Cicero, on theology as well. Diogenes of Oinoanda, like Lucretius, was a devoted follower of Epicurus. It was probably in the first half of the second century A.D. that Oinoanda, a small city in the mountains of Lycia in southwest Asia Minor, received a remarkable gift from Diogenes, who must have been wealthy and locally influential. The gift was a massive Greek inscription, carved on the limestone wall of a stoa or colonnade. Diogenes explains that he has "reached the sunset of life" and that, before he dies, he wants to advertise the benefits of Epicurean philosophy with the intention of

---

23. K. Kleve, "Lucretius in Herculaneum," *Cronache Ercolanesi* 19 (1989) 5–27, published sixteen tiny fragments of what he believed to be a papyrus text of *On the Nature of Things* from the Herculaneum library. In the revised Loeb edition of 1992 (p. liv) I commented that "the fragments are so minute and bear so few certainly identifiable letters that at this stage some scepticism about their proposed authorship seems pardonable and prudent." At the time of writing I hear that Mario Capasso claims to have proved that the fragments cannot be Lucretian, and that Kleve claims to have identified more pieces of Lucretius. At least until the relevant publications appear I shall continue to suspend judgment.

bringing moral salvation not only to his contemporaries, but also to generations to come ("for they belong to us, though they are still unborn"), and not only to the people of Oinoanda, but also to foreigners— or rather to "those who are called foreigners, though they are not really so, for . . . the whole compass of this world gives all people a single country . . . and a single home." In accomplishment of his philanthropic and cosmopolitan mission, he sets out Epicurus' teachings on physics, epistemology, and ethics in writings that may have contained about 25,000 words and filled about 260 square meters of wall space. The inscription is eloquent proof of the continuing existence of Epicureanism as a missionary philosophy whose adherents regarded it as the saving truth; moreover, it is a valuable addition to our sources: Diogenes' own exposition of Epicurus' philosophy is informative and reliable, and there is the bonus that he quotes some maxims and letters written by his master. He was unknown until late in the nineteenth century, when French and Austrian epigraphists found 88 pieces of the inscription. Between 1968, when I started a long series of investigations at Oinoanda, and 2012 another 211 fragments have been brought to light, but no more than a third of the complete work has been recovered so far.

The question of which work or works of Epicurus Lucretius used in writing *On the Nature of Things* has been much discussed. The obvious difficulty facing those who try to answer it is the loss of so much of what Epicurus wrote, but our state of knowledge about his writings, and especially about *On Nature*, is by no means static. Much progress with the decipherment, restoration, and interpretation of the papyrus texts from Herculaneum has been made in recent decades and indeed recent years, and David Sedley, who himself has made an outstanding contribution to this work, now argues that Lucretius' only Epicurean source for "the physical exposition in the main body of all six books" (not, it is to be noted, for all the material in the poem) was *On Nature*, especially the first fifteen of its thirty-seven books.[24] He is careful to stress that he is only talking about "the bare bones of the exposition," and he gives full credit to Lucretius for the original way in which he handled the material, rearranging it, elaborating it, illustrating it, and of course treating it poetically. Although Sedley probably goes too far in claiming that *On Nature* was Lucretius' only source in his exposition of Epicurean physics, he certainly succeeds in showing that it was his main source. It

---

24. See D. Sedley, *Lucretius and the Transformation of Greek Wisdom,* especially Chapters 4–5 (pp. 94–165).

is to be noted that Lucretius' title translates that of his master's chief work, though it is almost certainly also meant to recall Empedocles' poem *On Nature*.

Early Greek philosophers, from Thales at the beginning of the sixth century B.C. down to the second half of the fifth century, had been mainly concerned with the physical nature of the universe. They are often called the Presocratics, a name that implies that Socrates (469–399) was the introducer of a new kind of philosophy—moral philosophy. Socrates was indeed the first Greek thinker to devote himself to the systematic exploration of moral issues, though the change of interest from physical phenomena to human problems began with the independent teachers known as the sophists, some of whom, including Protagoras and Gorgias, were senior contemporaries of Socrates. After Socrates the main focus of philosophy was on ethics, though by no means all Postsocratics followed him in having no interest in natural science. The fourth century B.C. was dominated, philosophically, by the giant figures of Plato (c.428–347), founder of the Academy, and Plato's pupil Aristotle (384–322), founder of the Lyceum. The philosophers who followed them could not fail to take account of their views, as well as those of Socrates, even when they reacted against them rather than adopted them. So it was with Epicurus, who was born six years after Plato's death and was doing his military service in Athens when Aristotle died. His primary concern, like that of Socrates, Plato, and Aristotle, was with moral philosophy, though he had his own ideas about it and, as we shall soon see, natural science had an essential, though subordinate, part to play in his system.

Formulating his ideas at a time when Athens had ceased to be a great power and the Greek city-states, as a result of the Macedonian conquests, had lost much of their political autonomy, Epicurus offered individuals a different sort of independence—moral independence. Defining philosophy as "an activity, attempting by means of discussion and reasoning, to make life happy," he believed that happiness is gained through the achievement of moral self-sufficiency (*autarkeia*) and freedom from disturbance (*ataraxia*).

The main obstacles to the goal of tranquillity of mind are our unnecessary fears and desires, and the only way to eliminate these is to study natural science. The most serious disturbances of all are fear of death, including fear of punishment after death, and fear of the gods. Scientific inquiry removes fear of death by showing that the mind and spirit are material and mortal, so that they cannot live on after we die: as Epicurus neatly and logically puts it: "Death . . . is nothing to us: when we exist, death is not present; and when death is present, we do not exist. Consequently it does not concern either the living or the dead, since for the living it is non-existent and the dead no longer exist" (*Letter to Menoeceus* 125). As for fear of the gods, that disappears when scientific investigation proves that the world was formed by a fortuitous concourse of atoms, that the gods live outside the world and have no inclination or power to intervene in its affairs, and that irregular phenomena such as lightning, thunder, volcanic eruptions, and earthquakes have natural causes and are not manifestations of divine anger. Every Epicurean would have agreed with Katisha in the *Mikado* when she sings:

> *But to him who's scientific*
> *There's nothing that's terrific*
> *In the falling of a flight of thunderbolts!*

So the study of natural science is the necessary means whereby the ethical end is attained. And that is its only justification: Epicurus is not interested in scientific knowledge for its own sake, as is clear from his statement that "if we were not disturbed by our suspicions concerning celestial phenomena, and by our fear that death concerns us, and also by our failure to understand the limits of pains and desires, we should have no need of natural science" (*Principal Doctrines* 11). Lucretius' attitude is precisely the same as his master's: all the scientific information in his poem is presented with the aim of removing the disturbances, especially fear of death and fear of the gods, that prevent the attainment of tranquillity of mind. It is very important for the reader of *On the Nature of Things* to bear this in mind all the time, particularly since the content of the work is predominantly scientific and no systematic exposition of Epicurean ethics is provided.[25]

Epicurus despised philosophers who do not make it their business to improve people's moral condition: "Vain is the word of a philosopher by whom no human suffering is cured. For just as medicine is of no use if it fails to banish the diseases of the body, so philosophy is of no use if it fails to banish the suffering of the mind" (Usener *fr.* 221). It is evident that he would have condemned the majority of modern philosophers and scientists.

As Diogenes Laertius (10.30) tells us, the Epicurean system "is divided into three parts—canonic, physics, and ethics," though he adds that the Epicureans "usually merge the canonic with the physics."

---

25. Possible reasons for this imbalance are considered in the Loeb edition li–lii.

The canonic[26] consists of Epicurus' rules of investigation, his epistemology. It is understandable that it was often not treated separately from physics, because the two are interlinked and interdependent.

According to the canonic, there are three criteria of truth. The fundamental criterion is sensation (1.422–425). In cases where sensation seems to deceive us, as when a square tower viewed from a distance appears to be round (4.353–363) or a straight oar submerged in water appears to be bent (4.436–442), the fault lies not with the senses, but with the mind, which wrongly interprets the information received by the senses (4.379–386, 462–468). The mechanics of sensation belong to the sphere of physics, and we shall see that sight, hearing, and smell are accounted for by a theory of emanations. The sense organs faithfully record the emanations that they receive, and if, for example, an image of a distant tower is already distorted when it reaches our eyes, they are not to be blamed any more than a camera is to be blamed if it records an already distorted image. It is when we interpret sense impressions that mistakes can arise. When we are investigating things, the aim is to obtain, wherever possible, a near, clear view of them. If we obtain such a view of a round-looking tower, we can be sure that it is indeed round. But if we have a distant view of a round-looking tower, the proper procedure is not to assume that it is round, but to suspend judgment until we can go near and obtain either "confirmation" or "nonconfirmation" of our sense impression of the distant tower. In the case of celestial phenomena and certain terrestrial phenomena such as volcanic eruptions and earthquakes a near, clear view is not possible. However, in investigating such phenomena we must still be guided by sensation. Taking phenomena of our immediate experience as "signs" and making use of analogy, we may be able to make inferences about their nature and causes, though these inferences cannot usually be confirmed when we test them against the evidence of sensation: if the result of a test is not "contradiction," it may at best be "noncontradiction"; and if, as quite often happens, several theories pass the negative test of noncontradiction, all of them must be considered possible. This plurality-of-causes procedure was justified not only on the ground that suspension of judgment is necessary when one cannot determine which explanation of a phenomenon in our world is the correct one, but also on the ground that explanations that are not valid in our world may well be valid in other worlds. There is the further point that, since Epicurus was interested only in scientific knowledge that helps us to achieve the moral goal of tranquillity of mind, it did not bother him if he could not identify the precise cause of a particular

---

26. The derivation of the word is explained in the note on 4.513.

phenomenon, so long as he could show that the phenomenon was natural and not supernatural. Lucretius, in his explanations of celestial and terrestrial phenomena in Books 5 and 6, frequently suggests several possible causes, and in each book he justifies this procedure (5.526–533; 6.703–711).[27]

Sensation by itself is irrational and incapable of memory, but the repeated reception of sense impressions creates in the mind general conceptions of all classes of things. Both in Greek and in Latin these general conceptions are often (though not by Lucretius) called "preconceptions," because, once created in the mind, they remain there, and further sense impressions are referred to them for testing and identification. However, it is important to understand that the (pre)conceptions are not innate, but derived from sensation. Indeed it is because they are derived from sensation that they are valid. Without them, memory, thought, and knowledge would be impossible, and they are the second criterion of truth.

The third criterion of truth, like the second, is bound up with sensation. This is feeling, or rather feelings—the feelings of pleasure and pain that are the supreme test in matters of conduct and morality. Pleasure and pain will be discussed shortly, and here it is necessary only to point out that Epicurus' ethics, like his physics, is based on the validity of sensation.

We turn now to Epicurean physics, the first principles of which, established by Lucretius early in Book 1 (149–264), are that nothing can be created out of nothing, and that nothing can be reduced to nothing: compound bodies are formed and then are dissolved, but their constituent material has always existed and always will exist. The universe, which is therefore birthless and deathless, consists of just two ultimate realities— matter and void. The existence of matter is proved by sensation; and if there were no void, motion would be impossible, apparently solid objects could not be penetrated, and a ball of wool and a piece of lead of similar bulk would not have different weights, whereas sensation assures us that all these things occur (1.329–397). The extent of the universe, and that of each of its two ultimate components, is infinite, as Lucretius proves in 1.951–1051. One of his arguments (1.968–983) is justly famous. He invites us to assume that the universe is finite and to consider what would happen if someone went to the very edge of it and threw a spear. One of two things would happen: either the spear would be stopped, in which case there must be matter ahead; or the spear would fly on, in which case

---

27. See also Epicurus *Letter to Herodotus* 79–80, *Letter to Pythocles* 86–88; Philodemus *De Signis;* Diogenes of Oinoanda *fr.* 13.III.

there must be space ahead. In neither case has the boundary of the universe been reached. Elsewhere (2.1048–1089) Lucretius argues that the number of worlds in the universe must be infinite.

In what form does uncompounded matter exist? It exists in the form of an infinite number of absolutely solid, indivisible, unmodifiable, imperishable particles or atoms (1.483–634). The Greek word *atomos* means "indivisible," and so the modern atom, which has been split into subatomic particles, is really misnamed. The Epicureans argued that, unless the elements of matter were indivisible and indestructible, there could be no permanence for the universe, and indeed no existence, for everything would long ago have been reduced to nothing (1.540–550). The atoms are so small that they are individually imperceptible (1.265–328). They are uniform in substance but vary widely, though not infinitely, in shape, size, and weight, and it is these variations, as well as the variations in their movements and arrangements, that explain the diversity of things in the universe (2.333–729). Although every atom is minute, it has a certain magnitude and therefore, despite being *physically* indivisible, is *mentally* divisible into a limited number of "smallest parts," that is to say, parts that are the minima of extension and magnitude. This interesting, but rather difficult, doctrine is expounded by Lucretius in 1.599–634, and he returns to it in 1.746–752 and 2.478–499.

All atoms, whether unattached in the void or joined in compounds, are always in motion (2.80–141). Those moving freely through the void fall downward by reason of their weight, and fall at a uniform speed despite their varying weights. The idea that they move downward is naive: there can be no "up" or "down" in infinite space. However, the idea that objects of different weights falling in a vacuum move with equal velocity—an idea that Epicurus could not prove by experiment— is correct. But his brilliant inference created a problem: the formation of compound bodies cannot take place without atoms colliding and, if all the atoms are moving in the same direction and at the same speed, how can collisions occur? The answer (2.216–293) is that at unpredictable times and places the atoms swerve very slightly from their straight course. This assumption of an atomic swerve was ridiculed for two millennia: Cicero thought it "puerile" as well as unscientific, and Lord Macaulay pronounced it to be "the most monstrous absurdity in all Epicurus' absurd theory," but in the modern atomic age it has been treated with more respect. An extremely important point, which emerges clearly from Lucretius' account, is that the supposition of the swerve was made not only to explain how compound bodies can be formed, but also to account for free will, which Epicurus firmly believed in, but which the physical determinism of Democritus seemed to have excluded. Moreover, it would be a mistake to suppose that Epicurus argued that the irregular movement of atoms proves the existence of free will: rather, as Lucretius' account makes clear, the argument was that the fact of free will proves the existence of the atomic swerve. Unfortunately our surviving sources do not make clear exactly how a random atomic movement makes possible actions performed by choice, but Epicurus certainly believed that by his theory he had preserved the moral independence of the individual. The very great significance that he attached to this matter can be gauged from his statement that "it would be preferable to subscribe to the legends of the gods than to be a slave to the determinism of the physicists" (*Letter to Menoeceus* 134). Once again we see that his moral system was of paramount importance to him.

The motion of atoms enclosed in a compound body is not linear, but vibratory, as they continually collide and rebound at intervals that vary according to the density of the substance. Why, if the component atoms of objects are continually on the move, do we not perceive their movement? The answer is simple: since the atoms themselves are imperceptible, their movements too are imperceptible (2.308–322). Every compound body, however solid it may appear to be, contains a greater or lesser amount of void. Lucretius explains that differences in the shapes of the atoms explain the differences in the density of things as well as differences in the effects that they have on our senses of taste, hearing, smell, sight, and touch (2.381–477). Hooked and branchy atoms cohere more closely together than smooth and round ones and affect our senses more harshly.

Whereas atoms are uncreated, unchangeable, and imperishable, compound bodies, no matter how solid and bulky they may be, have a beginning, undergo change, and eventually are dissolved. This is true not only of ourselves and all the things around us, but also of the totality of the world (2.1105–1174). Like every one of the infinite number of worlds in the universe, our world had a beginning and will have an end (5.91–109, 235–415). Lucretius shows that it is a natural, not a divine, creation (2.167–183; 5.156–234, 416–508); and in his brilliant account of how plants and animals originated, of how primitive human beings lived, and of how civilization developed, divine intervention is wholly excluded (5.772–1457).

The continual vibration of the component atoms of objects causes the atoms on the surface to be thrown off constantly at high speed as extraordinarily fine films shaped like the objects from which they emanate. When these filmy images (most often called *eidōla* in Greek and *simulacra* in Latin) impinge upon the eyes, they produce sight; and when they enter the mind, they cause thought, if the body is awake, or dreams, if it is asleep (4.26–521, 722–822, 877–906, 962–1036). All sensation is explained by contact. In the case of touch and taste, the contact with the object perceived is obviously direct. In the case of sight, however, the contact is, as we have seen, indirect; and the same applies to hearing and smell: these sensations too are caused by effluences entering the relevant sense organs.

The mind and spirit, the two components of the soul, are corporeal. Being parts of the body, they are born with it and die with it. Both are composed of extremely small, round, and smooth particles, which accounts for their extraordinary mobility. The spirit (*anima* in Latin), the seat of sensation, is distributed throughout the whole body, while the mind (*animus*), the seat both of thought and of emotion, is located in the breast. At death both mind and spirit are dispersed at once, and there is no more sensation or consciousness. Lucretius, who devotes the bulk of Book 3 to explanation of the nature of the mind and spirit and to proof of their mortality (3.94–829), goes on to argue that "death is nothing to us" and that fear of death is unreasonable (3.830–1094). Fear of death is, as we have seen, one of the two main obstacles to tranquillity of mind, so that it is not surprising that Lucretius devotes a whole book to his attempt to dispel it. It is to be noted that the Epicureans regarded fear of death not only as a very bad thing in itself, but also as the root cause of that feeling of insecurity that leads people to compete for wealth and power and often to commit crimes or go to war in pursuit of these objectives. Lucretius, who presents this analysis in language that strongly suggests that contemporary events such as the Catilinarian conspiracy are at the front of his mind (3.59–86), makes the paradoxical but psychologically perceptive statement that fear of death sometimes drives people to suicide (3.79–82).

The gods, fear of whom is the other main obstacle to true happiness, exist, but not as popularly conceived. They are material beings, composed of exceedingly fine atoms, but, unlike other compound bodies, they continually gain new atoms to replace those they lose, so that they enjoy immortality. Occupying "the lucid interspace of world and world,"[28] they are perfectly self-sufficient, perfectly tranquil, and perfectly happy. Even if they had possessed the power to create and govern the world, to punish the wicked and reward the righteous, the whole business would have been much too troublesome for them to have undertaken it and, if they had undertaken it, the world and human beings would not have been as imperfect as they are (2.167–181; 5.156–234).

---

28. Tennyson's description of the homes of the gods, in imitation of Lucretius 3.18–22, is quoted in full in my note on that passage.

Since they have no interest in our affairs, can they be of any interest or value to us? Are they to be worshipped? One might suppose that the answer to these questions is an emphatic no, but in fact it is an emphatic yes. The gods, being perfect, do not need us, but, because they are perfect, we need them. Although they live out in space, the images that they, like all atomic compounds, discharge are able to penetrate our world. The images are so fine that they cannot be perceived by our senses, but only by our minds (5.148–149). Our visions of the gods, which we may have either when we are awake or when we are asleep, not only are proof of the existence of the gods and of their anthropomorphic character, but also convey to us something of their beauty and tranquillity (5.1169–1182). Such visions are most easily experienced by those whose minds are at peace and, although the gods cannot be influenced by prayer or sacrifice, worship of them is beneficial to the worshipper provided that the worshipper is free of popular misconceptions about them (6.68–78). Diogenes of Oinoanda, one of several writers to attest to the importance that the Epicureans attached to worship of the gods, criticizes Homer for representing them as physically or morally imperfect; and he also criticizes sculptors for portraying them as formidable and irascible: instead, he says, "We ought to make statues of the gods genial and smiling, so that we may smile back at them rather than be afraid of them" (fr. 19).[29]

As we have seen, Epicurus' ethical theory, like his physical theory, is based on the validity of sensation. Since our senses inform us that pleasure is good and pain is bad, we should aim to experience as much pleasure and as little pain as possible. But by no means every pleasure is to be taken, and by no means every pain is to be avoided, because pleasure (as anyone who drinks to excess can confirm) sometimes leads to pain, and pain (as anyone who has endured the dentist's drill knows) sometimes leads to pleasure (Letter to Menoeceus 129–130).

An important teaching is that pleasure is limited (5.1433), and that the limit of bodily pleasure is reached as soon as desire is satisfied and the

---

29. A. A. Long and D. N. Sedley, The Hellenistic Philosophers I 144–149, argue (and they are not alone in taking this line) that the gods are merely "our own instinctive thought-constructs," being "the projections of the ethical ideal of human beings." This theory is to be rejected: Epicurus himself calls god a "living being" and says that "the gods exist, because we have knowledge of them by clear perception" (Letter to Menoeceus 123), and, as Long and Sedley admit, Lucretius, Cicero, and Philodemus, who are the main surviving sources for Epicurean theology, agree that the gods are "a specially privileged extraterrestrial life-form." It would be extraordinary if all three had misunderstood Epicurus' teaching on such an important matter.

pain of want is removed: after that pleasure can only be varied, not increased (*Principal Doctrines* 18). Important too is the distinction made between kinetic pleasure (the pleasure of movement), derived from the process of satisfying desire (for example, eating to satisfy hunger), and katastematic or static pleasure (the pleasure of equilibrium), which comes when desire is satisfied and the pain of want has been removed. In sharp contrast to the hedonistic philosophers of the Cyrenaic school, who favored the pursuit only of kinetic pleasure and did not even recognize static pleasure as a pleasure at all, Epicurus, though he did not ignore kinetic pleasure, considered static pleasure to be much more desirable, partly because it is more long lasting, partly because it is pain-free, whereas kinetic pleasure, being derived from the process of satisfying desire, is necessarily preceded by pain—the pain of unsatisfied desire.

Certainly the desires of the body, and therefore kinetic pleasure, cannot be disregarded, but most bodily pleasure is achieved not by leading a life of sensual indulgence, but by strictly limiting one's desires and eliminating all those that are incapable of satisfaction and therefore bound to cause one pain. Desires are to be separated into three classes: natural and necessary; natural but unnecessary; neither natural nor necessary. The desires in the first class, the desires for essential food, drink, clothing, and shelter, are to be satisfied; those in the second class, including sexual desire, are to be satisfied, if they cannot be suppressed, in strict moderation and in the least disturbing way possible; and those in the third class, including the desires for wealth and status, must be eliminated because they can never be satisfied: they have no limit, so that one will always suffer the pain of want as well as anxiety that one will lose what one has acquired.

Much more important than bodily pleasure is mental pleasure. Whereas the body can feel pleasure only at the time of the pleasurable experience, the mind has the gifts of memory and anticipation: it can mitigate or eliminate present pain by the recollection of past pleasures or the expectation of pleasures to come; moreover, whereas the static pleasure of the body (freedom from pain) cannot be enjoyed all the time, because it is bound to be interrupted by the pain of physical want, it is possible, if one guides one's life by true principles, to experience without interruption the static pleasure of the mind (freedom from disturbance). Although the mind's ability to look back and forward is exploited by the wise to their advantage, it ruins the lives of those whose attitude to past events is bitter, and whose attitude to the future is dominated by unnecessary fears, especially of the gods and of death, and unnecessary and insatiable desires, especially for wealth and power.

The Epicureans have often been criticized for their hedonism and egoism. But their doctrine of pleasure turns out to be something much closer to asceticism than to self-indulgence. It was no advocate of *la dolce vita* who considered the addition of cheese to his normal bread-and-water diet a luxury (Diogenes Laertius 10.11), and who wrote to a friend concerning a young disciple, "If you wish to make Pythocles rich, do not increase his means, but diminish his desire" (Usener *fr.* 135). What of the charge of egoism? It is true that individuals should aim to obtain as much pleasure for themselves as possible. But, although virtue is the means to the end, which is pleasure, true pleasure is impossible without virtue and is also inseparable from friendship. The fact is that in Epicurean ethics, egoism and altruism merge.

Although Epicureanism did not offer its adherents a life after death, it did offer them a heaven on earth. "You shall live like a god among human beings," writes Epicurus in *Letter to Menoeceus* (135); Lucretius states that "there is nothing to prevent us from living a life worthy of the gods" (3.322); and Diogenes of Oinoanda looks forward to the time when "truly the life of the gods will pass to human beings" (*fr.* 56). These statements are to be taken literally: thanks to Epicurus, it is possible to obtain on earth the perfect tranquillity of mind and happiness that the gods enjoy out in space. It is true that, whereas the gods are immortal, humans are mortal, but perfect pleasure can be achieved in a limited time, and extension of time, even to infinity, would not produce any greater pleasure (*Principal Doctrines* 19–20), and what Lucretius strikingly calls "deathless death" (3.869) is nothing to us—of no more concern to us than the eternity of past time was to us before we were born (3.830–842, 972–977).

4. The Structure of Lucretius' Poem

On the Nature of Things is carefully structured.[30] The six books fall naturally into three pairs. Books 1 and 2 deal with atoms and void, Book 1 establishing the basic principles of atomism and Book 2 describing the movements, properties, and combinations of the atoms. In Books 3 and 4 the focus is on psychology: in Book 3 the material and mortal nature of the mind and spirit is demonstrated, and the bulk of Book 4 is devoted to explanation of sensation and thought. Books 5 and 6 are concerned with our world and its phenomena—Book 5 with its mortality, formation, and development, Book 6 with a variety of celestial and terrestrial phenomena.

---

30. The reader's attention is drawn to the translator's headnotes preceding the translation of each book of the poem.

It is noticeable that in each pair it is the odd-numbered book that presents the basic doctrines, whereas the even-numbered one, though essential to Lucretius' exposition of the Epicurean system, presents deductions from those doctrines and arguments that supplement and complement them. This pattern is certainly deliberate, and one would like to know whether it influenced the design of Virgil's *Aeneid,* where dramatic books alternate with less dramatic ones, though there it is the even-numbered books that stand out in higher relief.

There is not space to mention, let alone discuss, all the structural features and patterns of Lucretius' work, but it is important to give some attention to the opening and concluding passages of the books, not least because, as we shall see, consideration of them is relevant to the question of whether the poet is, as some think, a pessimist.

Each book has a carefully written preface. The preface to Book 1, which serves also as the preface to the whole poem, is the longest. Its sections include the opening invocation to Venus (1–43), praise of Epicurus as the moral savior of humanity (62–79), and disclosure of the philosopher-poet's pioneering and difficult task (136–145). The opening passages of the other five books develop themes of the first preface. Proud proclamation of the writer's mission is elaborated in the preface to Book 4.[31] Praise of Epicurus' achievement is repeated and expanded in the prefaces to Books 3, 5, and 6; and although the preface to Book 2 does not mention Epicurus, its theme is the indispensability of his philosophy. In no preface is there a trace of pessimism: in each passage Lucretius makes clear that, while those ignorant of Epicurean philosophy lead unsatisfactory and unhappy lives, those who embrace it find happiness. The message is consistently one of hope and optimism.

No book of the poem has a concluding passage, such as a modern scientific writer might provide, in which a final opinion, based on the preceding arguments, is presented. It is important to bear this point in mind, especially in connection with the concluding passage of the poem, which some have seen as evidence of Lucretius' pessimism and final despair. I shall return to this shortly.

The concluding sections of the books, like the books to which they belong, are paired.[32] Book 1 ends, if one disregards the last four lines (1114–1117), in which the poet addresses words of encouragement to

31. 4.1–25. The lines are almost identical to 1.926–950. As well as being poetically brilliant, the passage conveys an important message—a message that Lucretius wanted to reiterate at the beginning of the second half of his poem.
32. For discussion of the finales, see R. D. Brown, *Lucretius on Love and Sex* 47–60.

Memmius, with proof of the infinity of the universe (951–1113), Book 2 with proof of the infinite number of worlds that the infinite universe contains (1023–1174). In the closing sections of Books 3 and 4 Lucretius brilliantly deploys his poetical genius, his command of rhetoric, his satirical power, and his missionary fervor to deliver with maximum effect physics-based ethical messages: the passage in Book 3 (830–1094) is concerned with an unnecessary fear—fear of death; the passage in Book 4 (1058–1287) deals predominantly with an unnecessary desire—sexual desire. In the third pair of books the relationship between the final sections is less obvious than in the other two pairs, but is very real and very important. In order to understand it properly, we must take account of what Lucretius says in the preface to Book 6, a passage that (appropriately, in view of the close links between Books 5 and 6) has many similarities to the preface of Book 5.

Book 5 ends with an account of the development of civilization (1011–1457)—an account that makes clear that, while human beings were very successful in mastering their natural environment and in making technical and cultural advances, they were not so successful in mastering themselves: whereas primitive humans usually managed to satisfy their natural and necessary desires for food, drink, and shelter, "civilized" humans are too often disturbed by unnatural and unnecessary desires as well as by unnecessary fears. In the opening passage of Book 6 (1–42), which begins with mention of Athens, the place where cultural development reached "the peak of perfection" reported in the last line of Book 5, Lucretius describes how Epicurus, a citizen of Athens, correctly diagnosed the causes of the moral sickness from which people were suffering: he saw that they had all the things apparently necessary for a good life, but that they were unhappy because they did not understand the limits of fear and desire and did not know how to cope morally with situations of adversity.

This passage, with its mention of Athens and its emphasis on moral sickness and health, not only looks back to the closing section of Book 5, but also looks forward to the closing section of Book 6 (1138–1286), an account, modeled on that of Thucydides (2.47–52), of the terrible plague of Athens in 430 B.C. Lucretius represents the plague not only as a physical calamity, but also as a moral one: the plague-stricken Athenians, living before Epicurus' remedies were available, were philosophically, as well as medically, unequipped to deal with this situation of extreme adversity. There is the further point that the Epicureans were fond of representing the unenlightened as diseased or plague-stricken (see, for example, Cicero *De Finibus* 1.59; Diogenes of Oinoanda *fr.* 3), and there can be little doubt that the condition of the plague's victims symbolizes for Lucretius the moral condition of those ignorant of Epicurean philosophy.[33]

So the account of the plague does not reflect the poet's pessimism and despair. Rather "the prospect of salvation and of a heaven on earth which Lucretius offers . . . shines with a brighter and stronger light on account of this dark and hellish picture of what life is like without the guidance of Epicurus."[34]

---

33. See especially H. S. Commager Jr., "Lucretius' Interpretation of the Plague," *Harvard Studies in Classical Philology* 62 (1957) 105–118. See also my notes in the Loeb edition 492–493, 578–579.

34. Loeb edition 579.

SUGGESTIONS FOR FURTHER READING

(Confined, except for Greek and Latin texts, to works in English)

1. Lucretius

Algra, K. A., et al. (eds.), *Lucretius and His Intellectual Background* (Royal Netherlands Academy of Arts and Sciences: Amsterdam, 1997). The majority of the contributions are in English.

Clay, D., *Lucretius and Epicurus* (Cornell University Press: Ithaca, NY, 1983).

Dudley, D. R. (ed.), *Lucretius* (Routledge and Kegan Paul: London, 1965).

Gale, M. R., *Myth and Poetry in Lucretius* (Cambridge University Press: Cambridge, 1994).

Gillespie, S., and Hardie, P. (eds.), *The Cambridge Companion to Lucretius* (Cambridge University Press: Cambridge, 2007).

Greenblatt, S., *The Swerve: How the Renaissance Began* (Norton: New York; The Bodley Head: London, 2011).

Johnson, W. R., *Lucretius and the Modern World* (Duckworth: London, 2000).

Kenney, E. J., *Lucretius*, with Addenda by M. R. Gale (Oxford University Press: Oxford, 1995).

Sedley, D., *Lucretius and the Transformation of Greek Wisdom* (Cambridge University Press: Cambridge, 1998).

Segal, C., *Lucretius on Death and Anxiety: Poetry and Philosophy in De Rerum Natura* (Princeton University Press: Princeton, NJ, 1990).

West, D., *The Imagery and Poetry of Lucretius*, 2nd ed. (Bristol Classical Press: 1994).

2. Epicureanism

Algra, K., et al. (eds.), *The Cambridge History of Hellenistic Philosophy* (Cambridge University Press: Cambridge, 1999).

Annas, J. E., *Hellenistic Philosophy of Mind* (University of California Press: Berkeley, 1992).

Asmis, E., *Epicurus' Scientific Method* (Cornell University Press: Ithaca, NY, 1984).

Bailey, C., *The Greek Atomists and Epicurus* (Clarendon Press: Oxford, 1928).

Clay, D., *Paradosis and Survival: Three Chapters in the History of Epicurean Philosophy* (University of Michigan Press: Ann Arbor, 1998).

Jones, H., *The Epicurean Tradition* (Routledge: London, 1989).

Long, A. A., *Hellenistic Philosophy*, 2nd ed. (University of California Press: Berkeley; Duckworth: London, 1986).

Mitsis, P., *Epicurus' Ethical Theory: The Pleasures of Invulnerability* (Cornell University Press: Ithaca, NY, 1988).

O'Keefe, T., *Epicureanism* (Acumen: Durham; University of California Press: Berkeley, 2010).

Rist, J. M., *Epicurus: An Introduction* (Cambridge University Press: Cambridge, 1972).

Sharples, R. W., *Stoics, Epicureans and Sceptics: An Introduction to Hellenistic Philosophy* (Routledge: London, 1996).

Warren, J. (ed.), *The Cambridge Companion to Epicureanism* (Cambridge University Press: Cambridge, 2009).

Warren, J., *Facing Death: Epicurus and His Critics* (Oxford University Press: Oxford, 2004).

3. Epicurean Sources: Texts, Translations, Commentaries

(a) Epicurus

Arrighetti, G., *Epicuro: Opere*, 2nd ed. (Einaudi: Turin, 1973). Greek text with Italian translation and notes.

Bailey, C., *Epicurus: The Extant Remains* (Clarendon Press: Oxford, 1926). Greek text with English translation and commentary.

Inwood, B., and Gerson, L. P. (trans.) and Hutchinson, D. S. (introduction), *The Epicurus Reader: Selected Writings* (Hackett: Indianopolis, 1994). English Translation. Includes selections from Cicero, Lucretius, and Plutarch.

Long, A. A., and Sedley, D. N., *The Hellenistic Philosophers*, 2 vols. (Cambridge University Press: Cambridge, 1987). English translation of the principal sources, with philosophical commentary (vol. 1); Greek and Latin texts, with notes and bibliography (vol. 2).

Usener, H., *Epicurea* (Teubner: Leipzig, 1887). Text of Epicurus' extant works, including many fragments and testimonies.

(b) Lucretius

Bailey, C., *Titi Lucreti Cari De Rerum Natura libri sex*, 3 vols. (Clarendon Press: Oxford, 1947, 1950). Latin text with prolegomena, English translation, and commentary.

Brown, R. D., *Lucretius on Love and Sex: A Commentary on De Rerum Natura IV, 1030–1287 with Prolegomena, Text, and Translation* (Brill: Leiden, 1987).

Campbell, G., *Lucretius on Creation and Evolution: A Commentary on De Rerum Natura Book Five, Lines 772–1104* (Oxford University Press: Oxford, 2003).

Fowler, D., *Lucretius on Atomic Motion: A Commentary on De Rerum Natura Book Two, Lines 1–332* (Oxford University Press: Oxford, 2002).

Smith, M. F., *Lucretius, De Rerum Natura* (Loeb Classical Library, 1975, 1982, 1992). Latin text with the English translation (revised) of W. H. D. Rouse, introduction, and notes.

(c) Cicero

Rackham, H., *Cicero, De Finibus Bonorum et Malorum* [On the Ends of Good and Evil] (Loeb Classical Library, 1914). Latin text and English translation. Book 1 expounds Epicurus' ethical system; Book 2 criticizes it.

——, *Cicero, De Natura Deorum* [On the Nature of the Gods], *Academica* [Academics] (Loeb Classical Library, 1933). Latin text and English translation. *De Natura Deorum* Book 1 expounds and criticizes Epicurean theology.

(d) Philodemus

Obbink, D., *Philodemus: On Piety. Part 1: Critical Text with Commentary* (Clarendon Press: Oxford, 1996). Includes England translation.

(e) Plutarch

Moralia 1086c–1127e in Einarson, B., and De Lacy, P. H., *Plutarch Moralia* vol. 14 (Loeb Classical Library, 1967). Greek text and English translation.

(f) Diogenes of Oinoanda

Smith, M. F., *Diogenes of Oinoanda: The Epicurean Inscription* (Bibliopolis: Naples, 1993). Greek text with English translation, introduction, and commentary.

——, *Supplement to Diogenes of Oinoanda, The Epicurean Inscription* (Bibliopolis: Naples, 2003). Includes new texts discovered in 1994 and 1997.

Note. For more new Epicurean texts, discovered at Oinoanda in 2007–, see the articles of J. Hammerstaedt and M. F. Smith published annually in *Epigraphica Anatolica*, starting in vol. 40 (2007).

ABBREVIATIONS AND CONVENTIONS

(a) Abbreviations

Lucr.   Lucretius

Works of Epicurus:

Hdt.	*Letter to Herodotus*
Pyth.	*Letter to Pythocles*
Men.	*Letter to Menoeceus*
PD	*Principal Doctrines (Kyriai Doxai)*
VS	*Vatican Sayings*
Us.	H. Usener, *Epicurea*

Works of Cicero:

Div.	*De Divinatione (On Divination)*
DND	*De Natura Deorum (On the Nature of the Gods)*
Fin.	*De Finibus Bonorum et Malorum (On the Ends of Good and Evil)*
Tusc. Disp.	*Tusculanae Disputationes (Tusculan Disputations)*

(b) References to the Text of Lucretius

Numerical references are always, unless otherwise indicated, to the text of Lucretius; and where no book number precedes the line number(s), the reference is to the book to which the note relates.

ON THE NATURE OF THINGS

BOOK ONE

(The headnotes that precede each book are the translator's.)

Preface

Basic Principles of Atomism

Refutation of Non-Atomic Theories of Matter

---

* See note on these lines.

1

Mother of Aeneas' people, delight of human beings and the gods, Venus,[1] power of life, it is you who beneath the sky's sliding stars inspirit the ship-bearing sea, inspirit the productive land. To you every kind of living creature owes its conception and first glimpse of the sun's light. You, goddess, at your coming hush the winds and scatter the clouds; for you the creative earth thrusts up fragrant flowers; for you the smooth stretches of the ocean smile, and the sky, tranquil now, is flooded with effulgent light.

---

1. **1–43:** Venus in this opening passage is a remarkably complex figure. She is the goddess of love and fertility from whose union with Anchises Aeneas, the legendary ancestor of the Romans, was born (see line 1), and she is the lover of Mars, god of war and father of Romulus and Remus (see 31–40). In addressing her, Lucr. may be conscious also of her being the patron goddess of Memmius' *gens* (clan), and certainly he means us to think of the cosmic theory of Empedocles, his model as a philosopher-poet: Empedocles assumed the existence of two motive-forces, Love and Strife, under whose influence his four elements unite and separate, and in Lucr.'s preface Venus symbolizes the creative forces in the world, while Mars (whom he calls *Mavors,* probably in order to underline his connection with *mors,* death) represents the destructive forces. She also personifies pleasure, the attainment of which, according to Epicureans,

Once the door to spring is flung open and Favonius'[2] fertilizing   10
breeze, released from imprisonment, is active, first, goddess, the birds of
the air, pierced to the heart with your powerful shafts, signal your entry.
Next wild creatures and cattle bound over rich pastures and swim rushing
rivers: so surely are they all captivated by your charm and eagerly follow
your lead. Then you inject seductive love into the heart of every creature
that lives in the seas and mountains and river torrents and bird-haunted
thickets and verdant plains, implanting in it the passionate urge to repro-   20
duce its kind.

Since you and you alone stand at the helm of nature's ship, and since
without your sanction nothing springs up into the shining shores of light,
nothing blossoms into mature loveliness, it is you whom I desire to be
my associate in writing this poem *On the Nature of Things,* which I am
attempting to compose for my friend Memmius.[3] Through your will,
goddess, he is always endowed outstandingly with all fine qualities. So
with all the more justification, Venus, give my words charm that will
ensure their immortality.

Meanwhile, cause the barbarous business of warfare to be lulled to   30
sleep over every land and sea. For you alone have the influence to obtain
for mortals the blessing of tranquil peace, since barbarous war is the
province of Mars mighty in arms who often stretches himself back upon
your lap, vanquished by the never-healing wound of love; throwing back
his handsome neck and gazing up at you, in open-mouthed wonderment
he feasts his greedy eyes with love; and, as he reclines, his breath hangs
upon your lips. As he rests upon your holy body, bend, goddess, to enfold
him in your arms; and from your lips, worshipful lady, let a stream of   40

---

is the object of human life. It is to be noted that she is addressed not only as
the power of physical creation and as the source of physical beauty, but also
as the inspirer of poetic productivity and beauty (see 21–28), and it is significant that Lucr.'s proclamation of his originality as a poet with a philosophical
theme (1.921 ff.) includes several echoes of the invocation to Venus: see
my discussion in *Hermathena* 102 (1966) 73–83, at 80–81. In the same article I
draw attention also to parallelisms between the invocation to Venus and the
address to Epicurus at the beginning of Book 3 (1–30)—parallelisms which both
reflect and reinforce Lucr.'s view that, just as Venus is the bringer of life,
light, and calm into the physical world, so Epicurus is the bringer of light and
calm into the spiritual world. 1–25 are imitated by Spenser in *The Faerie Queene*
4.10.44–47; and the description of Venus and Mars influenced Byron in *Childe
Harold's Pilgrimage* 4.51 and probably, through Politian, Botticelli's *Mars and
Venus.*

2. **11:** West wind.

3. **26:** On Memmius, see pp. xiii–xiv, xvii.

sweet, coaxing words flow in an appeal on behalf of the Romans for placid peace. For at this tempestuous time in my country's history, I cannot tackle my task with tranquil mind, and the gravity of the situation is such that the noble descendant of the Memmii cannot fail the cause of public security.[4]

[For it is inherent in the very nature of the gods that they should enjoy immortal life in perfect peace, far removed and separated from our world; free from all distress, free from peril, fully self-sufficient, independent of us, they are not influenced by worthy conduct nor touched by anger.][5]

50   As for what follows, Memmius, lend open ears and an alert mind, released from cares, to true philosophy. My gifts have been arranged for you with steadfast zeal; be sure that you do not contemptuously discard them without having understood them. For I will proceed to explain to you the working of the heaven above and the nature of the gods, and will unfold the primary elements of things[6] from which nature creates, increases, and sustains all things, and into which she again resolves them when they perish. In expounding our philosophy I often call these elements "matter" or "generative particles of things" or "seeds of things";
60   and, since they are the ultimate constituents of all things, another term I often use is "ultimate particles."

When all could see that human life lay groveling ignominiously in the dust, crushed beneath the grinding weight of superstition, which from the celestial regions displayed its face, lowering over mortals with hideous scowl, the first who dared to lift mortal eyes to challenge it, the first who ventured to confront it boldly, was a Greek.[7] This man neither the reputation of the gods nor thunderbolts nor heaven's menacing rumbles could

---

4. **42–43:** A probable allusion to Memmius' praetorship of 58 B.C.

5. **44–49:** These lines occur also at 2.646–651. There they are well adjusted to their context, but in the present passage they come in abruptly and inappropriately. How is their appearance to be explained? There are two possibilities: one is that Lucr. himself wrote them here but did not live to use them or delete them (in the same way that he did not live to delete 4.45–53); the other is that an early commentator, considering the lines in Book 2 relevant to, and perhaps inconsistent with, the invocation to Venus, quoted them, and that the quotation then found its way into the text. The passage is closely related to Epicurus *PD* 1. On the Epicurean conception of the gods, see pp. xxviii–xxix.

6. **55:** The atoms.

7. **66:** Epicurus.

⟵ Explore? Intentions
↓

daunt; rather all the more they roused the ardor of his courage and made 70
him long to be the first to burst the bolts and bars of nature's gates. And
so his mind's might and vigor prevailed, and on he marched far beyond
the blazing battlements of the world,[8] in thought and understanding
journeying all through the measureless universe; and from this expedition he returns to us in triumph with his spoils—knowledge of what can
arise and what cannot, and again by what law each thing has its scope
restricted and its deeply implanted boundary stone.[9] So now the situation
is reversed: superstition is flung down and trampled underfoot; we are
raised to heaven by victory.

In this connection, I fear that you may perhaps imagine that you are 80
starting on the principles of an irreligious philosophy and setting out on a
path of wickedness. But in fact more often it is that very superstition that
has perpetrated wicked and irreligious deeds. Consider how at Aulis the
elite of Greece's chieftains, the flower of its manhood, foully polluted the
altar of the Virgin Goddess of the Crossroads with the blood of
Iphianassa.[10] As soon as the ribbon[11] had been fastened about her virgin
locks so that it flowed down either cheek in equal lengths, and as soon as
she had noticed her father standing sorrowfully before the altars, and 90
near him attendants trying to keep the knife concealed, and the people
moved at the sight of her to streaming tears, struck dumb with dread and
sinking on her knees, she groped for the ground. Poor girl! Little could it
help her at such a time that she had been the first to give the king the
name of father. For uplifted by masculine hands, she was led, trembling
with terror, to the altars. Instead of being escorted by the wedding
hymn's cheerful ring, when the solemn service of sacrifice had been
performed, she was to be immolated by her father and fall a sorrowful
and sinless victim of a sinful crime, cheated of the marriage for which

---

8. **73:** The reference is to the fiery envelope that, according to the Epicureans,
surrounds the world, but there is also the idea of Epicurus being a victorious
general, who, in storming the city, sets its walls ablaze.

9. **76–77:** Repeated at 595–596, 5.89–90, 6.65–66. The metaphor of the
boundary stone, which occurs also at 2.1087, is used to emphasize the fundamental Epicurean principle that the powers of everything are governed and limited by
an inviolable law of nature.

10. **84–86:** Agamemnon, commander-in-chief of the Greek expedition to Troy,
sacrificed his own daughter Iphianassa (or Iphigenia) to Artemis, the Roman
Diana (the Virgin Goddess of the Crossroads), in order to appease the anger of the
goddess, who was delaying his fleet with contrary winds at Aulis, a port of
Boeotia. Iphigenia was told that she was being brought to Aulis to marry Achilles.

11. **87:** The mark of a sacrificial victim.

100   she was just ready. And all to what purpose? To enable a fleet to receive
      the blessing of a prosperous and propitious departure. Such heinous acts
      could superstition prompt.[12]

      The time may come when you yourself, terrorized by the fearsome
      pronouncements of the fable-mongers,[13] will attempt to defect from us.
      Consider how numerous are the fantasies they can invent, capable of
      confounding your calculated plan of life and clouding all your fortunes
      with fear. And with reason; for if people realized that there was a limit set
      to their tribulations, they would somehow find strength to defy irrational
110   beliefs and the threats of the fable-mongers. As it is, they have no way,
      no ability, to offer resistance, because they fear that death brings punish-
      ment without end. They are ignorant of the nature of the soul: they do not
      know whether it is born with the body, or whether on the contrary it
      insinuates itself into us at the moment of birth; and they are uncertain
      whether it is dissipated by death and so perishes when we perish, or
      whether it visits the gloom and yawning wastes of Orcus,[14] or whether it
      miraculously steals its way into other creatures[15] as described by our
      own poet Ennius, who first brought down from lovely Helicon a garland
      of perennial leafage,[16] to send his fame flashing through all the peoples
120   of Italy. And yet in his immortal verses Ennius also declares that there are
      precincts of Acheron,[17] where neither soul nor body survives, but only a
      kind of wraith weirdly wan and pale. From these parts, so he relates, the
      apparition of Homer, of never fading genius, rose and appeared to him
      and began to shed briny tears and disclose nature's secrets.
      So it is imperative that I give a correct account of celestial phenomena,
      explaining what principle governs the courses of the sun and moon, and
130   also what force is responsible for all that happens on earth; above all, my

      ---

      12. **101:** A famous line (*tantum religio potuit suadere malorum*), which Voltaire
      predicted would last as long as the world.

      13. **102:** "Fable-mongers" here and at 109 translates the derogatory *vatum,*
      which refers to those who, whether poets or priests, are professional promoters of
      traditional religion and mythology.

      14. **115:** The lower world.

      15. **116:** A reference to the doctrine of metempsychosis, held by the
      Pythagoreans, Empedocles, and Ennius.

      16. **117–118:** On Ennius and Lucr.'s debt to him, see pp. x, xi. The typically
      Lucretian play on words "Ennius . . . perennial" (Latin *Ennius . . . perenni*)
      reflects and reinforces the point that Ennius' work is undying. Helicon is a
      mountain in Boeotia, sacred to the Muses.

      17. **120:** A river in the underworld; hence the underworld itself.

penetrative reasoning must reveal the nature of the mind and spirit,[18] and disclose what it is that visits us when we are buried in sleep or lie awake in the grip of sickness[19] and gives us the terrifying illusion of hearing and seeing face to face people who are dead, and whose bones are embosomed in the earth.

I am wide awake to the difficulty of the task of illuminating the obscure discoveries of the Greeks in Latin verse. The main obstacles are the inadequacy of our language[20] and the novelty of my subject—factors that entail the coinage of many new terms. But your fine qualities, 140 Memmius, and the hope of gaining the pleasure of your delightful friendship[21] spur me to make a success of my task, however laborious, and induce me to forego sleep and spend the still calm of the night in quest of words and verses that will enable me to light the way brightly for your mind and thus help you to see right to the heart of hidden things.

This terrifying darkness that enshrouds the mind must be dispelled not by the sun's rays and the dazzling darts of day, but by study of the superficial aspect and underlying principle of nature.[22]

The first stage of this study will have this rule as its basis: nothing ever 150 springs miraculously out of nothing. The fact is that all mortals are in the grip of fear, because they observe many things happening on earth and in the sky and, being at a complete loss for an explanation of their cause, suppose that a supernatural power is responsible for them. Therefore, as soon as we have seen that nothing can be created out of nothing, we shall have a clearer view of the object of our search, namely the explanation of the source of all created things and of the way in which all things happen independently of the gods.

If things could be created out of nothing, any kind of thing could be 160 produced from any source; nothing would need a seed. In the first place, human beings could spring from the sea, squamous fish from the ground, and birds could be hatched from the sky; cattle and other farm animals and every kind of wild beast would bear young of unpredictable species,

---

18. **131:** The bulk of Book 3 is devoted to demonstration of the corporeal and mortal nature of the mind (*animus*) and spirit (*anima*), the rational and irrational parts of the soul.

19. **132–133:** The reference is to the filmy "images" discharged from the surfaces of objects. Their existence and nature are demonstrated in Book 4. See pp. xxvii–xxviii.

20. **139:** Lucr. mentions this difficulty again at 832 and 3.260.

21. **140–145:** On the significance of these important lines, see p. xiii.

22. **146–148:** Repeated at 2.59–61, 3.91–93, 6.39–41.

and would make their home in cultivated and barren parts without
discrimination. Moreover, the same fruits would not invariably grow on
the same trees, but would change: any tree could bear any fruit. Seeing
that there would be no elements with the capacity to generate each kind
of thing, how could creatures constantly have a fixed mother? But as it is,
170 because all are formed from fixed seeds, each is born and issues out into
the shores of light only from a source where the right matter and the right
ultimate particles exist. And this explains why all things cannot be produced from all things: any given thing possesses a distinct creative
capacity.

A second point: why do we see the rose bursting out in spring, the corn
in scorching summer, the vine at autumn's coaxing, if it is not because,
only when the fixed seeds of things have streamed together at their
appropriate time, is any created thing uncovered, while the attendant
seasons assist the prolific earth to deliver the frail objects into the shores
180 of light in safety? But if they were produced from nothing, they would
suddenly spring up at unpredictable intervals and at unfavorable times of
the year, for there would be no ultimate particles that could be debarred
by the unpropitious season from entering into creative union. Moreover,
so far as growth is concerned, the lapse of time required for the confluence of seed would be unnecessary, if things could arise out of nothing. Children, too young to talk, in an instant would become young
adults, and trees would suddenly bound up out of the ground. But it is
evident that none of these things happens, since in every case growth is a
190 gradual process, as one would expect, from a fixed seed and, as things
grow, they preserve their specific character; so you may be sure that each
thing increases its bulk and derives its sustenance from its own special
substance.

There is the further point that, if there were no rain at regular times of
the year, the earth would be unable to thrust up her luxuriant produce;
and if deprived of food, animals naturally could not propagate their kind
and keep alive. Therefore the supposition that, as there are many letters
common to many words,[23] so there are many elements common to many
things, is preferable to the view that anything can come into being
without ultimate particles.

Furthermore, why has nature not succeeded in producing human
200 beings so huge that they could wade across the open sea, making it seem
shallow, and who could dismember mighty mountains with their hands

---

23. **196–198:** Lucr. is fond of this illustration: see 823–829, 907–914, 2.688–
699, 1013–1022. Conveniently, the Latin word *elementa* can mean "letters of the
alphabet" as well as "elements."

and outlive many generations? Surely the reason is that things are created
from a definite, appointed substance, and it is firmly laid down what this
substance can produce. Therefore we are bound to admit that nothing can
come into being from nothing, because a seed is essential as the source
from which each thing can be produced and committed to the care of the
air's soft breezes.

Finally, since we see that cultivated ground is superior to uncultivated
and rewards the labor of our hands with improved yield, it is evident that 210
the earth contains elements of things which we rouse from dormancy
when we turn up the fertile clods with the plowshare and trench the soil.
If this were not so, our labor would be unnecessary, because you would
see things everywhere improve considerably of their own accord.

The complement of the foregoing doctrine is the principle that, although nature resolves everything into its constituent particles, she never
annihilates anything. For if anything were subject to destruction in all its
parts, anything might be whisked out of sight in a flash and cease to exist:
no force would be needed to effect the dispersion of its parts by unravel- 220
ing its interlaced fabric. But as it is, because all things are composed of
imperishable seeds, nature does not allow us to witness the destruction of
anything until it has encountered a force that dashes it to pieces or works
its way inside through the interstices and so breaks it up.

Moreover, if time wholly destroys the things it wastes and sweeps
away, and engulfs all their substance, whence does Venus escort each
kind of creature back into the light of life? Or, when this is done, from
what store does the creative earth furnish the food to sustain and
strengthen each? From what source is the sea provided with an unfailing 230
supply of water by its native springs and by the rivers that rise far beyond
its bounds? Where does the ether find fuel to feed the stars? For everything of perishable substance must inevitably have been swallowed up
by the sweep of infinite time and days that are no more. But if through
that space of ages past the elements that compose and reshape the universe have survived, it is certain that they are endowed with an immortal
nature. Therefore it is impossible for anything to return to nothing.

Furthermore, the same force would cause the destruction of all things
without exception, if there were no imperishable substance, more or less 240
closely interwoven, to give them stability. The fact is that a mere touch
would be enough to cause their death, since there would be no imperishable elements to form a web that in each case could be unwoven only by
a real force. But as it is, because the elements are interwoven in various
ways, and their matter is imperishable, things survive intact until they
encounter a force sharp enough to unweave their particular fabric. Noth-

ing, therefore, returns to nothing, but everything dissolves and returns to
the elements of matter.

250   Lastly, the rains disappear, when father sky has sent them spurting
down into the lap of mother earth;[24] but crops spring up and show a
sheen, branches clothe themselves with green leaves, and trees grow and
become heavy with fruit. This is what provides the human race and
beasts with nourishment; this is what gives us the happy sight of cities
blooming with children, and leafy woodlands full of the song of new-
hatched birds; this is what causes cattle and sheep, exhausted by their
very plumpness, to lie down in luxuriant pastures, and white moist milk
260   to ooze from distended udders; this is what enables newborn creatures to
frisk and play on unsteady legs in the tender grass, their young minds
intoxicated with neat milk.[25]

And so no visible object ever suffers total destruction, since nature
renews one thing from another, and does not sanction the birth of anything unless she receives the compensation of another's death.

Now then, I have taught that things cannot be produced from nothing,
and also that, once born, they cannot be reduced to nothing. But in case
you are beginning to treat my words with skepticism because the elements of things are imperceptible to our eyes, let me draw your attention
270   to other particles that, though invisible, have undeniable reality.

In the first place, the wild wind awakened whips the waves of the sea,
capsizes huge ships, and sends the clouds scudding; sometimes it swoops
and sweeps across the plains in tearing tornado, strewing them with great
trees, and hammers the heights of mountains with forest-splitting blasts.
Such is the frenzied fury of the wind, when it shrieks shrill, rages, and
menacingly murmurs. Undoubtedly, therefore, there are invisible particles of wind that sweep the sea, sweep the lands, sweep the clouds in the
280   sky, buffeting and battering them with swirling suddenness. The flow of
their current and the devastation they deal is no different from that of a
river in sudden spate: water is by nature soft, but when swollen by a great
deluge racing down from high mountains after heavy rains, it rams
together debris of forests and whole trees; even sturdy bridges cannot
withstand the sudden shock of the advancing flood, so furious is the force

---

24. **250–251:** Lucr. again (as in the opening lines of the poem) exploits mythology for his poetic and philosophical purposes. The story of the marriage of earth
and sky is an old one. The poet returns to it in 2.991–998, a passage that seems to
have been influenced by Euripides.

25. **259–261:** Serious in his love of animals but lighthearted in his writing here,
Lucr. suggests that the reason for the unsteadiness and playfulness of the newborn creatures is that their mothers' milk has the intoxicating effect of neat wine.

with which the river, made to boil by bulk of rain, dashes against the piles; with thundering roar it deals destruction, rolling big boulders beneath its waves and sweeping away all that obstructs its course. This, 290 then, is the way in which currents of wind also must operate: when, with the strength of a river, they have pounced in any direction, they chase things before them and sweep them away in attack after attack and sometimes, swooping upon them in swirling eddy, whirl them around and carry them off in a swift tornado. So I insist that there are invisible particles of wind, since in their effects and behavior they are found to rival great rivers, whose substance is manifest.[26]

Then again, we smell the various odors of things, even though we never see them approaching our nostrils; we do not observe seething 300 heat, nor can we discern cold with our eyes, nor do we see sounds; and yet all these must be of a corporeal nature, since they have the power to act upon our sensory organs. For nothing can touch or be touched, unless it is corporeal.

Moreover, garments hung up on a wave-plashed shore grow damp, and the same garments spread out in the sun grow dry. Yet we do not see how the moisture has soaked them through, nor again how it has withdrawn under the influence of the heat. Therefore the moisture is sprayed out in the form of tiny particles that are completely invisible to our eyes. 310

Furthermore, as the sun completes many annual circuits, a finger ring is worn thin on the inside; the fall of water drop by drop hollows a stone; the curved plowshare, though made of iron, imperceptibly suffers attrition in the fields; we see the stone pavements of streets worn away by the feet of the crowd; and the bronze statues by city gates display right hands rubbed thin by the frequent reverential touch of passersby. We observe, then, that all these objects, being worn away, are losing substance; but 320 our inadequate faculty of sight has debarred us from being shown what particles are departing at any particular moment.

Lastly, whatever increase nature in course of time apportions little by little to things, duly curbing their growth, cannot be perceived by straining the keenest eyesight. Likewise, whenever things waste away, decayed by age, or cliffs beetling over the sea are devoured by the corroding brine, you cannot see what they lose at any single moment. Therefore it is by means of invisible particles that nature does her work.

---

26. **271–297:** The argument that the existence of invisible atoms is believable, because the invisible wind has visible effects equal to those of water, which is visible, is brilliantly conceived and presented. On the elaborate correspondences between the simile (the description of the river in flood) and the context (the description of the wind), see especially D. West, *Philologus* 114 (1970) 272–274.

Yet it is not true that everything is packed solid and confined on every
330 side by corporeal substance; for there is void in things. Knowledge of
this fact will stand you in good stead in many connections; it will prevent
you from straying in uncertainty, from continually questioning about the
universe, and from treating my words with skepticism. There is, then,
intangible space, void, and vacuity. Otherwise, movement would be
absolutely impossible. For the obvious province of matter, namely to
prevent[27] and obstruct, would operate against all things all the time, with
the result that nothing could advance because nothing would begin to
340 give way. But as it is, throughout the seas and lands and heights of
heaven we plainly perceive countless things moving in countless
different ways; whereas if void did not exist, things would not so much
be robbed and deprived of restless motion, as could never under any
circumstances have been produced at all, since on every side matter
would be packed solid in a motionless mass.

Moreover, no matter how solid things may appear to be, they are in
fact of a porous consistency, as you may perceive from the following
examples. In caverns moist streams of water seep through, making the
350 rocks all weep with an abundance of drops. Food distributes itself into
every part of an animal's body. Trees grow and produce a profusion of
fruit in season, because their sustenance is diffused right through them
from the deepest roots, up through the trunks, and into every branch.
Sounds penetrate partitions and wing their way through the walls of
houses. Numbing cold permeates to our very bones. But you could not
possibly perceive these things happening if there were no empty spaces
that the various particles could use as passages.

Lastly, why, in the case of objects of identical bulk, do we observe that
360 some weigh more than others? If a ball of wool and a lump of lead
contain an equal quantity of matter, the two ought to be of equal weight,
because it is the function of matter to press everything downward,
whereas void by nature is invariably weightless. So an object which is
evidently lighter than another of equal bulk without doubt shows plainly
that it contains more void; conversely, the heavier object indicates that it
contains more matter and much less vacuity. Therefore it is indisputable
that, as I have been seeking to prove by penetrative reasoning, what we
term void exists as an ingredient in things.

370 In this connection, I feel obliged to anticipate the false view of certain
theorists,[28] for fear it should divert you from the truth. They claim that

---

27. **336–337:** The translation "province . . . prevent" is an inadequate attempt to
reproduce the pun *officium . . . officere.*

28. **370–371:** The theory that Lucr. goes on to refute was held by Empedocles,

waters yield to the pressure of squamous creatures and open liquid paths
for them, because the fish leave behind them spaces into which the
waters that yield can stream together; and they maintain that other things
are able to move by the same reciprocal process and so exchange position, even though the universe is a plenum. Be sure that credence has
been given to this theory on totally false grounds. For how in the world
can the squamous fish advance when the waters have not given them
room? And again, how can the waters withdraw when the fish are unable 380
to move? So we have a choice of two alternatives: either we must deny
motion to all bodies, or we must say that void is an ingredient in things
and that this is what enables each thing to begin to move.

Lastly, suppose that two wide[29] bodies collide and quickly rebound:
obviously air must occupy all the void that is formed between them. But
no matter how swiftly the surrounding currents of air close in, it is
impossible for the whole space to be filled in an instant, because the air
must overrun each successive point of space before the whole area is 390
occupied. If by chance it is supposed that the rebound of the bodies has
the effect described because the air is condensed, the supposition is off
target, for it involves the creation of a vacuum that did not previously
exist and likewise the formation of a plenum from what was previously a
vacuum, whereas air cannot undergo condensation in this manner; and
even if it could, it is my view that in the absence of void it could not
contract into itself and concentrate its parts.

So, no matter how many objections you offer, you are only delaying
the time when you must admit that things contain void. Moreover, I 400
could supply you with many additional proofs in order to collect credit
for my words. But for a sagacious mind such as yours these few tracks
are sufficient to enable you to pick up the rest for yourself. For, as hounds
often track down by scent a mountain-prowling beast to its leafy covert
when once they have definitely struck the spoor, so in such matters as
these you will be able to see for yourself one thing after another, working
your way into every concealed hiding place and dragging out the truth.
But if you flag or shrink even a little from the task, Memmius, I can give 410
you this solemn pledge: my mellow tongue will pour forth from my
mind's rich store such liberal drafts, welling from deep springs, that I
fear halting age with stealing steps may occupy our limbs and loosen the

Anaxagoras, Plato (*Timaeus* 80c), Aristotle (*Physics* 213b-216b), and the Pe-
ripatetic philosopher Strato of Lampsacus, a contemporary of Epicurus. It is
mentioned by Cicero *Academica* 2.125.

29. **384:** In the Loeb I followed D. R. Shackleton Bailey in reading *late* for *lata,*
but see now I. Avotins, *Phoenix* 51 (1997) 38–43.

vital fastenings within us before the whole array of proofs on any one
subject has been dispatched in my verses through your ears.[30]

But now, to resume the work of weaving the web of my argument, the
420 universe in its essential nature is composed of two things, namely matter
and the void in which matter is located and moves in every direction. The
existence of matter is proved by universal sensation; and unless in the
first place trust in sensation is established as an unshakeable foundation,[31] there will be no criterion to which we can refer in the case of
things hidden from view in order to verify any matter by reasoning. Then
again, if there were no room and space—void, as we call it—matter
could not be located anywhere, and its movement in any direction would
be absolutely impossible. This is the point I explained to you a little
430 while ago.[32] Besides these nothing exists that you could declare to be
distinct and divorced from both matter and void, whose discovery would
involve the existence of a kind of third constituent. For whatever exists
must be something in its own right; and if it is susceptible of even the
lightest and faintest touch, its very existence ensures that it will increase
the aggregate of matter by an amount either great or small and augment
the total sum. But if it is intangible, having no ability to prevent anything
from passing through it in any direction, then undoubtedly it will be that
empty space which we call void.

440   Moreover, whatever exists as a separate entity will either act upon
something or submit to being acted upon by other things, or its nature
will be such that things can exist and happen in it. But nothing can act or
be acted upon, unless it is corporeal; and again, nothing except void and
vacuity can provide space.

Therefore, apart from void and matter, no third constituent with a
separate existence can be allowed to remain in the aggregate of things,
such as might at any time be perceived by our senses or apprehended by
the exercise of reason.

---

30. **410–417:** Engagingly, Lucr. makes gentle fun of his missionary zeal, though
one should not doubt that he is completely serious in his declared readiness to do
whatever is necessary in his attempt to convert Memmius to Epicureanism (see
140–145). Although this passage is Lucr.'s own, he may have taken his cue from
Epicurus, who at the end of *On Nature* 28 makes fun of his garrulity; and so may
Diogenes of Oinoanda, author of the massive Epicurean inscription (see pp. xx–
xxi), who humorously mentions the vast number of letters he has converted into
stone for the information and salvation of his readers (*fr.* 116).

31. **422–425:** Sensation, according to the Epicureans, is the primary standard of
truth. Cf. 693–700, 4.478–521, and see pp. xxiv–xxv.

32. **429:** 335–345, 370–383.

You will find that all predicable things are either properties or accidents   450
of matter and void.[33] A property is what cannot under any circumstances
be severed and separated from a body without the divorce involving
destruction: such is the relationship of heaviness to rocks, heat to fire,
liquidity to water, touch to all matter, intangibility to void. On the other
hand, to slavery, poverty and wealth, freedom, war, concord, and all
other things whose coming and going does not impair the essential nature
of a thing, we regularly apply the appropriate term accidents. Likewise
time has no independent existence: rather from events themselves is   460
derived a sense of what has occurred in time past, of what is happening at
present, and of what is to follow in the future; and it must be admitted
that no one has a sense of time as an independent entity, but only as
something relative to the movement of things and their restful calm.

Again, when people assert that the rape of Tyndareus' daughter[34] and
the subjugation of the people of Troy in war are facts, beware of possibly
being trapped by them into an acknowledgment that these events have an
independent existence, simply because those generations of human
beings, of whom they were accidents, have been swept away beyond
recall by ages past. For it could be said that any event is an accident   470
either of the whole earth or of the actual regions in which it occurred.
Moreover, if there had been no material substance, and no place and
space in which all things happen, the beauty of Tyndareus' daughter
would never have fanned into flame the fire of passion smoldering deep
in Phrygian Alexander's[35] heart, so kindling the blazing strife of savage
war; nor would the wooden horse, unknown to the Trojans, have
discharged from its pregnant womb under cover of night the Greeks who
filled Pergama[36] with flames. From this you may clearly see that all
events without exception have, unlike matter, no independent existence,
and cannot be said to exist in the same sense as void; rather you may with   480
justification term them accidents of matter, or of space in which all things
happen.

My next contention is that two kinds of bodies are to be distinguished:
there are primary elements of things, and objects compounded of primary elements. As for the primary elements, no force has power to
extinguish them, for the solidity of their substance assures them of victory in the end. And yet it seems difficult to believe that it is possible to

---

33. **449–482:** On properties and accidents, see also Epicurus *Hdt.* 40, 68–73.

34. **464:** Helen of Troy.

35. **474:** Paris.

36. **476:** The citadel of Troy.

find any body composed of solid matter. For the thunderbolt from the sky
490 penetrates the walls of houses, as do voices and sounds; iron grows
white-hot in the furnace, and rocks exposed to the ferocity of fervent fire
splinter apart; gold, for all its firmness, is dissolved and liquefied by heat,
and icy bronze, mastered by the flame, melts; warmth and penetrating
cold filter through silver, as is proved by our experience of first one, then
the other, when, in accordance with custom, we hold cup in hand while
sparkling water is poured in from above. Such is the strength of the
evidence that the universe seemingly contains nothing solid. But true
reasoning about the nature of things cannot be defied; so give me your
500 attention while in the space of a few verses I prove that bodies composed
of solid and indestructible matter do exist. It is these which, according to
our teaching, are the seeds and primary elements of things, the constituents and components of the universe.

In the first place, since our investigations have shown that the two
elements, matter and the void in which all things happen, have two
completely different natures, each must be an independent, uncompounded entity. For wherever there is empty space, which we term void,
there is no matter; and again, wherever matter is stationed, under no
510 circumstances is there empty void. It follows that the ultimate particles
are solid and contain no void.

Moreover, since created things contain void, the void must be surrounded by solid matter: nothing can be shown by valid argument to
contain void concealed in its substance, unless you concede that what
confines the void is solid; and the only thing capable of keeping in
confinement the void within objects is an aggregate of matter. Therefore
matter, which consists of solid substance, is able to be everlasting, even
though all compound bodies suffer dissolution.

520 There is the further point that, if there were no empty space, the whole
universe would consist of solid matter; conversely, if there were no
definite bodies to fill the places which they occupy, the whole universe
would be space, vacuum, and void. So it is evident that matter and void
are interspersed and alternate with one another, since the universe is
neither a complete plenum nor a complete vacuum. There are, therefore,
definite bodies that have the effect of interspersing empty space with
full space. These bodies cannot be shattered by the impact of blows
from without, nor can their fabric be penetrated and so unraveled from
530 within, nor can they be demolished by any other kind of assault; this
is a point I explained to you a little while ago.[37] For obviously it is

---

37. **531:** 215–264, 485–502.

impossible for anything containing no void to be crushed or smashed or cut in two, or for it to admit any of the forces fatal to all compound things—moisture, permeating cold, and penetrating fire. And the more void each thing holds within it, the more its internal structure is weakened by the assaults of these forces. So if the ultimate particles are, as I have taught, solid and without void, they must of necessity be everlasting.

Besides, if matter had not been everlasting, before now all things 540 would have returned to nothing, and everything we see must have been reborn from nothing. But since I have shown above[38] that nothing can be created out of nothing or, once born, reduced to nothing, the first elements must consist of imperishable substance, into which everything can be resolved at its last hour, so that a constant supply of matter may be available for the renewal of things. Therefore the primary elements are solid and simple; otherwise they could not have been preserved through the ages and so renewed things from infinite time past. 550

Again, if nature had appointed no limit beyond which things cannot be broken up, the particles of matter would already have been so pulverized by the destructive hand of past ages that nothing could within a specific length of time be conceived from them and win its way to the prime of life. For it is an observable fact that anything can be destroyed faster than it can be reconstructed; and so what eternity's long duration of days and all time past would already have disarranged and disintegrated could 560 never be repaired in the rest of time. But as it is, it is evident that a definite and permanent limit to the process of destruction has been established, since we observe that each thing is renewed, and that for every kind of being there is established a specific period of time in which it is able to attain the bloom of maturity.

There is the further point that, once it is allowed that void is an ingredient in things, the absolute solidity of the ultimate particles of matter can be reconciled with an explanation of the formation and behavior of all soft substances—air, water, earth, and fire.[39] On the other 570

---

38. **543:** 149–264.

39. **567:** The four elements of Empedocles, whose theory is criticized in 716–829. Their perishability is one of Lucr.'s objections in that passage, and it is also one of his arguments for the mortality of the world in 5.235–323. Here he may be thinking not only of Empedocles, but also of Anaxagoras (see 847–856) and those who, like Heraclitus (see 635–704), chose one of the four substances as the primary element.

hand, if the primary elements of things were soft, the origin of hard flintstones and iron would be inexplicable, because nature as a whole would be without any initial foundation. The elements therefore derive their power from their solidity and simplicity, and it is their concentration in denser union that enables all compound bodies to be closely compacted and display stalwart strength.

Moreover, even on the supposition that no limit to the division of matter has been established,[40] it must be admitted that particles corresponding to every kind of thing have survived to this day from time 580 everlasting, hitherto immune to the danger of any attack. But since such particles are by nature fragile, the supposition does not tally with the fact that they have succeeded in surviving from time everlasting in spite of having been battered through the ages by innumerable blows.

Furthermore, since in the case of each species, a fixed limit of growth and tenure of life has been established, and since the powers of each have been defined by solemn decree in accordance with the ordinances of nature, and since, so far from any species being susceptible of variation, each is so constant that from generation to generation all the variegated 590 birds display on their bodies the distinctive markings of their kind, it is evident that their bodies must consist of unchanging substance. For, if the primary elements of things could be overpowered and changed by any means, it would be impossible to determine what can arise and what cannot, and again by what law each thing has its scope restricted and its deeply implanted boundary stone;[41] and it would be equally impossible for the generations within each species to conform so consistently to the nature, habits, mode of life, and movements of their parents.

600   Then again,[42] since each of those ultimate particles that are beneath the ken of our senses has an extreme point, that point is evidently without parts and is the smallest existence; it never has had and never will be able to have an independent, separate existence, since it is itself a primary and unitary part of something else. Then rank upon rank of similar parts in

---

40. **577–583:** Lucr.'s main target here is Anaxagoras, for whom matter is infinitely divisible (see 843–844).

41. **595–596:** Identical to 76–77 (see note there), 5.89–90, 6.65–66.

42. **599–634:** The doctrine that each atom, though physically indivisible, has a limited number of inseparable "smallest parts," which are the minima of extension and magnitude, is expounded by Epicurus *Hdt.* 56–59. Lucr. introduces it again at 746–752, where he is criticizing Empedocles and others who think like him, and at 2.478–499, where he is arguing that the number of atomic shapes is not infinite.

close formation provide the ultimate particle with its full complement of substance and, since they cannot have an independent existence, they must cling so fast to the whole atom that they cannot by any means be wrenched apart from it. The primary elements are therefore solid and simple, being formed of smallest parts packed solid in a closely cohering 610 mass; they are not compounded as a result of the assembly of those parts, but rather derive their power from their everlasting simplicity; nature does not allow anything to be torn away or subtracted from them and so preserves the seeds of things.

Moreover, if there is no smallest point, every minutest body will be composed of an infinite number of parts, since a half of a half will always have a half and there will be no limit to the possibility of division. If this is the case, what will distinguish the whole universe from the smallest thing in it? Nothing; for, no matter how fully infinite is the whole 620 universe, the minutest objects will equally be composed of an infinite number of parts. But since sound judgment loudly protests against this conclusion and denies that the mind can believe it, you must admit defeat and acknowledge the existence of points that have no parts and are the smallest things; and this being so, you must also acknowledge the existence of solid and everlasting primary elements.

Lastly, if it had been creative nature's way to compel all things to be resolved into their smallest parts, she would no longer be able to renew 630 anything out of them, because objects that are insufficiently bulky to have any parts cannot possess the essential characteristics of generative matter, namely the variety of interlacements, weights, collisions, concurrences, and movements that cause all things to happen.

And so those who have thought that fire is the ultimate substance of things, and that fire is the sole constituent of the universe, have obviously deviated far from the path of sound judgment. The first to join battle as their leader was Heraclitus,[43] whose dark sayings gained him a bril-

---

43. **638:** Epicurean writers, like writers from other philosophical schools, devoted much space to refutation of rival theories and were often less than completely fair to their opponents. Lucr. is no exception: it has been calculated by K. Kleve, "The Philosophical Polemics in Lucretius," in O. Gigon (ed.), *Lucrèce* (Fondation Hardt: Geneva, 1978) 39–75, that more than 15 percent of his work is openly polemical, and, as the following treatment of Heraclitus, Empedocles, and Anaxagoras shows, he does not always fully and accurately present the views that he criticizes. Like Diogenes of Oinoanda (*fr.* 6), he begins his review of rival theories of matter (635–920) with Heraclitus of Ephesus (c.540–c.480 B.C.), who, believing that everything is in flux, and that equilibrium in the world is

640 liant reputation among Greeks noted for their frivolity rather than for
their serious pursuit of the truth. For fools always have a greater admira-
tion and liking for any idea that they see obscured in a mist of paradoxical language, and adopt as true what succeeds in prettily tickling their
ears and is painted with a specious sound.[44]
I demand to know how things can be marked by such variety, if they
are made of fire pure and simple. The condensation or rarefaction of hot
fire would be ineffectual if the parts of fire retained the same nature as
650 that of the whole mass of fire. For the result would simply be fiercer heat

maintained by a constant struggle of opposites, regarded fire, which exemplifies
these two central doctrines, as the controlling form of matter. Probably the main
reason why Lucr. and Diogenes make Heraclitus their first target is that he had
much influence on the physical theory of the Stoics, who were the chief philosophical opponents of the Epicureans in their day. Unlike Diogenes, Lucr. never
mentions the Stoics by name, and some influential modern scholars believe that
he never has them in mind. But apart from the intrinsic implausibility of the
supposition that one who shows himself keenly aware of the contemporary moral
and social scene (see, for example, 3.59–86, 1053–1075) and the contemporary
religious scene (see notes on 6.45, 86–89) should have no awareness of the
contemporary philosophical scene, it is indisputable that he does mention views
held by the Stoics: for example, in 5.156–234, where he argues that the world
was not made by the gods for the benefit of human beings, he makes points
identical to those made by Diogenes, who names the Stoics as his opponents (see
notes on 5.156–173, 200–203). How in such a case can one reasonably deny that
he too is targeting them? Even when he reproduces arguments that Epicurus was
directing not against the Stoics, but against other opponents (Plato, for example),
this does not necessarily mean that he is criticizing exactly the same opponents:
Epicurus' followers were quite capable of adopting their master's arguments
while intending them for different or wider targets. At 641, and again at 1068,
Lucr. calls his opponents *stolidi,* "fools," which is surely meant to suggest *Stoici,*
"Stoics": the word is not used by him elsewhere and, as well as involving the sort
of verbal play that is characteristic of him (see note on 117–118), is most
satisfyingly insulting, especially in view of the Stoic opinion that everyone
except the wise man as conceived by the Stoic is a fool.

44. **639–644:** Heraclitus was noted, or notorious, for his paradoxical and oracu-
lar pronouncements. Lucr., who prides himself on his clarity (136–137, 143–
145, 933–934 [identical to 4.8–9]), naturally disapproves of Heraclitus' deliberate obscurity, and the preposterous metaphor "painted with a specious sound"
(644) is the climax of his mockery of him and his admirers. In view of Heraclitus'
monistic theory, his riddling language, and his influence on the Stoics, Lucr.
would have dealt with him more harshly than with Empedocles in any case, but
there is also the consideration that, unlike Empedocles, he did not have the saving
grace of being a poet.

when the parts were concentrated, gentler heat wh
and dissipated. Beyond this there is no effect that
possible under such circumstances; still less could
things be derived from condensed and rarefied fi
and rarefaction of fire would be possible, only if v
an ingredient in things. But because these think
conflicting with their doctrines, and therefore shrin   ....ng the
existence of pure void in things, their fear of the steep path causes them
to miss the way of truth. They fail to perceive that, if things were   660
deprived of void, all would lose their individuality and condense into a
single body which could not radiate anything rapidly from itself, in the
way that burning fire radiates light and heat, showing you that its parts
are not packed solid.

But if by chance they suppose that fires in combination can be extinguished and alter their substance by some other means, it is evident that,
if they are thoroughgoing in the application of their theory, all heat
without exception will disappear utterly into nothing, and all created
things will come into being from nothing. For every change that involves   670
a thing outstepping its own limits means the instantaneous death of what
previously existed.[45] Therefore something must survive intact for the
creation of things: otherwise you would find everything without exception returning to nothing and the rich array of things being reborn and
growing in strength from nothing. In fact, since there are most definitely
certain particles whose nature always remains the same, but whose coming and going and rearrangement cause compound bodies to alter their
nature and undergo change, it is evident that these ultimate particles do
not consist of fire. The withdrawal and departure of some, the annexation   680
of others, and the rearrangement of some would be ineffectual, so long as
all retained the nature of fire: for whatever they formed would in every
case be fire. The true position, as I see it, is this: there are certain particles
whose concurrences, movements, order, position, and shapes produce
fires; different combinations of them form things of different nature, but
they themselves are unlike fire or any other thing capable of emitting
particles to our sensory organs and affecting our sense of touch by its
contact.

Moreover, to do as Heraclitus does and declare that all things are fire,   690
and that nothing in the aggregate of things has reality except fire, strikes
me as harebrained lunacy. For he uses the senses as a base for an attack
on the senses and, in so doing, undermines the foundation of all our
beliefs and the source of his own knowledge of the fire that he cham-

---

45. **670–671:** Repeated at 792–793, 2.753–754, 3.519–520.

He believes that the senses can correctly identify fire, but not other things which are no less distinct. I regard this attitude as both misleading and mad. For to what criterion shall we appeal? What can be more reliable than our own senses as the test of truth and falsehood?[46] Moreover, why should anyone dispense with everything else and wish to keep only the substance of fire rather than deny the existence of fire and acknowledge the existence of some other substance? It is plain that either course is equally preposterous.

And so those who have thought that the ultimate substance of things is fire, and that the universe can consist of fire, and those who have chosen air[47] as the original constituent material of things, or those who have thought that water[48] by itself forms things, or that earth[49] creates everything and converts itself into the substance of all things—all these thinkers have evidently strayed far from the path of truth. So have those who recognize two first principles, partnering air with fire[50] or earth with water,[51] and those who suppose that all things are developed from four elements—fire, earth, air, and water. Chief among them is Empedocles of Acragas,[52] a son of the triangular island around whose deeply indented coasts flows the Ionian deep, showering brine from gray-green waves; its fringe is divided from the coasts of the Aeolian land[53] by a narrow channel and the surge of an impetuous sea. Here is yawning

---

46. **693–700:** Cf. 422–425, 4.478–521.

47. **707:** Anaximenes and Diogenes of Apollonia.

48. **708:** Thales.

49. **709:** Pherecydes (?).

50. **713:** Oenopides (?).

51. **713:** Xenophanes.

52. **716:** Empedocles (c.493–c.433 B.C.) of Acragas (Latin Agrigentum) in Sicily ("the triangular island") expounded his philosophy in two hexameter poems, *On Nature* and *Purifications.* Considerable fragments of the poems survive, and some new fragments of *On Nature,* preserved on papyrus, have been published in A. Martin and O. Primavesi, *L'Empédocle de Strasbourg* (de Gruyter: Berlin, 1999). (The recent suggestion that *On Nature* and *Purifications* are alternative titles of a single work is unlikely to be correct: for the arguments against it, see D. Sedley, *Lucretius and the Transformation of Greek Wisdom* 2–10.) Although Lucr. rejects Empedocles' theory of matter, he much admires him as a poet and takes him as a model. Empedocles was not only a philosopher, but also a mystic: in one fragment he claims to be a god; and Lucr., in 733, may have this passage in mind.

53. **721:** Southwest Italy.

Charybdis;[54] here rumbling Etna threatens to reassemble her angry flames in readiness to belch fire from her throat in another violent eruption and once more shoot to the sky flakes of flame. There are many reasons why this country is regarded with awe and wonder by the peoples of the world and is reputed to merit a visit; it is rich in good things and bulwarked with a strong force of men; yet assuredly it has owned nothing more splendid than this man, nothing held in greater reverence, 730 wonder, and affection. Why, the verses molded by his divine genius give so magisterial an exposition of his splendid discoveries that it seems scarcely credible that he was born of mortal stock.

He and those very markedly inferior and far less important theorists whom I mentioned above made many fine and inspired discoveries and from the innermost shrine of their hearts delivered oracles more holy and much more reliable than those that the Pythia pronounces from the tripod and bay of Phoebus.[55] Yet in the matter of the primary elements of 740 things they came to grief; and on this point the fall of these great men was great and heavy.

In the first place, although they exclude void, they permit movement, and they acknowledge the existence of soft and porous things—air, sunlight, water, earth, animals, and plants—even though they fail to add void as an ingredient in their substance.

Secondly, they suppose that there is no limit at all to the divisibility of bodies, no stop set to their breaking, and no smallest part whatsoever in things, whereas our observation that each object contains an extreme point, which is the smallest part perceptible to our senses, justifies the 750 inference that invisible things too contain an extreme point which is their smallest part.[56]

There is the further point that, since they assume the primary elements to be soft things—things that we ourselves observe to be subject to birth

---

54. **722:** A dangerous whirlpool on the Sicilian side of the Straits of Messina, opposite Scylla (see note on 4.732).

55. **737–739:** The Pythia is the priestess of Apollo (Phoebus) at Delphi, who delivered the oracles. A tripod served as her throne. The bay or sweet laurel (*laurus nobilis*), not to be confused with the poisonous plant now known as laurel (*prunus laurocerasus*), was sacred to Apollo. In order to augment her inspiration, the Pythia may have chewed bay leaves. Lines 738–739 are repeated at 5.111–112, where Lucr. refers to his own pronouncements. Epicurus too compares himself to an oracle (*VS* 29); see also Philodemus *On Piety* (ed. D. Obbink) 2043–2046, Cicero *Fin.* 2.20, 102, *DND* 1.66; Diogenes Laertius 10.12.

56. **746–752:** See 599–634 and the note there. Here Lucr.'s point is that, just as each visible object has a visible minimum, so the invisible atoms must have a minimum.

and wholly of mortal substance—the universe must by now have returned to nothing, and the rich array of things must have been reborn and
grown in strength from nothing; and by this time you will have realized
how far both these notions are removed from the truth.

    Then again, their primary elements are in many ways hostile, indeed
760 poison, to one another; and so, when they clash, either they will perish or
they will disperse, just as we see lightning, rain, and wind disperse when
a tempest has gathered.

    Moreover, if everything is formed from four substances, and if every-
thing is resolved into them, how is it any more justifiable to call those
substances the primary elements of things than to suppose the reverse
and declare that things are the primary elements of those substances? For
the two come into being from one another and have been exchanging
their aspect and whole nature with one another from all eternity.

770 But if by chance you imagine that fire and the substance of earth and
breezy air and sparkling water combine in such a way that the union
involves no alteration of their nature, you will find that nothing can be
formed from them, whether animate, or of inanimate substance like a
tree. The fact is that in the mixture of this heterogeneous mass each
element will exhibit its own special quality: air will be seen to be intermingled with earth, and fire will be seen to remain with water. In reality,
for the creation of things the essential attribute of the primary elements is
780 an indeterminate and imperceptible quality, in order to preclude the
protrusion of any antagonistic feature that might prevent each created
thing from having its own distinctive character.

    Some[57] go so far as to make the sky and its fires their starting point,
claiming that fire first changes itself into breezy air, that air produces
water, that water creates earth, and that inversely all are changed back
from earth—first moisture, then air, finally heat; and they suppose that
these substances continually experience interchange as they pass from
heaven to earth, from earth to the stars in the sky. But under no circum-
790 stances should primary elements do this. Something must survive insus-
ceptible of change: otherwise everything would be utterly annihilated.
For every change that involves a thing outstepping its own limits means
the instantaneous death of what previously existed.[58] Therefore, since
the four substances which I mentioned just now are transmuted into one
another, they must be composed of other elements that cannot ever

---

57. **782:** Aristotle (*De Generatione et Corruptione* 2.4) and the Stoics (Cicero
DND 2.84, 3.30–31).

58. **789–793:** Repeated at 2.750–754. Lines 792–793 occur also at 670–671
and 3.519–520.

undergo transformation: otherwise you would find everything being utterly annihilated. Why not rather assume the existence of certain particles endowed with such a nature that, if they happen to have created fire,
they can also, after experiencing a few gains and a few losses together   800
with modification of order and movement, produce breezy air, and that
this is how all other things are changed into one another?

"But," you object, "the plain facts clearly show that all things derive
their nourishment from the earth and grow from it up into the breezy air;
and unless the season is generous with rain at the proper time, making the
vegetation quiver beneath the melting storm clouds, and unless the sun
for its part cherishes things by imparting heat, growth is impossible for
crops, trees, and animals." This is true: indeed, if we ourselves were not
supported by solid food and soft liquid, we should suffer loss of sub-   810
stance, and all the life would be drained from all our sinews and bones.
For unquestionably we, like other things and others again, are sustained
and nourished by specific substances. Undoubtedly the reason why
different things are nourished by different substances is that many primary elements common to many things are combined in things in many
ways. And it is often of great consequence in what groupings and positions the same primary elements are combined, and what motions they
reciprocally impart and receive.[59] For the same atoms constitute sky, sea,   820
lands, rivers, and sun; the same compose crops, trees, and animals;[60]
only they differ in their combinations and movements. Similarly,
throughout these verses of mine you see many letters common to many
words, even though you must concede that the verses and the words
differ both in sense and in resonant sound. Such is the power letters
derive from mere alteration of order.[61] But the primary elements have at
their disposal several other means of variation to enable them to create
the whole multiplicity of things.

Now let us move on to examine the theory of Anaxagoras.[62] The   830
Greeks term it "homoiomereia," but the inadequacy of the Latin lan-

---

59. **817–819:** Cf. 908–910, 2.760–762, 883–885, 1007–1009.

60. **820–821:** Cf. 2.1015–1016.

61. **823–829:** See note on 196–198.

62. **830:** Anaxagoras (c.500–c.428 B.C.), a native of Clazomenae in Ionia (western Asia Minor), lived in Athens from c.456 until c.436, when he was banished
for impiety. His theory is subtle and difficult. Like the atomists, he believed that
matter exists in the form of an infinite number of separate particles; unlike them,
he regarded the particles as heterogeneous in substance, and matter as infinitely
indivisible. The Greek *homoiomereia* (a term probably not used by Anaxagoras

guage[63] denies us a name for it in our own tongue; nevertheless an
exposition of the actual theory presents no difficulties.

First, you must understand that, when he speaks of the "homoiomereia" of things, what he means is this: bones are composed of infinitesimally small particles of bone, and flesh of infinitesimally small
particles of flesh; blood is formed by the confluence of many drops of
840   blood; gold is composed of grains of gold, and earth is a concretion of
tiny particles of earth; fire consists of particles of fire, water of particles
of water; and everything else he supposes to be produced in the same
way. And yet he refuses to recognize the existence of any void in things,
or of a limit to the divisibility of matter. So I consider that on both these
points he goes as far astray as the theorists of whom we spoke above.[64]

There is the further point that his primary elements are too fragile, if
indeed the term "primary elements" can be applied to particles that are
endowed with the same nature as the very things they form, and that, like
850   them, are subject to strain and to death and have nothing to rein them
back from destruction. For which of them will defy grinding force, so as
to elude destruction in the very teeth of death? Fire or water or air?
Which of these? Blood or bones? None, in my opinion: for all without
exception will be essentially as perishable as perceptible objects whose
destruction, when they succumb to some force, we witness with our own
eyes. In fact, nothing can return to nothing or grow from nothing; for
proof of this I refer you to the demonstrations already provided.[65]

860   Moreover, since food strengthens and nourishes our bodies, presumably our veins, blood, bones, and sinews are composed of heterogeneous
particles;[66] alternatively, if it is claimed that every kind of food is of
composite substance and contains tiny pieces of sinew together with
particles of bones, veins, and blood, then all food, whether solid or
liquid, must be supposed to consist of heterogeneous elements and to be
compounded of bones, sinews, serum, and blood. Furthermore, if the
particles of all things that grow from the earth are contained in the
particles of earth, the earth must be composed of heterogeneous sub-
870   stances that spring up out of it. Apply this reasoning to other objects, and

---

himself) means "similarity of parts." Anaxagoras thought that each substance is
divisible into parts like each other and like the whole.

63. **831–832:** Cf. 139, 3.260.

64. **846:** Heraclitus, Empedocles, and company. See 658, 742–752.

65. **858:** See 149–264.

66. **860:** A line has been lost after 860. I have translated Lambinus' stopgap *et
nervos alienigenis ex partibus esse.*

you may use the very same phraseology. If flame, smoke, and ash are concealed in logs, logs must be composed of heterogeneous substances that spring up out of them. Moreover, all the bodies that the earth sustains and strengthens . . . .[67]

At this stage there remains a faint chance of evading the hand of justice; and Anaxagoras seizes it by supposing that everything is mixed imperceptibly in everything, but that the only visible substance is the one that contributes to the mixture most particles and those stationed most conspicuously in the foremost positions. But this supposition is far re- 880
moved from the true explanation. For if it were correct, we should expect corn, when bruised by the pestle's formidable force, often to emit a trace of blood or one of those substances that are nourished in our bodies; and when we grind the corn with stone on stone, we should expect a trickle of blood to appear. In the same way grass and water ought often to exude drops with the sweet flavor of milk from the udders of a fleecy ewe; and when lumps of earth are pulverized, surely different kinds of grasses and cereals and leaves should often be revealed, dispersed in minute particles 890
in the earth that conceals them; and (my last example) when wood is snapped, ash and smoke and minute, hidden particles of fire should be visible. Since experience clearly teaches that none of these things happens, you may be sure that things are not mixed in this way in other things, but hidden seeds common to many things must be combined in things in many ways.

"But," you object, "it is a common occurrence on mighty mountains for the topmost points of neighboring tall trees to be rubbed together under the stress of southerly gales until they burst into a flashing flower 900
of flame." This is true; but there is no fire implanted in the wood: rather there are many seeds susceptible of combustion that cause conflagrations in the forests, when friction has made them stream together.[68] If ready-made flame were secreted in the wood, the fire could not remain latent for an instant: it would consume the forests everywhere and reduce the trees to ashes. Do you see now that, as I said a little earlier,[69] it is often of very great consequence in what groupings and positions the same primary elements are combined, and what motions they reciprocally impart 910
and receive, and do you see that a slight change in arrangement enables the same atoms to produce fires and wood? It is the same with the words

---

67. **873–874:** The text of the manuscripts does not make sense. I follow those editors who invert the order of the lines and assume a lacuna after them.

68. **897–903:** Cf. 5.1094–1100.

69. **907:** At 817–819. See note there.

themselves when, with a slight rearrangement of the letters, we designate "fires" and "conifers"[70] by distinct sounds.

Lastly, if you cannot explain what you see happening in the perceptible world without supposing that the particles of matter possess the same nature as the objects they compose, this is the way to destroy your primary elements: the consequence will be that they will shake and
920 tremble with uncontrollable laughter and moisten their faces and cheeks with briny tears.[71]

Now then, learn what follows and hear it more clearly.[72] I am fully sensible of the obscurity of my subject; but a high hope of glory has struck my heart sharply with its inspiring thyrsus, and at the same time has injected into my breast sweet love of the Muses; this is what impels me now to penetrate by power of intellect the remote regions of the Pierian maids,[73] hitherto untrodden by any foot. Joyfully I visit virgin springs and draw their water; joyfully I cull unfamiliar flowers, gathering
930 for my head a chaplet of fame from spots whence the Muses have never before taken a garland for the brows of any person: first because I teach about important matters and endeavor to disentangle the mind from the strangling knots of superstition, and also because on an obscure subject I compose such luminous verses, overspreading all with the charm of the Muses. For obviously my actual technique does not lack a motive. Doctors who try to give children foul-tasting wormwood[74] first coat the rim of the cup with the sweet juice of golden honey; their intention is that the
940 children, unwary at their tender age, will be tricked into applying their lips to the cup and at the same time will drain the bitter draught of wormwood—victims of beguilement, but not of betrayal, since by this means they recover strength and health. I have a similar intention now:

70. **914:** "Fires and conifers" represents Lucr.'s *ligna atque ignes* (pieces of wood and fires), where the two nouns share the letters *ign.*

71. **915–920:** The reductio ad absurdum is characteristic of Lucr., especially when he is ending an argument. Cf. e.g. 2.973–990, a passage that includes two lines (976–977) very similar to 1.919–920; cf. also 3.367–369, 776–783.

72. **921:** Or the meaning may be "and hear a clearer theme." The passage 921–950, most of which (926–950) is repeated (with minor alterations) at the beginning of Book 4 (1–25), is poetically brilliant and also of the greatest importance for its revelation of Lucr.'s philosophical mission and of his firm belief that his poetic art can help him to fulfill that mission.

73. **926:** The Muses.

74. **936:** Wormwood (*Artemisia absinthium*), one of the bitterest of plants, is efficacious as a vermifuge and is recommended by the medical writer Celsus for the treatment of sore throat (4.7.3) and various stomach problems (4.12.2, 4, 6).

since this philosophy of ours often appears somewhat off-putting to those who have not experienced it, and most people recoil back from it, I have preferred to expound it to you in harmonious Pierian poetry and, so to speak, coat it with the sweet honey of the Muses. My hope has been that by this means I might perhaps succeed in holding your attention concentrated on my verses, while you fathom the nature of the universe and the 950 form of its structure.

Now then, since I have demonstrated that indestructible particles of absolutely solid matter fly about incessantly throughout eternity, let us reveal whether there is a limit to their sum or not; let us establish also whether the void whose existence we have discovered, the place and space in which everything happens, is essentially finite, or whether it opens out to boundless breadth and abyssal depth.

In fact, the universe is not bounded in any direction; otherwise it would inevitably have an extremity. Now it is plain that nothing can have 960 an extremity, unless there is something on the farther side to bound it, so that there is seen to be a point beyond which our vision cannot trace the object. And since we must admit that there is nothing outside the aggregate of things, it has no extremity and therefore has no end or limit.[75] It makes no difference in which area of it you take up your position, because, no matter what place anyone may occupy, the infinite extent of the universe in every direction is not diminished.

Then again, just suppose that all the existing space were finite, and that someone ran forward to the edge of its farthest border and launched a 970 spear into flight: do you favor the view that the spear, cast with virile vigor, would fly far and reach its target, or do you suppose that something could check it by obstructing its course? You must grant and adopt one or the other of these hypotheses, and yet both deny you a subterfuge and compel you to acknowledge that the expanse of the universe is infinite. For whether there is something to check the spear and prevent it from hitting its mark and lodging in its target, or whether it flies on, it did not start from the end of the universe. In this way I will dog you: 980 wherever you locate the farthest border, I will ask about the ultimate fate of the spear. Our conclusion will be that nowhere can a boundary be fixed: no escape will ever be found from the limitless possibility of flight.

Moreover, if the whole extent of the entire aggregate of things were hemmed in on all sides and had fixed borders, so that it was finite, the fund of matter, impelled by its solid weight, would have streamed together from all sides to the bottom; nothing could happen beneath the

---

75. **958–964:** Cf. Epicurus *Hdt.* 41.

pavilion of the sky: indeed there would be no sky at all and no light of the
990   sun, since from time everlasting all matter would have been subsiding
into an inert mass. But, in fact, the ultimate particles are assuredly given
no respite from movement, because there is no bottom at all where they
can congregate and settle. All activity on all sides always takes place in
perpetual motion, and the particles of matter are supplied from below,
darting out of infinite space.

Lastly, before our eyes one thing is seen to bound another: the air sets
1000   a boundary to the hills, and the mountains to the air; the land delimits the
sea, and the sea delimits every land; but the universe has nothing beyond
to bound it.

Therefore the nature of space and the unfathomable depth of its abyss
is such that not even streaks of lightning, gliding through the desert of
eternity, could career through it in their course, nor could their progress
diminish at all the distance that remains to be traveled. Such is the
immensity of the area of space that everywhere lies open to things,
infinite in every direction on every side.

Furthermore, nature denies the aggregate of things the power of con-
fining itself within limits, since she compels matter to be bounded by
1010   void, and void by matter, so that by their alternation she makes the
universe infinite; or else, even if one of the two component parts were
not bounded by the other, the extent of its own simple substance would
be measureless. [But, if space were finite, it could not contain an infinite
amount of matter; and if the aggregate of matter were finite,][76] neither
sea nor land nor the lambent precincts of the sky nor the race of mortals
nor the sacred bodies of the gods[77] could subsist for one short hour of
time. For the fund of matter, wrenched apart from union, would be
disaggregated and carried through the vast void; or, to be more precise, it
1020   would never have concreted to create anything, since its disconnected
elements could not have been united.[78]

Certainly the primary elements did not intentionally and with acute
intelligence dispose themselves in their respective positions, nor did they
covenant to produce their respective motions;[79] but because throughout
the universe from time everlasting countless numbers of them, buffeted
and impelled by blows, have shifted in countless ways, experimentation
with every kind of movement and combination has at last resulted in

---

76. **1013:** A lacuna must be assumed after 1013. The words in brackets give the
likely sense of the missing lines.

77. **1015:** On the Epicurean gods, see pp. xxviii–xxix.

78. **1014–1020:** Cf. Diogenes of Oinoanda *fr.* 67.

79. **1021–1023:** Repeated at 5.419–421.

arrangements such as those that created and compose our world;[80] and
the world, guaranteed preservation through many long years once it had   1030
been directed into harmonious movements, in its turn ensures that the
rivers replenish the insatiable sea with plentiful streams of water, that the
earth, warmed by the sun's fostering heat, renews her produce, that the
family of animals springs up and thrives, and that the gliding ethereal
fires have life. But they could not possibly do this, unless an abundance
of matter were able to issue from infinite space, so that they constantly
make good all their losses in due season. For just as animals, deprived of
food, naturally lose substance and dwindle away, so all things are bound
to disintegrate as soon as their supply of matter, diverted somehow from   1040
its course, has failed. And external blows on all sides cannot conserve the
whole of any world formed by the combination of atoms. By dint of
repeated hammering, the atoms can keep part of it in check temporarily
until reinforcements arrive to make up the sum. Sometimes, however,
they are forced to rebound and thereby give the primary elements of
things ample space and time to escape, enabling them to break loose
from union. So I insist that multitudinous atoms must rise up [out of
space];[81] in fact, there could not even be a succession of blows, if there   1050
were not infinite resources of matter on all sides.

In this connection, Memmius, give a wide berth to the belief of those
who say that all things gravitate toward the center of the world, that
this gravitation enables the world to stand firm without the help of
external blows, and that top and bottom cannot disperse in any direction
because of the universal centripetence—if indeed you believe that anything can be self-supported.[82] They suppose that all heavy objects in the
antipodes press upward and rest on the earth in a reversed position, like   1060
the reflections of things that we observe in water. Similarly they argue
that animals roam upside down and cannot drop off the earth into the
regions of the sky below any more than our bodies can of their own
accord shoot up into the celestial precincts; that inhabitants of the antipodes see the sun when we are looking at the stars of the night; that they
share the seasons with us alternately, and that their nights correspond to
our days.

---

80. **1024–1028:** Cf. 5.187–194, 422–431.

81. **1049:** I have supplied the words in brackets to make the sense clear.

82. **1052–1113:** Although D. J. Furley, *Bulletin of the Institute of Classical
Studies* 13 (1966) 16–23, argues that Lucr. is arguing here only against the
Peripatetics, I have no doubt that he is targeting the Stoics as well. See my note on
this passage in the Loeb edition and the note above on 638.

But[83] these [are fallacies] that fatuous [error has commended] to fools
1070   who cling to [their doctrine with topsy-turvy reasoning. Since the universe is] infinite, there can be no center; and, even if [there were a
center], there is no reason why anything at all should settle there [rather]
than on the contrary [be repelled] far from it. For all room and space—
void [as we term] it—whether at the center or away from the center,
[must] always be nonresistant to heavy bodies, no matter where their
movements carry them. Moreover, bodies do not have access to any
place where they can lose the pull of their weight and come to rest in the
1080   void; and again void, so far from being able to support anything, by
virtue of its own nature must give way at once. Therefore this hypothesis
that things maintain their cohesion through submission to a passion for
the center is impossible.

Furthermore, the same theorists do not imagine that all bodies gravitate toward the center, but only those of earth and moisture—the water of
the sea and the mighty mountain-torrents, and whatever things are, as it
were, embedded in earthy substance; on the other hand, they declare that
the gossamer breezes of air and hot fires fly off from the center, and the
1090   reason why the whole surrounding ether coruscates with stars and the
flaming sun feeds in the azure meadows of the sky is that all the heat
assembles there after its flight from the center; and they deny that the
topmost branches of trees could burst into leaf, if [an internal fire did]
not [mount up] gradually from the earth, [providing] each with nourishment. . . . [But if air and fire have a natural tendency to rise upward,
1102   there is nothing][84] to prevent the ramparts of the world from flying
apart with the volatility of flames and being dispersed throughout the
vast void. Everything else would suffer the same fate: the thunderous
precincts of the sky would rush upward, the earth would suddenly withdraw from beneath our feet, and amid the commingled debris and
disintegration of heaven and earth the whole world would disappear
into the unfathomable void. Thus in an instant nothing would re-
1110   main except deserted space and invisible atoms. For, in whatever part
you suppose that matter first fails, that part will serve as a gate of

---

83. **1068–1075:** A tear in the page of the archetype has robbed us of the ends of
the lines. I have translated Munro's restorations. The same tear was responsible
for the disappearance of 1094–1101.

84. **1094–1101:** The contents of the lacuna (see note on 1068–1075) are
disputed.

death for the world through which the whole throng of matter will sally out.

So a little effort will lead you to a mastery of these problems. Light will be shed on one thing after another, and blinding night will not blot out your path. Truth will illumine truth until you gain a clear insight into nature's profoundest principles.

BOOK TWO

It is comforting,[1] when winds are whipping up the waters of the vast sea, to watch from land the severe trials of another person: not that anyone's distress is a cause of agreeable pleasure; but it is comforting to see from what troubles you yourself are exempt. It is comforting also to witness mighty clashes of warriors embattled on the plains, when you have no share in the danger. But nothing is more blissful than to occupy the heights effectively fortified by the teaching of the wise, tranquil sanctuaries from which you can look down upon others and see them wander- 10 ing everywhere in their random search for the way of life, competing for intellectual eminence, disputing about rank, and striving night and day with prodigious effort to scale the summit of wealth and to secure power.[2] O minds of mortals, blighted by your blindness! Amid what deep darkness and daunting dangers life's little day is passed! To think that you should fail to see that nature importunately demands only that the

---

1. **1–13:** Of these lines C. Bailey says that "to almost all readers [they] have an unpleasant taste of egoism and even of cruelty." In reply, two points may be made. One is that Lucr. is careful to stress that pleasure is derived not from the suffering of other people, but from the thought that one is not sharing it, and surely what he says is true. The other point is that, although the Epicureans experienced enhanced pleasure when they compared their own tranquillity and happiness with the discontent and unhappiness of the unenlightened, they made it their business to bring the message of truth and salvation to those in ignorance of it, and of course Lucr. was no exception. It is to be noted that his views in this passage are in line not only with those of Epicurus (see Cicero *Fin.* 1.62), but also with those of some eminent thinkers of more recent times, including David Hume and Edmund Burke, the relevant passages of whom are quoted by W. A. Merrill, *T. Lucreti Cari De Rerum Natura libri sex* (American Book Company: New York, 1907) 398–399.

2. **12–13:** Repeated at 3.62–63.

body may be rid of pain, and that the mind, divorced from anxiety and
fear, may enjoy a feeling of contentment![3]

20   And so we see that the nature of the body is such that it needs few
things, namely those that banish pain and, in so doing, succeed in be-
stowing pleasures in plenty. Even if the halls contain no golden figures of
youths, clasping flaring torches in their right hands to supply light for
banquets after dark,[4] even if the house lacks the luster of silver and the
glitter of gold, even if no gold-fretted ceiling rings to the sound of the
lyre, those who follow their true nature never feel cheated of enjoyment
30   when they lie in friendly company on velvety turf near a running brook
beneath the branches of a tall tree and provide their bodies with simple
but agreeable refreshment, especially when the weather smiles and the
season of the year spangles the green grass with flowers.[5] Fiery fevers
quit your body no quicker, if you toss in embroidered attire of blushing
crimson, than if you must lie sick in a common garment.

Therefore, since neither riches nor rank nor the pomp of power have
any beneficial effect upon our bodies, we must assume that they are
40   equally useless to our minds. Or when you watch your legions swarming
over the spacious Plain[6] in vigorous imitation of war, reinforced with
numerous reserves and powerful cavalry, uniform in their armor, uniform in their spirit, can it be that these experiences strike terror into your
irrational notions, causing them to flee in panic from your mind? Can it
be that the fears of death leave your breast disburdened and eased of
care? But if we recognize that these suppositions are absurd and ridiculous, because in reality people's fears and the cares at their back dread
50   neither the din of arms nor cruel darts, and strut boldly among kings and
potentates, respecting neither the glitter of gold nor the brilliant luster of
purple raiment, how can you doubt that philosophy alone possesses the
power to resist them? All the more so, because life is one long struggle in

---

3. **16–19:** For the Epicurean doctrine that the aim is to maximize pleasure and
minimize pain both for the body and, more importantly, for the mind, see pp.
xxix–xxxi.

4. **24–26:** Lucr. is imitating Homer *Odyssey* 7.100–102.

5. **29–33:** Repeated, with minor alterations, at 5.1392–1396. There Lucr. is
describing how primitive human beings amused themselves, and the purpose of
the repetition is to emphasize that human beings today would do well to go for the
simple and wholesome pleasures enjoyed by their primitive ancestors. Most
pleasure is achieved by limiting one's desires: see pp. xxix–xxxi.

6. **41:** The Campus Martius or "Plain of Mars" beside the Tiber was used by the
Romans for assemblies, recreation, and military exercises. Julius Caesar spent
three months there before marching to Gaul early in 58 B.C., and Lucr. may well
have watched exercises of his army. Cf. 2.323–332.

the gloom. For, just as children tremble and fear everything in blinding
darkness, so we even in daylight sometimes dread things that are no more
terrible than the imaginary dangers that cause children to quake in the
dark.[7] This terrifying darkness that enshrouds the mind must be dispelled   60
not by the sun's rays and the dazzling darts of day, but by study of the
superficial aspect and underlying principle of nature.[8]

Now then, by what motion do the generative particles of matter produce different things and then disintegrate them? By what force are they
compelled to do this? What speed of movement through the vast void has
been granted to them? I will explain; as for you, be sure to lend attentive
ears to my words.

Certainly matter does not cohere in a solid mass, since we observe that
everything loses substance, and we perceive that all things ebb, as it
were, through length of days, as age steals them from our sight. Nev-   70
ertheless the aggregate of things palpably remains intact, because, although the particles that withdraw from each object diminish it by their
departure, they join another object and favor it with increase. They cause
some things to decline, others to mature, but never stay with them. So the
aggregate of things is constantly refreshed, and mortal creatures live by
mutual exchange. Some species grow, others dwindle; at short intervals
the generations of living things are replaced and, like runners, pass on the
torch of life from hand to hand.[9]

If you suppose that the primary elements of things can stay still, and   80
by staying still can produce new motions in compound bodies, you are
straying far from the path of sound judgment. Since they are wandering
through the void, the primary elements of things must all be propelled
either by their own weight or by a chance blow from another atom. For
the consequence of the frequent meetings and collisions that occur as
they move is that they rebound instantly in different directions—not
surprisingly, since their solid weight makes them absolutely firm and
there is no obstruction behind them.

---

7. **55–58:** Francis Bacon, who was well acquainted with Lucr., begins his essay
Of Death thus: "Men fear death as children fear to go into the dark; and as that
natural fear in children is increased with tales, so is the other."

8. **55–61:** Identical to 3.87–93, 6.35–41. Lines 59–61 are identical also to
1.146–148.

9. **79:** Metaphor, already used by Plato *Laws* 776b, from the lampadedromy, a
relay race, either on horseback (as described by Plato *Republic* 328a) or on foot,
in which a lighted torch was passed from competitor to competitor. The race was
associated with certain Athenian festivals.

To grasp more firmly the restless movement of all the particles of
90   matter, remember that the whole universe has no bottom and thus no
place where the ultimate particles could settle; space is infinite and
measureless, being of boundless extent in every direction on every side,
as I proved by sound argument in the course of a lengthy demonstration.[10] Since this is an established fact, it is certain that the ultimate
particles are allowed no rest anywhere in the unfathomable void; rather
they are harried by incessant and various movement, some rebounding to
considerable distances after they have clashed, others leaving short inter-
100 spaces when they have been jerked back from collision. And all those
that are concentrated in closer union and rebound only a very short
distance apart, entangled by the interlacement of their own shapes, form
the basis of tough rock, the bulk of stern steel, and other such substances.
Of the rest that pursue their roving course through the vast void, a few
spring far apart and rebound to considerable distances, thus furnishing us
with unsubstantial air and radiant sunlight; but there are many other
110 atoms roaming the vast void whose inability to adapt their movements to
those of any compound bodies has debarred them from gaining
admittance.

It occurs to me that this activity is mirrored and reflected in a phenomenon of our everyday experience.[11] Watch carefully whenever shafts of
streaming sunlight are allowed to penetrate a darkened room. You will
observe many minute particles mingling in many ways in every part of
the space illuminated by the rays and, as though engaged in ceaseless
120 combat, warring and fighting by squadrons with never a pause, agitated
by frequent unions and disunions. You can obtain from this spectacle a
conception of the perpetual restless movement of the primary elements
in the vast void, insofar as a trivial thing can exemplify important matters
and put us on the track of knowledge.

A further reason why you should devote particular attention to these
particles that are seen to be in commotion in the sun's rays is that such
commotion also implies the existence of movements of matter that are
secret and imperceptible. For you will observe many of those particles,
130 under the impulse of unseen blows, changing course and being forcibly
turned back, now this way, now that way, in every direction. It is evident
that they all derive this random movement from the atoms. First, the
primary elements of things move of their own accord; next, the smallest
atomic aggregates, which are, one might say, nearest in force to the

---

10. **92–94:** See 1.958–1007.

11. **112–124:** This illustration, brilliantly embellished by Lucr., goes back to
Democritus (see Aristotle *De Anima* 404a).

atoms, are impelled by the impact of the unseen blows of the atoms; and they themselves in their turn assail slightly larger compounds. So the scale of movement ascends from the atoms and by degrees passes within the range of our senses, so that eventually movement is extended to those 140 particles that we can perceive in the sun's light, although the blows that cause their movement are imperceptible.

Now, Memmius, the brief account that follows will enable you to understand what swiftness of movement has been granted to the particles of matter. In the first place, when dawn sprinkles the earth with fresh light, and the variegated birds flit through the delicate air, filling the pathless woods with liquid notes, the suddenness with which the rising sun at this time arrays everything with overspreading radiance is manifest and plain for all to see. And yet the heat and crystal light radiated by 150 the sun do not traverse empty space; thus they are compelled to travel more slowly while they cleave their way (so to speak) through billows of air. Moreover, the particles of heat do not move individually, but interwoven with one another in a rounded mass. Thus they are simultaneously hampered by one another and impeded by external circumstances, and these factors compel them to move more slowly. But the primary elements, which are solid and simple, travel through empty void with nothing to retard them from without; they consist of parts combined into a single unity, and their exertions carry them in the same direction that 160 they took in the beginning. Undoubtedly therefore they must be unrivaled in swiftness, and must move much more rapidly than sunlight, racing through a space many times as wide as the expanse of sky that the sun's lightning rays pervade in the same time.

. . . nor[12] [can] they follow up every individual atom and thus observe its behavior.

And yet, in defiance of these facts, certain theorists,[13] ignorant of the properties of matter, believe that, in the absence of divine direction, nature could not conform so obligingly to human requirements by chang- 170 ing the seasons of the year, by producing crops and indeed all the other gifts to which mortals are beckoned by divine pleasure, the leader of their life, their escort, who entices them through the acts of Venus to reproduce their kind so that the human race may be saved from extinc-

---

12. **164:** A passage, probably of considerable length, has been lost after 164. In it Lucr. will have completed his proof of the speed of the atoms, and, in view of what he says in 167 ff., he may have gone on to explain how ever-moving atoms formed and form the world and everything in it.

13. **167:** Plato and the Stoics.

tion. In supposing that the gods have arranged everything for the benefit of humanity, these thinkers have obviously deviated far from the path of sound judgment in every respect. For even if I had no knowledge of the primary elements of things, I would venture to deduce from the actual
180 behavior of the sky, and from many other facts, evidence and proof that the world was by no means created for us by divine agency: it is marked by such serious flaws. Later, Memmius, I will make this plain to you;[14] but now I will complete my explanation of the movements of atoms.

I feel that I have now reached the point in my argument when I should establish for you the further principle that no corporeal thing can by its own force be carried upward or travel upward. In this connection, do not be deceived by the particles of flames. Certainly flames tend upward at their birth and as they increase, and lustrous crops and trees grow upward
190 too, though all bodies, left to themselves, are drawn downward by their weight. But when fires leap up to the roofs of houses and lick beams and rafters with darting flame, it must not be supposed that they do this spontaneously and shoot up without any external constraint. The situation is similar to that when blood let from our body springs spurting up in the air and sprinkles gore. Do you not observe too with what force water spits out beams and timbers? When a team of us has struggled to depress them with all our might, the more we have thrust them straight down, the more impetuously the water spews them up and returns them to the
200 surface, causing the greater part of their bulk to emerge with a leap. And yet we do not doubt, I think, that all these substances, left to themselves, are carried downward through empty space. Flames must be no exception: when subjected to pressure, they are able to mount upward through the breezy air; but the natural tendency of their weight is to fight to pull them down. Again, do you not observe the high-flying torches of the nocturnal sky trailing long trains of flame in whatever direction nature
210 has given them passage? Do you not perceive stars falling to earth? The sun from the zenith distributes its heat in every direction, and broadcasts its radiance upon the fields; thus the sun's heat, also, inclines toward the earth. You perceive lightning flashes streaking crosswise through rainstorms, when, now from this side, now from that, the fires tear out of the clouds and dart together; frequently the force of their flame falls upon the earth.

In this connection, I am anxious that you should grasp a further point: when the atoms are being drawn downward through the void by their

---

14. **182:** The reference is to 5.195–234. Lines 2.177–181 are almost identical to 5.195–199.

property of weight, at absolutely unpredictable times and places they deflect slightly from their straight course, to a degree that could be 220 described as no more than a shift of movement. If they were not apt to swerve, all would fall downward through the unfathomable void like drops of rain; no collisions between primary elements would occur, and no blows would be effected, with the result that nature would never have created anything.[15]

Anyone who happens to believe that heavier atoms are carried straight through the void more swiftly than lighter ones, fall on them from above, and so cause the blows capable of producing the movements necessary for creation, is diverging far from the path of sound judgment. Every- 230 thing that drops through water and unsubstantial air falls with a velocity proportional to its weight, because the body of water and air with its fine nature are unable to retard all bodies equally, but yield more quickly to the superior power of heavier objects. On the other hand, empty void cannot offer any resistance to any object in any part at any time: it must give way at once in conformity to its own nature. Thus all the atoms, despite their unequal weights, must move with equal velocity as they shoot through the unresisting void. The heavier will therefore never be 240 able to fall on the lighter from above, or of themselves cause the blows determining the varied movements that are the instruments of nature's work.

So I insist that the atoms must swerve slightly, but only to an infinitesimal degree, or we shall give the impression that we are imagining oblique movements—a hypothesis that would be contradicted by the facts. For it is a plain and manifest matter of observation that objects with weight, left to themselves, cannot travel an oblique course when they plunge from above—at least not perceptibly; but who could possibly 250 perceive that they do not swerve at all from their vertical path?

Moreover, if all movements are invariably interlinked, if new movement arises from the old in unalterable succession, if there is no atomic swerve to initiate movement that can annul the decrees of destiny and prevent the existence of an endless chain of causation, what is the source of this free will possessed by living creatures all over the earth? What, I ask, is the source of this power of will wrested from destiny, which enables each of us to advance where pleasure leads us, and to alter our movements not at a fixed time or place, but at the direction of our own 260 minds? For undoubtedly in each case it is the individual will that gives the initial impulse to such actions and channels the movements through the limbs.

---

15. **216–293:** On the theory of the atomic swerve, see pp. xxvi–xxvii.

Have you not observed too that, at the very moment when the starting gates are opened,[16] the horses, despite their strength and impatience, cannot burst forward as suddenly as their minds desire? The reason is that the whole mass of matter throughout the whole body must be actuated: only when the whole frame has been actuated can it respond with energy to the eagerness of the mind. So you can see that the initial
270 movement is produced by the mind: it originates from the act of mental will, and is then diffused through every part of the body.

But it is a quite different matter when we are thrust forward by a blow delivered with formidable force and powerful pressure by another person; for in that event it is transparently clear that the whole bulk of our body moves and is swept along involuntarily until the will has reined back[17] all our limbs. So do you now see that, even though an external force pushes a crowd of us, often compelling us to move forward against
280 our will and sweeping us along precipitately, there is in our breasts something with the ability to oppose and resist it? At its bidding the mass of matter through every member and limb at times is compelled to change direction or, when thrown forward, is reined back and brought back to rest.

Thus you are obliged to acknowledge that the seeds have the same ability, and that, besides blows and weight, they have another cause of motion from which this innate power of ours is derived, since we see that nothing can come into being from nothing. Weight ensures that all movements are not caused by blows, that is to say by external force. But the
290 factor that saves the mind itself from being governed in all its actions by an internal necessity, and from being constrained to submit passively to its domination, is the minute swerve of the atoms at unpredictable places and times.[18]

---

16. **262–263:** Before a race in the circus the horses and chariots were drawn up in stalls. At the start of the race the gates of the stalls were flung open. Cf. 4.990.

17. **276:** The metaphor "reined back" here and at 283 may well have been prompted by the racecourse illustration just above (263–265); and in the present paragraph Lucr. may be thinking of a crowd at the races. See M. F. Smith, *Hermathena* 102 (1966) 76–77. See also notes on 5.1290, 1436.

18. **289–293:** Diogenes of Oinoanda, after criticizing Democritus for believing that all movements of atoms are controlled by necessity, and after commending Epicurus for discovering that atoms have "a free, swerving movement," says: "The most important consideration is this: if fate is believed in, all admonition and censure are nullified, and not even the wicked [can justly be punished since they are not responsible for their wrongdoings]" (*fr.* 54).

At no time was the fund of matter either more solidly packed or more sparse than it is now. It experiences no gains and no losses. Thus the movement of the ultimate particles now is identical to what it has been in ages past, and it will always be so in the future. Things that have 300 always been produced will continue to be produced under the same conditions, and each will exist, grow, and prosper in its strength, insofar as it is permitted by the ordinances of nature. No force can transform the aggregate of things: there is no place outside the universe into which any kind of matter could escape, or from which a new force could emerge to burst into the universe and change the whole nature of things by disarranging their movements.

In this connection, there is no need to wonder why, despite the movement of the primary elements of things, their entirety seems to stand 310 entirely still, except when compound bodies move as unities. All the ultimate particles lie far beneath the range of our senses. Since they themselves are imperceptible to you, their movements too must be hidden from sight—an inference confirmed by the fact that even perceptible objects often conceal their movements when they are separated from us by a wide space. Often on a hillside fleecy sheep crop the luxuriant pasture and inch forward wherever the tempting grass, pearled with fresh dew, summons them, while their lambs, replete with food, gambol and 320 gently butt. Yet to us in the distance the whole scene seems indistinct, appearing only as a motionless white blur on the green of the hill. Again, great legions fill a spacious plain[19] with rapid movement in vigorous imitation of war: the glitter of arms glances to the sky, as the earth on every side reflects the gleam of bronze; the ground resounds to the tramp of strong men's feet;[20] shouting strikes the mountains and re-echoes to the starry firmament; cavalry gallop round the flanks and suddenly career through the center, making the plain tremble beneath the vigor of 330 their charge. And yet high in the mountains there is a spot from which all seems to be stationary, appearing only as a motionless pool of bright light upon the plain.

Now then, next I want you to grasp the nature of the elements of all things, the great diversity of their forms, and the variety of their manifold shapes. Not that only a few share the same form, but in general they are

---

19. **323–332:** As in 2.40–43 (see note on 2.41), Lucr. seems to be thinking of an exercise on the Campus Martius.

20. **325–327:** These lines recall Homer *Iliad* 2.457–458, 19.362–363, *Odyssey* 14.267–268.

not all alike.[21] This need occasion no surprise: since the supply of atoms
340 is, as I have taught,[22] so huge as to be infinite and incomputable, it is of
course inevitable that they should not all conform to one pattern and be
characterized by the same shape.

Consider too the human race, the mute swimming shoals of squamous
fish, the sleek herds, the wild beasts, and the various sorts of birds that
haunt the smiling water-regions around banks and springs and pools or
flit flocking through the pathless woods: even if you take successively all
the individual members of these species, you will find that they differ in
shape from one another. Indeed, if this were not so, the offspring could
350 not recognize its mother, nor the mother her offspring, whereas we see
that they can do so, and that they are known to one another no less than
human beings.

For example, often before a god's gracefully ornamented shrine a calf
falls a victim beside the incense-smoking altars, and with its last breath
spurts a hot stream of blood from its breast. Meanwhile the bereaved
mother ranges through green glades searching the ground for the imprint
of those cloven hoofs. With her eyes she explores every place in the hope
that she will be able to spy somewhere the young one she has lost. Now
she halts and fills the leafy grove with her plaintive calls. Time after time
360 she returns to the cowshed, her heart transfixed with longing for her calf.
Tender willow shoots, and grass freshened by dew, and those familiar
streams brimming their banks as they slide by, fail to soothe her mind
and remove the pang of anguish; and the sight of other calves in the
luxuriant pastures is equally powerless to divert her thoughts into a new
channel and disburden her of care. So deeply does she feel the loss of
something that she knows as her very own.

Furthermore, tender, tremulous-voiced kids recognize their horned
mothers, and frolicsome lambs the flocks of bleating ewes: thus, in
370 obedience to nature, each usually[23] races to its own udder of milk.

Lastly, take any kind of corn and you will not find that all the individual grains of that variety are identical, but that some difference of form
marks off one from another. We observe the same diversity of form in the
family of shells that mosaic the lap of the earth, where the waves of the
sea gently plash the thirsty sand of the incurving shore.

So I insist that the same must apply to the primary elements of things:

---

21. **336–337:** Identical to 723–724 and very similar to 692–694.

22. **339:** 1.1008–1051.

23. **370:** Not "invariably," as *fere* is often mistranslated. Lucr., a keen observer
of animal behavior, knew that lambs and kids sometimes run to the wrong udder
of milk.

since they are natural formations and are not modeled by hand after a
single, fixed pattern, some of these particles are bound to be marked by   380
differences of shape as they fly about.

It is a simple matter for us to explain by reasoning of the mind why the
fire of lightning has a far more penetrating current than the fire that
emanates from our torches on earth. You could say that the fire of
lightning, being of celestial origin, is composed of smaller atomic shapes,
and that its subtlety enables it to pass through interstices impenetrable to
this fire of ours that emanates from logs and is produced by the torch.

Again, light permeates horn, but rain is repelled.[24] Why is this, if it is
not because the constituent atoms of light are smaller than those of liquid   390
water, the sustainer of life? Similarly we see that, whereas wine flows
through a filter in no time, olive oil dawdles, evidently because oil's
constituent atoms are larger or more hooked and more closely intertwined, with the result that they cannot so rapidly be separated from one
another and so percolate individually through the pores of the filter.

There is the further point that the liquids of honey and milk taste
pleasant to the tongue, when they are rolled in the mouth; on the other   400
hand, foul wormwood and styptic centaury have such a repulsive savor
that they make us grimace. So you will have no difficulty in recognizing
that substances capable of affecting our senses pleasantly are composed
of smooth and round atoms; on the other hand, all that are perceived as
bitter and harsh consist of an interlacement of more hooked atoms, and
for that reason are apt to tear open the passages leading to our senses and
to force their way through the body in effecting their entrance.[25]

In fact, the contrast between things that affect our senses pleasantly
and unpleasantly always reflects the difference between the shapes of
their elements. You must not suppose that the spine-chilling rasp of a   410
squeaking saw is caused by atoms as smooth as those of the tuneful
melodies that instrumentalists rouse from dormancy, shaping them with
supple fingers on the strings. Nor must you suppose that primary elements of the same form penetrate our nostrils, when foul carcasses are
being burned, and when the stage of a theater is freshly sprayed with
Cilician[26] saffron, while the altar nearby is exhaling perfumes of Pan-
chaea.[27] Again, you must not assume that the same seeds produce pleas-

---

24. **388–389:** The picture is of a horn lantern being carried on a wet night.

25. **398–407:** For a more detailed treatment of taste, see 4.615–672.

26. **416:** The Cilician city of Corycus was famous for its production of saffron.

27. **417:** A mythical or semimythical island in the Arabian Sea, reputedly rich in
incense.

420 ing hues upon which we can feast our eyes, and colors that sting the pupil
and force us to weep or whose ugliness makes them a horrible and
hideous sight. The truth is that the component atoms of every object that
soothes our senses must have some degree of smoothness; and con-
trariwise the constituent material of anything displeasing and harsh must
have some degree of roughness.

There are also atoms that cannot legitimately be regarded as smooth
nor yet as entirely hooked and barbed, but rather as somewhat angular, so
that they are able to titillate our sensory organs rather than hurt them:
430 tartar and piquant elecampane are in this class.

Furthermore, scorching fire and icy frost prick our bodily senses with
different kinds of denticles, as is proved to us by the touch of each. For
the holy gods are my witnesses that touch, yes touch, is the sense of the
body, when something extraneous insinuates itself into it, or when something born within affects it (either inflicting pain, or giving pleasure
when emitted in the creative acts of Venus), or again when, in consequence of a collision, the atoms are disturbed within the body itself and
440 the commotion confuses our senses; you can test this yourself by striking
any part of your body with your hand.

So the atoms must vary widely in shape, when they can produce such
different sensations.

Moreover, things that seem to us hard and firm must be composed of
atoms more hooked together—atoms that interlace their ramifications to
form a deeply compacted[28] structure. The substances stationed in the
very first rank of this class include diamonds, which defy the attack of
450 every blow, tough flintstones, inflexible iron, and bronze sockets that
complain noisily as they withstand the force of the bolts. On the other
hand, those things whose substance is liquid and fluid must be composed
of smoother and rounder atoms; indeed poppy seed is scooped up just as
easily as water, for the individual spherical particles do not impede one
another and, if you spill them, they go rolling downhill just as freely as a
liquid. Lastly, all things that you see being dissipated in an instant—
smoke, clouds, and flames, for example—though not composed entirely
of smooth and round atoms, yet must not have a closely knit structure to
460 hamper them: they can sting the body and penetrate stones without
clinging together. So it is easy for you to grasp that whatever substances
have a biting effect on our senses are composed of atoms that are sharp,
but not interlaced.

The fact that you perceive some things, such as briny sea water, to be

---

28. **446:** Or, if my tentative conjecture *arte* for *alte* is correct, "closely
compacted."

bitter as well as fluid should not cause you any surprise. Intermingled with the smooth and round atoms, to which the brine owes its fluidity, are rough particles that cause pain. But, in spite of their roughness, these particles cannot be hooked together: their ability to advance with a 470 flowing motion and at the same time irritate the senses indicates that they are spherical as well as rough. And so that you will be more firmly convinced that it is a mixture of smooth and rough elements that constitutes the bitter substance of Neptune,[29] there is a method of separating them and observing them apart: when the water is filtered several times through the earth into a pit, it loses its harshness and flows in a fresh stream; for it leaves behind the elements of nauseous brine, which, because of their roughness, can more easily stick in the earth.

Now that I have demonstrated this truth, I will at once append a proposition that is a corollary of it and an inference from it: the number 480 of atomic shapes is limited.[30] If this were not so, the bulk of some seeds would inevitably be of infinite magnitude. For within the narrow compass of any single atom, there cannot be scope for much variety of shape.[31] Suppose that the ultimate particles consist of three smallest parts, or even increase this number by a few more. Try all those parts of a single atom in every combination, interchanging top and bottom, right and left, so that you see what form is given to the whole atom by each 490 arrangement. Thereafter, if you should wish to vary its shape further, you must add more parts. Subsequently, if you should wish to vary its shape still further, the arrangement will call for more parts, as before. So acquisition of new shapes involves increase of bulk. Therefore you cannot believe that the seeds differ in form to an infinite degree, or you will compel some of them to be of immeasurable magnitude, which, as I have demonstrated above,[32] is inadmissible.

Be sure that, if the shapes were infinite in number, exotic robes of 500 glistening purple from Meliboea,[33] steeped in the dye of Thessalian mollusks, and the regiments of gilded peacocks, imbued with radiant

---

29. **472:** The sea. For Lucr.'s attitude to such personifications, see 2.655–660.

30. **478–480:** Epicurus disagreed with Democritus, who had thought that the variety of atomic shapes is infinite. Lines 478–479 are identical to 522–523.

31. **481–499:** Lucr. returns to the theory of "smallest parts," which he expounded in 1.599–634. See note there.

32. **499:** The reference is almost certainly to 1.599–634, and especially to 1.619–622, not to a proof that, in the opinion of some editors, preceded 2.478 and has been lost.

33. **501:** A town on the coast of Thessaly. The dye was obtained from the murex, a gastropod mollusk.

loveliness, would be surpassed and obscured by things adorned with new colors; the aroma of myrrh and the taste of honey would be scorned; likewise the song of the swan[34] and the subtle melodies from the strings of Phoebus' lyre would be smothered and silenced. Something would always emerge to excel all others. And in the same way that all good things, as I have said, would be outdone in goodness, so, inversely, all

510 bad things would be outdone in badness, for there would always be something to surpass everything else in its repulsiveness to our nostrils, ears, eyes, and taste. Since this is not the case, but things are restricted by a definite limit that encloses the sum total of them at either extreme, you must acknowledge that there is also a limit to the number of different atomic shapes. Again, the path that extends from fire to icy frosts is of limited length, as is the distance back again. For all the degrees of heat and cold and moderate warmth lie between these two extremes, and their succession makes up the complete scale. So they are created in a

520 range of limited extent, since they are marked by an extreme point at either end, hemmed in on one side by flames, on the other by freezing frosts.

Now that I have demonstrated this truth, I will at once append a proposition that is a corollary of it and an inference from it:[35] the atoms of each shape are infinite in number. For, since the range of different forms is limited, either the atoms of each shape must be infinite in number, or the aggregate of matter must be limited, which, as I have proved,[36] is not the case: for I have shown in my verses that an infinite

530 supply of the minute particles of matter continually maintains the aggregate of things with an uninterrupted succession of blows from all sides.

Although you see that some animals are rarer than others and have a less prolific nature, in some other region and place, in far-off lands, they may be so common that the total is made up. Among quadrupeds the most conspicuous example of such a species is snake-handed[37] elephants: whereas many thousands of these beasts fortify India with an

---

34. **505:** For the reputedly beautiful song of the swan, see also 3.6–7, 4.181–182 (identical to 4.910–911), and perhaps 4.547–548 (where the text is doubtful). The belief that swans sing just before they die is found first in Aeschylus *Agamemnon* 1444–1445, and next in Plato *Phaedo* 84e–85a.

35. **522–523:** Identical to 478–479.

36. **528:** 1.1008–1051.

37. **537:** "Snake-handed" is a wonderful epithet for elephants. It may be noted that a nineteenth-century Thai treatise on elephants in the British Library (Or. 13652.f.6) contains a fine illustration of a mythical elephant, which is composed of twenty-four minor deities and has a naga (divine snake) as its trunk.

ivory palisade,[38] and the strength of their numbers is such that the interior of the country is impenetrable, we see very few specimens.   540
Nevertheless I will concede this point to you: let us imagine that there
is some created thing that is absolutely unique, having no counterpart in
the whole world; and yet, unless there are infinite resources of material
from which it can be conceived and produced, it will not be able to be
created nor, for that matter, will it be able to grow and obtain nourishment. For indeed, if at this stage I were to grant you[39] that a limited
number of the particles capable of creating that unique thing are tossed
about the universe, from what source, in what place, by what force, and
in what way will they meet and combine in this mighty ocean of matter,   550
this multitude of alien atoms? It is my opinion that they have no means of
achieving union. Compare what happens when many mighty vessels
have been wrecked: transoms, ribs, yardarms, prows, masts, and buoyant
oars are tossed this way and that by the vast sea; floating stern-fittings are
seen along every coast—a lesson to mortals that they should resolve to
avoid the shifty sea with its snares and violence and deceit, and always
mistrust it when with seductive serenity it wears a treacherous smile.[40]
Similarly be sure that, once you lay down that the elements of a certain   560
class are limited in number, they will be scattered and tossed this way
and that by contrary tides of matter throughout all time; thus they could
never be driven together and enter into union, let alone remain united and
grow by gaining further atoms. But everyday experience plainly teaches
us that both these things happen: objects can be created and, once created, can grow. It is obvious therefore that there is an infinite number of
elements of every class, so that there is an abundant supply of material
for everything.

And so the destructive motions cannot hold sway eternally and bury   570
existence forever; nor again can the motions that cause life and growth
preserve created things eternally. Thus, in this war that has been waged
from time everlasting, the contest between the elements is an equal one:
now here, now there, the vital forces conquer and, in turn, are conquered;

38. **538:** It is not absolutely clear whether "palisade" is metaphorical, or whether
there was supposed to be an actual barrier made of ivory. The former alternative
is much more probable.

39. **547:** The text is manifestly corrupt in the middle of the line. In *Classical
Quarterly* 51 (2001) 617–20 I propose *si iam hoc tibi dem* for *sumant oculi,* and I
have translated this.

40. **552–559:** For the treachery of the sea and the folly of sailing it, see also
5.1004–1006 and, for example, Plautus *Rudens* 485–486, Virgil *Eclogues* 4.31–
32, *Georgics* 1.254, Horace *Odes* 1.3, Propertius 3.7.37, Tibullus 1.3.35–50.

with the funeral dirge mingles the wail that babies raise when they reach
the shores of light; no night has followed day, and no dawn has followed
580 night, which has not heard mingled with those woeful wails the lamentations that accompany death and the black funeral.

In connection with this topic, it is advisable to keep this further truth
under seal and retain it in the depository of your memory: no object
whose substance is plainly visible consists only of one class of atoms;
each is composed of a mixture of different seeds. The extent of the
properties and powers that an object possesses indicates the multiformity
of its constituent atoms.
590 First and foremost, the earth contains the ultimate particles that enable
bubbling springs of cool water to replenish the boundless sea. She contains too the atoms that generate fire: for in many places her crust blazes
up in flames, while from her bowels bursts the fury of Etna. She also
contains seeds that enable her to raise up lustrous crops and exuberant
trees for the races of humanity and to supply the mountain-prowling tribe
of wild beasts with rivers, foliage, and luxuriant pastures. Consequently
she has at the same time been titled Great Mother of the gods,[41] mother
of wild beasts, and parent of human beings.

600 She it is whom the erudite poets of ancient Greece represented as
enthroned in a chariot drawn by a pair of lions, thereby teaching that the
world, for all its vastness, is suspended in airy space, because earth
cannot rest on earth. They gave her a team of wild beasts to show that
every offspring, no matter how savage, is bound to be softened and
tamed by parental kindness. They encircled the top of her head with a
turreted crown, because earth in prominent places is fortified, and so
protects cities. Even today this diadem adorns the image of the divine
Mother, as she is processioned through great countries, striking awe into
610 the people. She it is whom many different nations, in accordance with the
ritual usage of ancient times, call Mother of Ida;[42] and they provide her
with an escort of Phrygians, because they declare that the production of
cereals originated in Phrygia and spread from there to every region of the
earth. They assign her eunuch-priests, because they wish to indicate that

41. **598:** The cult of the Phrygian goddess Cybele, the Great Mother, was
brought to Rome from Pessinus (southwest of the Turkish capital Ankara) in
205–204 B.C. She was generally represented wearing a mural crown (606–609)
and accompanied by lions (601).

42. **611:** Mt. Ida in Phrygia. There is also a Mt. Ida in Crete—a coincidence that
contributed to the confusion of the cult of Cybele with that of Rhea (see note on
629).

those who have profaned the divinity of the Mother, and have been found
wanting in gratitude to their parents, must be judged unworthy to bring
forth offspring into the shores of light and life. All around the statue rolls
the thunderous percussion of taut timbrels; concave cymbals clash,
raucous-voiced trumpets snarl, and the Phrygian rhythm of the hollow   620
pipe goads on the devotees, who brandish before them weapons that
symbolize their violent frenzy, to terrorize the ungrateful minds and
irreverent hearts of the populace with the power of the goddess. And so,
as soon as her silent figure is processioned into great cities to bless
mortals with mute benediction, the people strew her path all through the
streets with bronze and silver, enriching her with liberal offerings, and
shade the Mother and her escort with showers of snowy rose-blossoms.
From time to time during the ceremony an armed company, whom the
Greeks call Curetes,[43] caper among the Phrygian retinue, leaping rhyth-   630
mically in ecstasy at the shedding of blood and shaking their terrifying
plumes with the nodding of their heads. Their antics recall the Curetes of
Dicte in Crete, who, according to the legend, once upon a time drowned
that famous wailing of Jupiter; it was the occasion when around the baby
boy those boys clad in armor danced swiftly, rhythmically clashing
bronze on bronze, to prevent Saturn from finding his son and devouring
him in his jaws, thus inflicting a never-healing wound in the Mother's
heart. This may explain why armed men accompany the Great Mother;   640
alternatively, the significance of their presence is that the goddess demands that men should be determined to defend their native land with
valiant feats of arms and should prepare to be both a shield and an honor
to their parents.

But although these ideas are conceived and expressed in a fine and
impressive manner, they are far divorced from the true explanation. For it
is inherent in the very nature of the gods that they should enjoy immortal
life in perfect peace, far removed and separated from our world; free
from all distress, free from peril, fully self-sufficient, independent   650
of us, they are not influenced by worthy conduct nor touched by
anger.[44] The fact is that the earth is at all times destitute of sensation,
and the reason why it brings forth many things in many ways into the

43. **629:** The Curetes, who lived in Crete, were said to have protected the infant
Jupiter by drowning his cries in a cave on Mt. Dicte. Jupiter's mother, Rhea, had
hidden him there, to save him from being swallowed by his father, Saturn. The
cult of Rhea came to be confused with that of Cybele, and Lucr. here confuses the
Curetes with Cybele's attendants, the Corybantes.

44. **646–651:** These lines occur also, perhaps erroneously, at 1.44–49. See note
there.

light of the sun is that it is possessed of the primary elements of many substances.

In this connection, if people choose to call the sea Neptune and corn Ceres, and prefer to misapply the name of Bacchus rather than use the proper term for liquor of grapes,[45] let us concede that they may designate the earth as Mother of the gods, on condition that they really and truly
660 refrain from tainting their minds with the stain of superstition.[46]

Although fleecy flocks and warlike steeds and horned herds often graze the same grassy sward beneath the same pavilion of sky and drink their fill from the same stream of water, they differ in appearance, retain the character of their parents, and reproduce the habits of their respective species. So great a diversity of matter is there in every kind of grass and in every stream.
670 Then again, each individual animal is composed of bones, blood, veins, heat, fluid, flesh, and sinews, and these too have wide differences between them corresponding to the differences in the shapes of their constituent elements.

Moreover, all inflammable and combustible objects conceal in their substance, if nothing else, at least the particles that enable them to shoot out flames, radiate light, throw off sparks, and scatter glowing ashes far and wide.

Go through all other things by the same method of reasoning, and you will find that they hide in their substance the seeds of many things and contain atoms of various shapes.
680 Furthermore, you see many objects that are endowed with the qualities of color, taste, and smell together: in the first place, most offerings . . . .[47] These, then, must be composed of atoms of various shapes. For the burning smell penetrates the body by a route that is impassable for the color; likewise, the color and the taste steal their way into the senses by separate entrances—a clear indication for you that there are differences between the shapes of their elements. Therefore atoms of dissimilar shapes unite to form a single mass, and compound bodies consist of a mixture of seeds. Similarly, throughout these verses of mine, you see
690 many letters common to many words, even though you must concede

---

45. **655–656:** Lucr. himself calls the sea Neptune (472) and wine Bacchus (3.221).

46. **659–660:** This emphatically worded proviso is of course extremely important.

47. **681:** At least one line, describing offerings burned upon altars, is lost after 681.

that different verses and words are composed of different letters. I do not
mean to suggest that they have only a few letters in common, or that no
two words are composed of the very same letters, but only that in general
they are not all alike.[48] This analogy is equally applicable to other things:
although many objects have many primary elements in common, as
aggregates they can differ from one another. So it can legitimately be
said that the human race, crops, and exuberant trees consist of different
atoms.

However, it must not be imagined that all kinds of atoms can be linked   700
together in all kinds of combinations; otherwise you would witness the
creation of prodigious things everywhere: monsters, half-human, half-
brute, would appear;[49] sometimes tall branches would sprout from the
trunk of a living creature; often the limbs of terrestrial and marine animals would be united;[50] and Chimaeras,[51] belching flame from their
hellish throats, would be nourished by nature throughout the all-
producing earth. In fact, it is apparent that none of these things happens,
since we observe that everything is created from definite seeds and a
definite parent and is able to preserve its specific character as it grows. It   710
is evident that this must happen according to a fixed law. For whenever a
body takes in food, the assimilable elements in the food are absorbed into
the system, unite, and perform the appropriate motions. On the other
hand, we observe that nature rejects alien matter and returns it to the
earth; moreover, many invisible particles escape from the body under the
impact of blows: these particles failed to form connections anywhere or
to respond sympathetically to the vital motions within the body and
imitate them.

Do not imagine that animals alone are governed by these laws: all
things are subject to the same restriction. Just as all created things differ   720
from one another in regard to their whole nature, so each must consist of
primary elements of different shapes; not that only a few atoms share the
same form, but in general they are not all alike.[52] Furthermore, since the
seeds differ, there must be differences between their interspaces, courses,
interlacements, weights, collisions, concurrences, and motions—
differences that account not only for distinctions between the bodies of

---

48. **688–694:** See note on 1.196–198.

49. **702:** Centaurs. See note on 4.732 and cf. 5.878–891.

50. **704:** Scylla. See note on 4.732 and cf. 5.892–893.

51. **705:** The Chimaera is described by Lucr. in 5.904–906.

52. **723–724:** Identical to 336–337.

animals, but for the division of the earth from the entire sea, and the
partitionment of the whole heaven from the earth.

730   Now then, pay heed to words won by labor I delight in.[53] You must not
suppose that these white objects glistening before your eyes are composed of white elements, or that black things spring from black seeds;
nor must you believe that objects arrayed[54] in any other color are so
attired because their constituent particles are imbued with that color. The
particles of matter have absolutely no color, either like or unlike that of
compound bodies.

If by chance you think that the mind is unable to become cognizant of
740   such particles, you are wandering far astray. Blind-born people, who
have never discerned the light of the sun, recognize by touch objects that
they have never connected with color from the moment of their birth. It is
evident therefore that our minds too can form a conception of particles
not painted with any color. In fact, when we ourselves touch objects in
blinding darkness, we do not feel that they are imbued with any color.

Now that I have proved this point, I will proceed to teach you [that the
atoms are colorless]. All colors without exception change, and all things
750   [that change color, change themselves].[55] But under no circumstances
should the primary elements do this. Something must survive insuscept-
ible of change: otherwise absolutely everything would be reduced to
nothing. For every change that involves a thing outstepping its own
limits means the instantaneous death of what previously existed.[56] So
beware of daubing the seeds of things with color, or you will find everything without exception returning to nothing.

Moreover, if the elements are destitute of any color, but are endowed
with various shapes by means of which they produce every kind and
760   variation of color, it being of great consequence in what groupings and
positions all the seeds are combined, and what motions they reciprocally
impart and receive,[57] you can easily explain at once why something that

---

53. **730:** For the pleasurable nature of the poet's task, see also 1.927–930 (identical to 4.2–5), 3.419–420.

54. **734:** I prefer Lambinus' *induta* to *imbuta*. Cf. *nullo velata colore* in 797.
With *imbuta* the accusative *colorem* is a problem.

55. **748–749:** At least one line has certainly been lost after 748; and unless we
are prepared to make an improbable textual emendation, another lacuna must be
assumed after 749. I have adopted Bailey's suggestion concerning the contents of
the missing lines.

56. **750–754:** Identical to 1.789–793. Lines 753–754 are identical also to
1.670–671 and 3.519–520.

57. **760–762:** Cf. 1.817–819, 908–910, 2.883–885, 1007–1009.

was dark a little while ago can suddenly become as white as marble: as
the sea, when mighty winds have disturbed its smooth surface, is turned
into white-flecked billows of gleaming marble. You could say that, when
something we often see as dark has had its substance thoroughly mixed
up, so that the relative position of its primary elements is changed and it   770
experiences a number of gains and losses, it immediately assumes a
shining white appearance. But if the smooth stretches of the ocean were
composed of azure seeds, under no circumstances could they turn white:
no matter how you jumble together azure seeds, they can never pass into
the color of marble.

And if the component seeds of the uniform, unbroken glitter of the sea
are imbued with different colors, in the same way that a single square
figure is often composed of different figures of various forms, it would   780
be natural that, as we distinguish the different figures in the square, so we
should distinguish the wide variety of different colors in the smooth
surface of the sea or in the uniform, unbroken glitter of anything else.
Moreover, whereas the different component forms in no way debar and
prevent the complete figure from being square in its outline, the presence
of a variety of hues is incompatible with the uniformity of the color of the
whole object.

Furthermore, the reason that sometimes leads us on and inveigles us
into attributing color to the primary elements of things is knocked on the   790
head, since, [according to this hypothesis,][58] white things are not created
from white atoms, nor black things from black atoms, but both from
atoms of various colors. In fact, white things will arise much more easily
from colorless atoms than from black atoms or from atoms of any other
color that clashes and conflicts with it.

Besides, since colors depend upon light for their existence, and the
primary elements of things do not emerge into the light, it is evident that
they are not robed in any color. For what color can there be in blinding
darkness? Why, even in the light color varies according as the incident   800
ray that it reflects is perpendicular or oblique. Consider the iridescence
imparted by sunlight to the plumage that rings and garlands the neck of
the dove: sometimes it is glossed with red garnet, sometimes, as seen
from a different angle, it appears to blend green emeralds with blue
lazuli. Likewise, when the tail of a peacock is drenched in a flood of
light, it exhibits changing colors as it is turned about. Since these colors
are produced by a certain incidence of light, obviously we must not
suppose that they can be produced without it.

Moreover, since one kind of impingement on the pupil of the eye gives   810

---

58. **790:** Words in brackets supplied to make the sense clear.

rise to the perception of white, while a different kind of impingement gives rise to the perception of black or some other color, the significant factor being not the color of the objects you happen to touch, but rather their shape, it is evident that the primary elements have no need of colors, but produce varying impressions by the variety of their shapes.

Furthermore, since specific colors are not linked to specific atomic shapes, and any configuration of primary elements can have any hue, 820 why, [if the atoms are colored,][59] are not compound bodies of every kind steeped likewise in every kind of color? It would be natural that crows in flight should often radiate whiteness from white wings, and that swans should be born black from black seeds or should spring from seeds of any other simple or composite color.

Here is another point: the more minute the pieces into which anything is broken up, the more you can perceive the color gradually fading away and being extinguished. This is what happens when purple stuff is picked 830 into tiny pieces: when it is shredded thread by thread, all the purple or scarlet color, in spite of its unsurpassed brilliance, is shed. So you may infer from this that the small shreds exhale all their color before they are resolved into their constituent atoms.

Lastly, since you admit that not all objects emit sound or smell, you do not attribute sound and smell to everything. Similarly, since our eyes cannot discern all things, it is evident that there are some objects destitute 840 of color, just as there are some devoid of smell and sound; and an intelligent mind can have cognizance of these objects no less surely than it can distinguish those deprived of other qualities.

But do not suppose that color is the only quality of which the ultimate particles are permanently despoiled: they are also absolutely devoid of warmth, cold, and burning heat; they move barren of sound and drained of taste and exhale no intrinsic odor from their substance. When you are preparing to compound the exquisite scent of marjoram or myrrh, or the 850 bouquet of nard that respires nectar to our nostrils, the first requisite is an oil that as nearly as possible is odorless and wafts no aroma to our nostrils, the object being that it should have as little power as possible to interfere with and destroy by its own pungency the scents blended with its substance and steamed with it. For the same reason the primary elements, in creating things, cannot contribute an odor or sound of their own, since they are unable to emit anything from themselves; similarly they cannot communicate any taste or cold or heat, whether fierce or gentle, or any other such qualities. Since these qualities are of a perish- 860 able nature, being either soft and pliant, or fragile and crumbling, or

---

59. **820:** Words in brackets supplied to make the sense clear.

hollow and porous, all must be extraneous to the primary elements—that is, if we wish things to be underlaid by indestructible foundations upon which the totality of existence can rest; otherwise you will find everything without exception returning to nothing.

Now you must acknowledge that even those things that we perceive to be sensible are all composed of insensible elements. The phenomena of our everyday experience, so far from refuting this hypothesis and conflicting with it, themselves lead us by the hand and oblige us to believe that animate beings are produced, as I say, from insensible elements. In 870 fact, we can see worms emerging alive from fetid slime, when the earth, sodden after untimely rains, has undergone putrefaction.[60]

Moreover, we can see all things being transmuted in the same manner: rivers, leaves, and luxuriant pastures are transmuted into cattle, cattle are transmuted into human bodies, and our bodies often increase the strength of wild beasts and the bodies of strong-winged birds. Thus nature transmutes every kind of food into living bodies and so engenders all the 880 senses of animate beings, in much the same way that she resolves dry logs into flames and transforms them wholly into fire. Do you not see now that it is of great consequence in what order all the primary elements are placed, in what way they are combined, and what motions they reciprocally impart and receive?[61]

But then what is it that impresses your mind, prompting and compelling it to express conflicting opinions that prevent you from believing that the sensible is produced from the insensible? Undoubtedly it is the fact that stones, wood, and earth, even when blended together, cannot yield 890 vital sensation. So, in this connection, you will do well to remember this: I am not suggesting that every substance capable of creating sensible things produces sensations as a matter of course, but that the supremely important factors are, first, the size and shape of the particles that produce the sensible, and, secondly, their motions, order, and positions. We see that logs and clods do not fulfill any of these conditions; but when they have become putrid as a result of the rains, they engender tiny worms, because their constituent elements are displaced from their old 900

---

60. **871–872:** Belief in spontaneous generation of certain kinds of plant and animal life, including worms and maggots, from putrefied matter, dung, etc., was held by several philosophers in antiquity, including Aristotle. Lucr. returns to it at 898–901, 928–929, 3.719–736, 5.797–798.

61. **879–885:** Cf. 1.901–910, where Lucr. is criticizing Anaxagoras. There can be little doubt that he is thinking mainly of the same philosopher in much of the present section (865–930, 973–990).

arrangements by a new force and are so combined that animate beings are bound to be born.

Those who suppose that the sensible can be produced from sensible particles, which in their turn derive their sensation from other sensible [particles, make the seeds of sensation perishable],[62] since they make them soft. For sensation is wholly bound up with the flesh, sinews, and veins, all of which we see to be soft and therefore to be formed of a perishable substance.

Nevertheless, let us suppose for a moment that such particles could subsist eternally: presumably it must be assumed that they have sensation either like that of some part of the body or like that of the whole
910 animate being they compose. But parts cannot possibly have independent sensation, because all the sensation of our limbs is dependent upon something else: if the hand or any other part is severed from the body, it cannot continue to have sensation by itself. We are left with the conclusion that the particles have sensation like that of the whole animate being; in which case they must have the same sensations as the whole body, so as to harmonize everywhere with the vital feeling. How, then, can they qualify for the description "primary elements of things" and avoid the paths of death, when they are animate things and animateness
920 implies mortality? But even if they can, their union and assemblage will produce nothing more than a jumbled mass of animate creatures, in the same way that human beings, cattle, and wild beasts obviously could not engender anything by mutual coition. If by chance it is supposed that in the body they abandon their own sensation and assume another, what is the use of granting them this power that is then withdrawn? Then again there is our earlier argument:[63] since we perceive that the eggs of birds change into live chicks, and that worms come seething out of the earth when untimely rains have caused putrefaction, it is evident that the
930 sensible can be produced from the insensible.

If by chance someone claims that the sensible can certainly arise from the insensible by a process of change or, as it were, by a kind of parturition that brings it into being, it will be sufficient to explain and prove to this person that parturition cannot take place before a combination has been effected, and that change is impossible without a previous union.

In the first place, no body can have sensation before the birth of the animate being itself for the obvious reason that its constituent materials

---

62. **903:** At least one line has almost certainly been lost after 903.

63. **926:** I translate *quod diximus ante,* a proposal first made by H. A. J. Munro, *Journal of Classical and Sacred Philology* 1 (1854) 43, and recently revived by W. S. Watt, *Philologus* 140 (1996) 250–251.

are still scattered and contained in the air, rivers, earth, and products of 940
the earth: they have not yet united and combined those mutually appropriate vital motions that kindle the vigilant senses, the sentinels of every
animate creature.

Moreover, when any animate being is suddenly struck down by a blow
too severe for its nature to endure, all the sensation of body and mind is at
once confounded. The arrangements of the primary elements are upset,
and deep within the organism the vital motions are impeded, until the
shock affects the substance in every limb, unties the vital knots that bind 950
spirit to body, and ejects the spirit, dispersing it through every pore. For
what more are we to suppose that the impact of a blow can do than
disaggregate and disintegrate everything?

It can also often happen that, after the impact of a less sharp blow, the
surviving vital motions triumph, yes triumph, by quelling the violent
disturbances caused by the impact, by summoning every element back
into its proper course, by frustrating the motion of death that was already
lording it in the body, and by reviving senses that were almost snuffed
out. For by what other means could a living creature, already standing 960
upon the very threshold of death, rally its consciousness and return to life
rather than pass on to the goal almost reached and pass away?

Furthermore, since pain occurs when the particles of matter in the
living flesh of the limbs are disturbed by some force and reel in their
places within the body, and seductive pleasure is produced when they
return to their position, it is evident that the primary elements are immune to all pain and cannot feel any pleasure by themselves. The fact is
that they do not consist of atoms whose displacements could cause them 970
pain or bless them with pleasure, the sustainer of life. Therefore they
cannot be endowed with sensation.

Again, if we cannot explain the ability of each animate being to
experience sensation without attributing sensation to its constituent elements, what are we to say of the special atoms that compose the human
race? Doubtless they shake and tremble with uncontrollable laughter and
sprinkle their faces and cheeks with dewy tears;[64] doubtless they are
qualified to discourse at length on the structure of compounds, and even
investigate the nature of their own constituent atoms. After all, if they 980
resemble whole human beings, they themselves too must consist of other
elements, and those others of others again: you dare not stop anywhere,
for I will dog you and insist that whatever, according to you, speaks and

---

64. **976–977:** These lines are very similar to 1.919–920, and the whole reductio
ad absurdum in 973–990 is to be compared with 1.915–920. In both passages the
argument is directed against Anaxagoras.

laughs and shows intelligence must be composed of elements that do the same. But if we recognize that this hypothesis is preposterous and crazy, and if one can laugh without being formed of laughing atoms, and can possess intelligence and expound philosophy in words of wisdom without being composed of intelligent and eloquent seeds, why should it not

990 be equally possible for things that we see endowed with sensation to be composed of seeds that are absolutely devoid of sensation?

To conclude, all of us are sprung from celestial seed; all are begotten by that same father, from whom mother earth, the giver of life, receives the limpid drops of moisture.[65] So she becomes pregnant and gives birth to lustrous crops, exuberant trees, and the human race; she gives birth also to all the species of wild beasts, providing them with the sustenance that enables them all to feed their bodies, lead a pleasant life, and reproduce their kind. So she has deservedly gained the name of mother.[66]

1000 Likewise everything that originated from the earth passes back into the earth, and everything that emanated from the ethereal regions is returned to the precincts of the sky that receive it once more. Death does not destroy things so completely that it annihilates the constituent elements: it merely dissolves their union. Then it joins them in fresh combinations and so causes all things to alter their forms and change their colors, to acquire sensation and resign it in an instant. It all goes to show that it is important in what groupings and positions the same primary elements are combined, and what motions they reciprocally impart and receive.[67]

1010 You must not imagine that the fluctuating qualities that we perceive on the surfaces of things, sporadically appearing and suddenly disappearing, are permanently inherent in the ultimate particles. Why, even in these verses of mine it is important in what groupings and order all the letters are placed. For the same letters denote sky, sea, lands, rivers, and sun, the same denote crops, trees, and animals; although not all the letters are alike, the great majority are so, and it is their position that is the

1021 distinguishing factor.[68] It is the same with physical objects: when the

---

65. **991–1001:** This passage, which is to be compared with 1.250–264, where, as here, Lucr. exploits the story of the marriage of earth and sky, seems to have been influenced by Euripides *Chrysippus fr.* 839. Euripides in turn was influenced by Anaxagoras.

66. **998:** For the motherhood of the earth, see also 598–599, 658–659, 1.251, 5.795–836.

67. **1007–1009:** Cf. 1.817–819, 908–910, 2.760–762, 883–885.

68. **1013–1022:** On the comparison between letters and atoms, see note on 1.196–198.

concurrences, motions, order, position, and shapes of the atoms are
changed, the objects too must change.

Now I beg you to concentrate your attention on true reasoning. A
novel topic is struggling strenuously to fall upon your ears, a novel
aspect of nature to reveal itself. But nothing is so simple that it is not
rather difficult to believe at first, and likewise nothing is so great or so
wonderful that our wonder at it does not diminish little by little. First and   1030
foremost, consider the pure splendor of the sky and all within its
confines—the random-roaming stars, the moon, and the sun radiant with
dazzling light. Suppose that all these marvels were now revealed to
mortals for the first time and were suddenly and unexpectedly thrust
before their eyes, what more wonderful spectacle than this could be
imagined, what spectacle that people would be less prepared to conceive
as credible, if they had not yet witnessed it? None in my opinion; so
marvelous would this sight have been.[69] As it is, however, the spectacle
has so satiated us that it has palled, and no one thinks it worth gazing up
at the lambent precincts of the sky. So no longer let dismay at mere   1040
novelty cause you to reject a theory from your mind, but rather weigh it
with penetrative judgment; then, if you consider it to be true, concede
victory or, if it is false, equip yourself to fight it. For, since the totality of
space out beyond the ramparts of our world is infinite, my mind seeks the
explanation of what exists in those boundless tracts which the intelligence is eager to probe and into which the mind can freely and spontaneously project itself in flight.

In the first place, we have a universe without any limit anywhere in
any direction, whether to left or to right, upward or downward. I have   1050
demonstrated this,[70] and indeed the fact is self-evident, for the nature of
the unfathomable abyss is conspicuously clear. Now, since the extent of
space is infinite in every direction, and in the unfathomable universe
seeds numberless in number, harried by incessant movement, fly about in
many ways, under no circumstances must it be considered likely that this

---

69. **1030–1037:** These lines seem to have been influenced by a passage of
Aristotle's dialogue *De Philosophia* (*fr.* 13 Ross). The Greek original is lost, but
the passage is translated by Cicero *DND* 2.95 in his exposition of Stoic theology.
An important difference between Aristotle and Lucr. is that the former sees the
glories of the sky as evidence of divine handiwork, whereas the latter does not.
Like Lucr., Cicero (*DND* 2.96) goes on to make the point that familiarity blinds
us to the wonders of nature.

70. **1050:** See 1.958–1001.

one earth and heaven alone has been formed, and that all those particles of matter outside it achieve nothing; and all the more so since our world is the creation of nature: the atoms themselves collided spontaneously 1060 and fortuitously, clashing together blindly, unsuccessfully, and ineffectually in a multitude of ways, until at last those atoms coalesced which, when suddenly dashed together, could always form the foundations of mighty fabrics, of earth, sea, and sky, and the family of living creatures. So I insist that you must acknowledge the existence elsewhere of other aggregations of matter similar to this world of ours which the ether hugs in a greedy embrace.[71]

Moreover, when an abundant supply of matter is available, when space is at hand and there is no obstruction from any object or force, 1070 things most certainly must happen and objects must be created. And if the fund of seeds is so vast that the sum of the lives of all living creatures would not suffice to count it, if the same force of nature is still operative and possesses the power to assemble all the seeds of things in the same order in which they have been assembled in our world, you are bound to admit that in other parts of the universe there are other worlds inhabited by many different peoples and species of wild beasts.

There is the further consideration that in the totality of created things there is nothing solitary, nothing that is born unique and grows unique and singular: everything belongs to some family, and each species has 1080 very many members. To begin with, direct your attention to living creatures: you will find that this is true of the race of mountain-prowling wild beasts, the double breed[72] of human beings, the dumb shoals of squamous fish, and all creatures that fly. Therefore, in accordance with the same principle, you must admit that the sky and the earth and the sun, the moon, the sea, and the rest, are not unique, but rather of numberless number. The fact is that they are restricted by the deeply driven boundary stone[73] of life and are composed of substance subject to birth no less than every class of terrestrial things that comprises very many members.

1090 Once you obtain a firm grasp of these facts, you see that nature is her

---

71. **1064–1066:** For the Epicurean belief that the infinite universe contains an infinite number of worlds, see also Epicurus *Hdt.* 45, 73–74, *Pyth.* 88–90, Us. *fr.* 301–307, Cicero *DND* 1.53, Diogenes of Oinoanda *fr.* 63.

72. **1082:** Male and female. Both here and in 1081 ("the race of mountain-prowling wild beasts") Lucr. is translating Empedocles, the relevant lines of whom, part of a passage which has only recently come to light, are a(ii)26–27 in A. Martin and O. Primavesi, *L'Empédocle de Strasbourg* (de Gruyter: Berlin, 1999) 139 (text and translation), 231–235 (commentary).

73. **1087:** See note on 1.76–77.

own mistress and is exempt from the oppression of arrogant despots, accomplishing everything by herself spontaneously and independently and free from the jurisdiction of the gods. For—and here I call to witness the sacred, peacefully tranquil minds of the gods, who pass placid days and a life of calm—who has the power to rule the entirety of the immeasurable? Who has the power to hold in his hand the strong reins needed to govern the unfathomable? Who has the power to revolve all the skies together and fumigate with ethereal fires all the fertile earths? Who has the power to be in every place at every time, so as to form darkness with the clouds and to shake the serene tracts of the sky with thunder, and then to launch bolts, often demolishing his own temples or retiring to the deserts for furious practice with the missile that often passes by the guilty and destroys the unoffending and undeserving?[74]   1100

Since the time of the world's creation and the birthday of the sea and land and the formation of the sun, multitudinous particles have been added from without: on every side they have been added—seeds that the vast universe has cast together. These enabled the sea and lands to increase, the pavilion of the sky to encroach further on space and hoist its lofty roof far above the earth, and the air to mount upward. For all the particles from all quarters are distributed by blows to their appropriate objects, and they go separate ways to their own kind: water joins water, earthy substance increases earth, fires forge fire, and ether ether, until nature, the creatress of things, has perfected her work and guided everything to the extreme limit of its growth; this point is reached, when the influx of material into the vital arteries no longer exceeds the outflow and loss. Here the development of all things must cease; here nature by her own agency arrests growth. All things you see growing up with sprightly increase, and rung by rung ascending the ladder of maturity, are admitting more particles than they are ejecting; this happens so long as the food is readily assimilated into all their veins, and so long as their bulk is not so dilated that they discard many particles and lose more than they need to absorb for their development. For you must certainly concede that many particles flow away and withdraw from things; however, still more must be acquired by them, until they have attained the zenith of their growth. From then onward by degrees their powers and mature strength are undermined by age, which declines into degeneracy. And indeed, once growth has been arrested, the bulkier and broader the object is, the more particles it throws off from its substance and scatters in every direction on every side; moreover, the food is not readily channeled into   1110   1120   1130

---

74. **1099–1104:** For detailed refutation of the view that thunderbolts are instruments of the gods, see 6.387–422.

all its veins and does not suffice to produce a supply of substance large enough to compensate for the copious emanations being discharged. So with reason all things perish, when they are rarefied by the efflux of
1140 particles, and succumb to external blows; for ultimately food fails them in old age, while particles never stop hammering them from without, enfeebling them and overcoming their resistance with hostile blows.

In just the same way the ramparts that surround the mighty world will be taken by storm and will collapse and crumble into ruins. In every case food must repair and renew the body; in every case food must be the body's prop and stay; but its task is impossible, since the veins are unable to absorb a sufficient quantity of it, and nature does not provide all that is
1150 required. Why, even now the world's life is in decline, and the earth is so exhausted that she has difficulty in producing tiny animals, though she once produced creatures of every kind and bore wild beasts of huge size.[75] For, in my opinion, the species of mortal creatures were not lowered from the heights of heaven to the fields by a golden rope,[76] nor were they created by the sea and the waves that plash the rocks;[77] they were generated by the same earth that now nourishes them from her own substance.

Moreover, in the beginning the earth herself spontaneously produced lustrous crops and exuberant vines for mortals; she herself gave them
1160 pleasant fruits and lush pastures, which now scarcely grow in spite of our toilsome tendance. We exhaust our oxen, sap the strength of our farmers, and wear out our iron implements in fields that scarcely afford subsistence: so ungenerous is their yield, and so surely do they demand increasing toil.[78] Now the aged plowman shakes his head and time after time sighs that his hard labor has all come to nothing; and when he

---

75. **1150–1152:** See 5.783–836, where Lucr. describes how the earth, when she was young, was able to produce from her body not only plants, but also all kinds of birds and animals, but how later her fertility, like that of a woman, declined, so that the only animals which she herself can produce now are tiny ones, such as worms. On the spontaneous generation of worms, etc., see note on 2.871–872.

76. **1153–1154:** The idea of a golden rope suspended from heaven goes back to Homer *Iliad* 8.19. The passage was often interpreted allegorically, in one way or another, by philosophers, including the Stoics (e.g., Marcus Aurelius 7.9). It is not recorded that anyone believed (as Lucr. humorously implies) that animals were actually lowered to earth on a rope. In 5.793, where he repeats that animals cannot have come from the sky, the rope is not mentioned.

77. **1155:** A probable allusion to the theory of the sixth-century B.C. philosopher Anaximander of Miletus. Cf. 5.794.

78. **1160–1163:** For the difficulties faced by those who cultivate the soil, see also 5.206–217.

compares present times with times past, he often extols his father's
fortune. His gloomy sentiments are echoed by the planter of the old and
shriveled vine who deplores the tendency of the times, heaps abuse upon
the age, and growls that the people of olden days, paragons of piety, 1170
supported life comfortably on their narrow plots, even though the portion
of land owned by each man was formerly much smaller than now. Only
he fails to grasp that all things gradually decay and head for the reef of
destruction, exhausted by long lapse of time.

BOOK THREE

Preface

The Nature and Composition of the Two Parts of the Soul—The Mind (the Seat of Thought and Emotion) and the Spirit (the Seat of Sensation)

Proofs That Mind and Spirit Are Subject to Birth and Death

When a person dies slowly, the gradual departure of the spirit shows that it
  is divisible and therefore mortal (526–547)
The mind is part of the body and cannot exist without it (548–557)
Mind and body can exist only in union (558–579)
Further proofs that the spirit suffers dissolution at death (580–614)
The mind has a fixed place in the body (615–623)
Divorced from the body, the spirit cannot be sentient or exist (624–633)
The spirit is divisible and therefore mortal (634–669)
If the spirit is immortal, we should have some recollection of our earlier
  existence (670–678)
The mind and spirit, being closely integrated with the body, cannot have
  been slipped into it at birth and cannot leave it without perishing (679–
  712)
Parts of the spirit remain in the body after death; therefore, being divisible,
  the spirit must be mortal (713–740)
The permanence of characteristics in species proves that the mind and spirit
  do not undergo transmigration and are not immortal (741–775)
The preposterous notion that immortal souls squabble with one another for
  possession of mortal bodies (776–783)
The mind and spirit cannot exist outside the body, and the union of a
  mortal body and an immortal soul is impossible (784–805)
The soul does not have the attributes of an immortal thing (806–829)

Fear of Death Is Unreasonable

Death is nothing to us (830–869)
Fears for the fate of the body after death are irrational (870–893)
The grief of mourners is unjustified (894–911)
In death there is no longing for sensual pleasures or for anything else (912–
  930)
Nature's rebuke to those who complain about death (931–977)
Hell and its torments exist only in our life (978–1023)
Why should you be reluctant to die, when far greater people have died
  before you? (1024–1052)
Restlessness and discontent can be banished only by study of Epicurean
  philosophy (1053–1075)
Why cling to life? Death is inevitable and will be eternal, no matter how
  long you live (1076–1094)

You, who out of such deep darkness first found a way to raise such
a brilliant light and illumine life's comforts, you, glory of the Greek

people,[1] I follow, and in your footsteps I now tread boldly[2]—less from a
desire to rival you than because of love, which inspires me to imitate you.
In any case, how could a swallow compete with a swan? Or how could an
unsteady-legged kid match in a race the strength of a mettlesome horse?
10 You are our father and the discoverer of truth: you supply us with fatherly
precepts; and from your pages, illustrious master, like the bees which in
flowerful vales sip each bloom, we feed on each golden saying—golden
and ever most worthy of eternal life.

As soon as your philosophy begins to proclaim the true nature of
things revealed by your divine mind, the terrors of the mind are dispelled, the walls of the world dispart, and I see what happens throughout
the whole void.[3] Plainly visible are the gods in their majesty, and their
calm realms which, buffeted by no wind, sprinkled by no storm cloud's
20 shower, sullied with no white fall of snow crystallized by biting frost,
are ever pavilioned by a cloudless ether that smiles with widespread
flood of radiance.[4] All the needs of the gods are supplied by nature, and
nothing at any time detracts from their peace of mind. On the other hand,
nowhere are the precincts of Acheron[5] visible, even though the earth
does not prevent me from discerning all that happens down in the expanse of space beneath our feet. At this experience, at this realization that
30 by your power nature has been so completely exposed and unveiled
on every side, I am thrilled by a kind of divine ecstasy and quaking awe.

Well, now that I have demonstrated the nature of the primary elements
of all things, the diversity of their forms, the spontaneous manner in
which they fly about under the impulse of incessant movement, and their
ability to create everything, it is obvious that my next task is to illuminate

---

1. **3:** Epicurus. For similarities between this eulogy of Lucr.'s master (1–30)
and the invocation to Venus at the beginning of the poem, see note on 1.2.

2. **3–4:** Cf. 5.55–56.

3. **14–17:** Epicurus enables Lucr. to follow where his master pioneered the
way: see 1.62–79, especially 72–77.

4. **18–22:** This description of the abodes of the gods is in imitation of Homer's
description of Olympus in *Odyssey* 6.42–46, and is in turn imitated by Tennyson
in his poem *Lucretius* 104–110: "The gods, who haunt / The lucid interspace of
world and world, / Where never creeps a cloud, or moves a wind, / Nor ever falls
the least white star of snow, / Nor ever lowest roll of thunder moans, / Nor sound
of human sorrow mounts to mar / Their sacred everlasting calm!" See also *The
Passing of Arthur* 427–429. Lucr. explains in 5.146–155 why the gods cannot
live in our world.

5. **25:** The underworld.

in my verses the nature of the mind and the spirit,[6] and send packing that fear of Acheron which disturbs human life from its deepest depths, suffusing all with the darkness of death, and allows no pleasure to remain   40 unclouded and pure.[7]

To be sure, people often claim that they dread illness or a life of infamy more than Tartarus[8] and death, and that they know the mind to be composed of blood, or even of wind if that happens to catch their fancy; they claim too that they have absolutely no need of our philosophy. But you may see from what follows that all these claims are a display of bravado to win applause rather than prompted by true conviction. For the same people, though banished from their homeland, driven far from the sight of other human beings, branded with the stigma of some foul crime, and afflicted, in a word, with every kind of tribulation, continue to live.   50 Wherever they bring their troubles, they offer sacrifices to their ancestors, immolate black victims,[9] dispatch oblations to the infernal deities, and in their bitter plight turn their minds much more zealously to superstition. The lesson is this: it is advisable to appraise people in doubt and danger and to discover how they behave in adversity; for then and only then is the truth elicited from the bottom of their hearts: the mask is ripped off; the reality remains.

Furthermore, avarice and blind lust for status, which drive wretched   60 people to encroach beyond the boundaries of right and sometimes, as accomplices and abettors of crime, to strive night and day with prodigious effort to scale the summit of wealth[10]—these sores of life are nourished in no small degree by dread of death.[11] For as a rule the ignominy of humble position and the sting of penury are considered to be incompatible with a life of enjoyment and security, and are thought to imply a sort of premature loitering before the portals of death from which people, under the impulse of unfounded terror, desire to flee far away and be far removed. To this end, they swell their fortune through the blood-   70 shed of civil war[12] and greedily multiply their wealth, heaping up murder

---

6. **35–36:** On the distinction between the mind and the spirit, the two components of the soul, see p. xxviii and what Lucr. says in 136–160.

7. **38–40:** The image is of clouding water by disturbing the mud at the bottom of a pool or spring.

8. **42:** Hell.

9. **52:** Black victims were regularly sacrificed to chthonian deities.

10. **62–63:** Repeated from 2.12–13.

11. **59–64:** See p. xxviii.

12. **70:** For the disturbed times through which Lucr. lived, see p. ix.

on murder; they take cruel delight in a brother's death that should be
mourned, and their relatives' tables are objects of abhorrence and fear.[13]

Similarly it is often the same fear that makes them fret with envy that
before their eyes another person possesses power and, parading in the
brilliant array of office, attracts the gaze of all, while they complain that
their own lot is to wallow in murk and mire. Some throw away their lives
in an effort to gain statues and renown. And often, in consequence of
80 dread of death, people are affected by such an intense loathing of life and
the sight of the light that with mournful hearts they sentence themselves
to death, forgetting that the source of their sorrows is this very fear,
which prompts one person to outrage decency, another to break bonds of
friendship, and, in short, to overthrow all sense of natural duty: often in
the past people have betrayed their country and beloved parents in attempting to avoid the precincts of Acheron.

Just as children tremble and fear everything in blinding darkness, so
we even in daylight sometimes dread things that are no more terrible than
90 the imaginary dangers that cause children to quake in the dark. This terrifying darkness that enshrouds the mind must be dispelled not by the
sun's rays and the dazzling darts of day, but by study of the superficial
aspect and underlying principle of nature.[14]

In the first place, I declare that the mind, or the intelligence as we
often term it, in which the reasoning and governing principle of life
resides, is part of a person no less than the hand and foot and eyes are
seen to be parts of a whole living creature.

[Some theorists imagine][15] that the sensibility of the mind is not
located in any specific part, but that it is a sort of vital condition of the
100 body—a "harmony"[16] as the Greeks call it; this, they suppose, endows us
with life and sensation, without the mind residing in any part of the body,
in the same way that one commonly speaks of the good health of the body,

---

13. **73:** Fear of poison.

14. **87–93:** Identical to 2.55–61, 6.35–41. Lines 91–93 are also identical to
1.146–148.

15. **97:** At least one line has been lost after 97.

16. **100:** The Greek *harmonia* means "attunement" rather than what we call
"harmony." The origin of the theory that the soul is an attunement of the bodily
constituents, a theory presented by Simmias and refuted by Socrates in Plato's
Phaedo (85e–86d, 91c–95a), is uncertain. It is likely to have been influenced
both by Pythagoreanism and by Sicilian medical theory. It was developed in the
fourth century B.C. by two pupils of Aristotle, Aristoxenus and Dicaearchus, the
former of whom began his philosophical studies with Pythagoreanism and was a
musician as well as a philosopher.

even though this health is not an organ of the strong person. Thus they do not locate the sensibility of the mind in any specific part; and here I consider that they go far astray. Often, although the plainly perceptible parts of the body are sick, elsewhere in some hidden part we feel pleasure; often too quite the opposite happens: a person who is miserable in mind may feel pleasure throughout the body. The situation is no 110 different from that when a sick person has a painful foot, but happens to have no pain in the head at the same time. Moreover, even when we have resigned our limbs to gentle slumber and our sprawling body lies heavy and insensible, there is something within us that at that time is stirred by many kinds of emotion, experiencing all the movements of pleasure and the heart's unreal anxieties.

Now, what follows will enable you to grasp that the spirit too resides in the limbs, and that the body does not owe its power of sensation to a "harmony." In the first place, even when a considerable portion of the body has been removed, it is a common occurrence for life to linger in 120 our limbs. On the other hand, when a few particles of heat have escaped from the body and a little air has been exhaled through the mouth, this same life at once abandons the veins and quits the bones. You may gather from this that not all particles have equal functions or safeguard the body to an equal degree; it is mainly these seeds of wind and warm heat that ensure that life lingers in our limbs. The body itself, then, contains vital heat and wind, which abandon our frame at the moment of death.

So, since the mind and spirit have been found to be a natural part of the 130 human body, repudiate this term "harmony," which was brought down to musicians from lofty Helicon—or maybe the musicians themselves borrowed it from some other source and transferred it to that quality that previously had no distinctive name. In any case, let them keep it; as for you, listen to the rest of my arguments.

Next I declare that, although mind and spirit are intimately connected and together form a single substance, the head, so to speak, and supreme ruler of the whole body is the reason, which we term the mind or intelligence; and this has its seat fixed in the middle region of the breast. Here 140 we feel the palpitation of throbbing fear, here the soothing touch of joy: here, then, is the intelligence and mind. The rest of the soul is disseminated through all the body and moves in obedience to the will and impulse of the mind. The mind quite independently possesses intelligence and experiences joy at times when no stimulus affects either the body or the spirit. And in the same way that the head or eye can smart under a painful attack without our whole body being agonized as well, so our mind sometimes by itself suffers pain or is animated with joy, when 150

the rest of the soul, scattered through the limbs of the body, is not roused by any new stimulus. But when the mind is disturbed by a more intense fear, we observe that the whole spirit throughout the limbs sympathizes with it: sweating and pallor break out all over the body; the tongue stutters and the voice falters; the eyes grow blear, the ears buzz, and the limbs give way:[17] in fact we often see people collapse in consequence of the mind's terror. It is a simple matter for anyone to infer from this that the spirit is intimately linked with the mind, and that the spirit, once
160   shaken by the mind's force, in its turn strikes the body and sets it in motion.

The same method of argument teaches us that the mind and spirit have a material nature. For it is an observable fact that they impel the limbs, wrench the body from sleep, transform the countenance, and pilot and steer the whole person; and since we perceive that all these operations imply touch, and touch in its turn implies matter, are we not bound to acknowledge that the mind and spirit consist of material substance?

Moreover, you notice that the mind suffers in concert with the body
170   and sympathizes with it. Even if a spear fails to strike the vitals when it is driven into the body with quivering force and severs bones and sinews, it induces faintness and a blissful[18] sinking to the ground, and on the ground a dizziness of mind and now and then a vacillating inclination to rise up again. So the mind must have a material nature, since it is affected by the painful blows of material spears.

Now I will continue my discourse with an exposition of the nature of the mind's substance and its component elements.
180   In the first place, I declare that the mind is exceedingly subtle, being composed of the minutest particles. If you pay attention, what follows will convince you that this is true. It is an observable fact that there is nothing that happens as swiftly as the mind imagines it happening, and as it actually initiates it.[19] So the mind rouses itself to activity more rapidly than anything whose nature is patent to our sight. The component seeds of such a mobile substance are bound to be extremely round and extremely minute: otherwise they could not be set in motion by the impulse

17. **154–156:** These lines seem to have been influenced by Sappho *fr.* 31, a poem adapted by Lucr.'s contemporary Catullus in his poem 51.

18. **173:** "The epithet *suavis* [blissful], rejected by some editors, will surprise only those who have never fainted." I quote from my Loeb note, where I cite supporting evidence from other writers, including Seneca and Montaigne.

19. **182–183:** Lucr. explains in 4.877–906 how mental visualization activates the body.

of a slight stimulus. Compare how water is made to move and flow by ever such a gentle impulse, since it is formed of small particles shaped so 190 that they can roll. On the other hand, the substance of honey is more cohesive, its fluid more viscous, and its flow more dilatory; and the reason why the whole mass of its matter has closer cohesion is undoubtedly that its constituent particles are less smooth, less subtle, and less round. Compare, too, how even a gentle, checked puff of breath can spill a high heap of poppy seed from the top downward, whereas it can make no impression on a pile of stones or ears of corn. Therefore the smaller and smoother bodies are, the more mobility they enjoy; conversely, the 200 heavier and rougher any are found to be, the more stability they have. Now, therefore, since the substance of the mind has been discovered to be exceptionally mobile, its component particles must be extremely small, smooth, and round. If you grasp this fact, my good friend, you will find that it will stand you in good stead in many connections.

The following fact too is indicative of the subtle texture of the mind's substance and the smallness of the space that it would occupy if it could 210 be gathered into a compact mass. As soon as a person is wrapped in the peaceful sleep of death and the substance of the mind and spirit has withdrawn, the body suffers no perceptible loss either in appearance or in weight: death leaves all intact, save the vital sensibility and heat. Therefore the entire soul is composed of very small seeds, which form a chain throughout the veins, flesh, and sinews; this must be so, because, even when all the soul has quit the whole body, the external contour of the frame is preserved in its integrity, and not one grain of weight is wanting. 220 It is like the case of a wine whose bouquet has evaporated, or of a perfume whose exquisite scent has dispersed into the air, or of some object whose flavor has departed: the substance itself suffers no visible diminution of size or loss of weight, undoubtedly because the flavors and odors that permeate the bodies of things are produced by many minute seeds. So I insist that the substance of the mind and spirit evidently is composed of extremely tiny seeds, since in its flight it carries off not one 230 grain of weight.

However, we must not suppose that the substance of the soul is simple. At death a sort of light breath impregnated with heat leaves the body, and heat draws air with it; indeed there is no heat that is not impregnated with air, because the rarity of its substance means that it must be interpenetrated by many primary particles of air. Already, then, the substance of the soul has been found to consist of three elements. But a combination of these three is not sufficient to produce sensibility, since the mind refuses to accept that any one of them is capable of producing sensory 240

motions and the thoughts that it itself revolves. Therefore a fourth element must be added to their number. This is entirely nameless;[20] it surpasses every existing thing in its mobility, in its subtlety, and in the smallness and smoothness of its atoms; this it is that initiates the channeling of the sensory motions through the limbs. It is the first to be stirred, because of the smallness of its component atoms; then the heat and the invisible power of the wind take up the motions, then the air; then everything is put in motion: the blood is actuated, and every part of the
250 flesh is pervaded by the sensation; the bones and marrow are the last to be affected, whether it be by pleasure or by the opposite emotion. But pain cannot penetrate so far, and intense agony cannot pierce so deep, with impunity: if they succeed, they cause general commotion of such violence that no place is left for life, and the particles of the spirit disperse through every pore of the body. For the most part, however, these motions are checked virtually on the surface of the body; and this is why we are able to preserve life.

Now, eager though I am to explain the way in which these elements[21] are intermingled, and the manner in which their functions are coordi-
260 nated, I am hampered by the inadequacy of our native tongue.[22] Nevertheless, I will touch upon the subject briefly to the best of my ability.

The atoms of the elements interpenetrate one another in their motions in such a way that it is impossible for any single element to be isolated or for its function to be separated spatially from that of the others; rather, all are, one might say, the many qualities of a single body. Compare how, although every part of a living creature's flesh has a distinct smell, color,[23] and taste, these qualities together constitute the bulk of a single
270 body. In the same way, a single substance is formed by a mixture of the heat and the air and the invisible power of the wind, together with that mobile force that gives rise to the initial motion and imparts it to the other elements and that is the ultimate source of sensory motion in every

---

20. **241–242:** Cf. Aëtius 4.3.11 (Us. *fr.* 315): "Epicurus regards the soul as a mixture of four things—something fiery, something airy, something windy, and a fourth nameless element." As Lucr. makes clear, the nameless element, an element more subtle than any element of our experience, was added in order to account for the extraordinarily subtle processes of thought and sensation. The idea of the fourth element may owe something to Aristotle's concept of the fifth element or quintessence.

21. **258:** The four elements of the soul.

22. **260:** Cf. 1.136–139, 832.

23. **267:** Reading *color* (Lambinus) rather than *calor.*

part of the flesh. This fourth element is deep-buried and deep-hidden;[24] indeed there is nothing in our body more impalpable: it is the very soul of the whole soul. Just as the force of the mind and the power of the spirit, owing to the smallness and fewness of their constituent particles, imperceptibly interpenetrate our limbs and every part of our body, so this nameless force, by reason of the minuteness of its component atoms, lies 280 hidden; it is, one might say, the very soul of the whole soul, and it is the supreme ruler of the whole body.

Similarly the wind and the air and the heat must function in an intermixture throughout the limbs and, although a particular element is bound to be more or less prominent than the others, all must be so intermixed that they are seen to form a unity: otherwise the heat and the wind and the power of the air would destroy sensation by their independent action and dissolve it by their divorce.

The mind contains as well the element of heat, which it displays when it seethes with anger and fire flashes fiercely from the eyes. It also 290 contains an abundance of that chill breath, the attendant of fear, which provokes shuddering in the limbs and makes the frame tremble. It contains too that still, calm air, which is in evidence when the breast is tranquil and the countenance unclouded. But heat is the element that predominates in those creatures whose hearts are fierce and whose irascible minds readily seethe with anger. First and foremost in this class are lions, so strong and ferocious: often they growl and roar until they burst their bellies, since they are unable to repress their tempestuous rage. On the other hand, the chill minds of deer contain more wind and are quicker 300 to send icy currents of air blowing through the flesh, thus inducing a trembling motion in the limbs. Again, the predominant element in the vital principle of cows is placid air: these beasts are never unduly inflamed and impassioned by the smoky torch of anger or blinded by its murky shadow; nor are they pierced and paralyzed by icy shafts of fear: they stand midway between deer and savage lions.

It is the same with human beings. Although education may give certain people equal refinement, it cannot obliterate the original traces of each individual's natural disposition. We must not suppose that faults of 310 character can be extirpated, and that it is possible to stop one person from being excessively prone to sudden fits of rage, another from succumbing a little too readily to fear, and a third from accepting certain situations more meekly than one should. And in many other respects people must

---

24. **273:** In this context "deep-buried" and "deep-hidden" do not express remoteness from the surface of the body, but, as P. M. Brown, in his edition of Book 3 (Aris and Phillips: Warminster, 1997), puts it, "remoteness from perceptibility."

differ in character and consequently in behavior. But for the moment I
cannot explain the secret causes of this variety or find names for all the
atomic conformations that give rise to it. What I see that I can affirm in
320 this connection is that the surviving traces of our natural dispositions,
which philosophy is unable to erase, are so very faint that there is nothing
to prevent us from living a life worthy of the gods.[25]

Now, the substance of the soul is encased by the whole body and is in
its turn the custodian of the body and the cause of its safety;[26] for the two
are twined together by common roots and evidently cannot be disen-
330 tangled without being destroyed. It is no easier matter to extricate the
substance of the mind and spirit from the whole body without causing
general disintegration than it is to extract the scent from lumps of incense
without destroying the substance in the process. Having their constituent
atoms inextricably intertwined from the moment of their creation, body
and soul are copartners in life; and it is evident that neither of them is
capable of experiencing sensation independently, without the help of the
other: rather it is by the united motions of both together that sensation is
kindled and fanned into flame in every part of our flesh. Besides, the
body is never born without the soul, never grows up without it, and
manifestly never lives on without it after death. For, unlike water, which
340 often releases the heat that has been imparted to it without undergoing
dissolution or diminution in consequence, never, I say, never can the
limbs survive when they are divorced from the spirit and abandoned
by it: they suffer decomposition, dissolution, and total destruction. So
from the beginning of their existence, even when they are nestling in
the mother's womb, body and spirit in mutual association learn the
motions necessary to life; and this is why they cannot be divorced without meeting with disaster and destruction. You may see then that, since
their lives are bound up together, their substances also are firmly bound
together.

350   Furthermore, anyone who tries to refute the notion that the body has
sensation, and believes that only the spirit in its interpenetration of the

---

25. **322:** See p. xxxi.

26. **323–324:** Cf. Diogenes of Oinoanda *fr.* 37.I. "The soul furnishes nature with
[the ultimate] cause [both of life and of] death. It is true that the number of its
constituent atoms, both its rational and irrational parts being taken into account,
does not equal that of the body; yet it girdles the whole person and, while being
itself confined, in its turn binds the person, just as the minutest quantity of acid
juice binds a huge quantity of milk."

whole body experiences this motion that we term sensation, is challenging a patent truth. For who will ever explain what bodily sensation is, if it is not what the actual facts of experience have shown and taught us? It is true that, once the spirit is released, the body is utterly destitute of sensation; but then what it loses was not its peculiar property in life, but one of many accidents[27] that it loses when it is expelled from life.

Moreover, to affirm that the eyes cannot perceive anything, but are the 360 means through which the mind sees, as though through open doors, is no easy matter when the sensory experience of our eyes leads us to the opposite conclusion, dragging and driving us to the pupils themselves; especially so, since we often fail to perceive glittering objects because our eyes are dazzled by their brightness. This does not happen to doors: those through which we really do see experience no pain when they are opened wide. Moreover, if our eyes act as doors, obviously the mind ought to have a clearer view when they are removed and doorposts and all have been taken up.[28]

In this connection, you certainly cannot accept the revered hypothesis 370 of the great Democritus,[29] that the elements of body and spirit are placed in juxtaposition, succeed one another alternately, and so weave the fabric of our frame. For the component atoms of the spirit are not only much smaller than those of our body and flesh; they are also outnumbered by them[30] and are scattered thinly through our limbs. So at least you may confidently assert that the intervals separating the primary particles of the spirit correspond to the size of the smallest objects whose impact is 380 able to awaken sensory motions in our bodies.[31] Sometimes we are not conscious of dust clinging to our bodies, or of a sprinkling of chalk that

---

27. **358:** Including color, heat, motion.

28. **359–369:** The theory that the eyes, ears, and nose are "doors" or "windows," through which the soul sees, hears, or smells, is described by Cicero *Tusc. Disp.* 1.46. It may have originated with Heraclitus and was adopted by the Stoics. For the characteristic reductio ad absurdum with which Lucr. concludes his refutation, compare 1.915–920.

29. **371:** Democritus (c.460–c.370 B.C.) developed the atomic theory invented by Leucippus. Despite important differences between his system and the Epicurean one, Lucr. respected him: see also 1039–1041, 5.622 (identical to 3.371).

30. **376:** The same point is made by Diogenes of Oinoanda in the passage quoted in the note on 323–324.

31. **377–380:** I quote my note in the Loeb: "An object that impinges on us and is not felt is smaller than the interval between two soul-particles. However, there is a problem below; for, among the examples of objects whose impingement we do

settles on our limbs; we do not feel a mist at night, or the spider's filmy
threads in our path that ensnare us as we move, or the same creature's
withered vesture[32] alighting on our heads, or birds' feathers, or floating
thistle down whose exceptional lightness often makes falling a heavy
390 task; nor do we feel the tread of each and every creeping creature, nor
each separate footstep that gnats and suchlike insects plant upon our
bodies. It all goes to show that many particles must be stirred up within
us before the seeds of spirit that interpenetrate every part of our bodies
begin to feel that the elements have been disturbed, and before they can
buffet their way across such great intervals, dash together, unite, and
spring apart again.

Powerful though the spirit is, the mind does more to keep secure the
vital fastenings and exercises more dominance over life. For without the
intellect and mind not one particle of the spirit can remain in the body for
400 the briefest moment of time; rather the spirit obediently follows the
mind's lead, dispersing into the air and leaving the limbs in the icy grip of
chill death. But, if a person's intellect and mind are preserved, life is
preserved. It does not matter how much the trunk is mutilated: even if all
the limbs have been amputated, so that the spirit that occupied those
members has been removed and separated from the body, the amputee
lives and draws in the ethereal breath of life. Though deprived, admit-
tedly not of all, but still of a considerable portion of the spirit, the person
lingers in life and clings to it.[33] Here is a parallel: even though an eye is
lacerated all around, so long as the pupil has survived unimpaired, the
410 living power of sight is preserved provided that you do not mutilate the
whole orb of the eye and so pare around the pupil as to leave it isolated;
for if you do that, the destruction of both orb and pupil is inevitable. But
once that central spot of the eye, minute as it is, suffers damage, the light
sets and gives way to darkness, no matter how sound the rest of the
shining orb may be. Such is the compact whereby spirit and mind are
ever conjoined.

---

not feel, Lucr. mentions cobwebs, feathers, and thistle-down—all of which obviously extend over more space than the interval between two soul-particles, and
are not felt because of their lightness rather than because of their smallness.
Either, as Bailey suggests, Lucr. failed to see any difference between his examples; or, as Giussani thinks, he may have believed that there are no soul-particles
on the absolute surface of the body."

32. **385–386:** The spider's molt.

33. **403–407:** The same point is made by Diogenes of Oinoanda *fr.* 37.I.13–
III.10.

Now then, to enable you to grasp that the minds and light spirits of living creatures are subject to birth and death, I will proceed to set forth verses that are the product of long research and the fruit of joyful labor[34]— verses worthy of your[35] manner of life. See to it that you couple spirit 420 and mind together under one name, and when, for example, I proceed to speak of the spirit and demonstrate its mortality, assume that my words apply to the mind as well, since the two are identical in structure and constitute a unity.

To begin with, I have demonstrated[36] that the spirit is subtle, being composed of minute particles. Its constituent atoms are much smaller than those of the clear moisture of water or those of mist or smoke, for it far surpasses them in mobility and a much slighter impulse suffices to set it in motion: indeed even images of smoke and mist set it in motion. 430 Compare how, when we are wrapped in sleep, we perceive altars exhaling columns of steam and giving off smoke; for unquestionably such perceptions are caused by images that are carried to us.[37] Now therefore, since, when vessels containing water are shattered, you perceive that the liquid flows out on all sides and disperses, and since mist and smoke dissolve into the breezy air, you must assume that the spirit too is dissipated, perishing much more quickly and being resolved more speedily into its ultimate particles, once it has been dislodged from the limbs and has withdrawn. For if the body, which is, as it were, the vessel of the 440 spirit,[38] is shattered by some force and made porous by the withdrawal of blood from the veins, so that it is no longer able to retain it, how can you believe that the spirit can ever be retained by air, which is a more porous container than our body?

Moreover, we are aware that the mind is born with the body, develops with it, and declines with it. A toddling child possesses a feeble intellect

---

34. **419:** Cf. 2.730–731.

35. **420:** "Your" = Memmius'.

36. **425:** 177–230.

37. **428–433:** The theory of images is explained in Book 4. See also pp. xxvii–xxviii. Lucr. mentions steam and smoke, because these, being fine substances, would discharge particularly fine images.

38. **440:** For the idea that the body is the "vessel" of the soul, cf. 555, 793 (identical to 5.137). For the idea that the mind itself is a vessel, see 936–937, 1003–1010, 6.17–21. On the vessel metaphor, especially, but not only, in reference to the mind or soul, see W. Görler, "Storing up Past Pleasures: The Soul-Vessel-Metaphor in Lucretius and in His Greek Models," in K. A. Algra et al. (eds.), *Lucretius and His Intellectual Background* 193–207.

that matches the weakness and delicacy of its body. Then, when maturity
450 is attained and strength is robust, judgment and mental power are corre-
spondingly more fully developed. Later, when the body is shaken by the
stern strength of time and the frame droops with forces dulled, the
intellect halts, the tongue raves, the mind staggers; everything fades and
fails at once. So it is natural to infer that the substance of the spirit too is
all dissolved, like smoke, into the breezy air aloft, since we observe that
it is born with the body, develops with it, and, as I have shown, succumbs
with it to the stress and strain of age.

460   There is the further point that, just as the body suffers dreadful
diseases and pitiless pain, so the mind manifestly experiences the gripe
of cares, grief, and fear; so the natural inference is that it has an equal
share in death.[39]

       Even during the body's sicknesses the mind often wanders from the
path of reason: patients are demented and mutter deliriously and sometimes, severely comatose, sink with drooping eyelids and nodding head
into a deep and endless sleep, from which they do not hear the voices and
cannot recognize the features of those who, with faces and cheeks be-
470 dewed with tears, stand around and implore them to return to life. Therefore, seeing that the mind is susceptible to the infection of disease, you
are bound to admit that it suffers dissolution like the body. For pain and
disease are the architects of death—a lesson that the fate of millions in
the past has inculcated upon us.
       Again, when the piercing potency of wine has penetrated into people,
and its warmth has been distributed and channeled into the veins, the
limbs become heavy; they reel about with staggering steps; the tongue
480 drawls, the mind is sodden, and the eyes swim; they bawl, belch, and
brawl more and more violently. What is the reason for these and all the
other similar symptoms of drunkenness,[40] if it is not that the potent
punch of the wine invariably has the effect of confounding the spirit
within the body? And the very fact that things can be confounded and
crippled always signifies that, if a slightly stronger force were to insinu-

39. **459–462:** The Stoic Panaetius (c.185–109 B.C.) is another who argued that
the soul's susceptibility to pain is evidence of its mortality: see Cicero *Tusc. Disp.*
1.79. The argument is an interesting one. No less interesting is Lucr.'s contention
below (510–525) that another indication of the soul's mortality is that it responds
to medical treatment.

40. **481:** E. J. Kenney, in his edition of Book 3 (Cambridge University Press:
Cambridge, 1971), notes Lucr.'s "unwillingness to describe the more disgusting
phenomena of drunkenness in his poetry."

ate itself into them, the result would be destruction and debarment from further life.

Often too people are seized before our very eyes by a sudden fit of epilepsy and fall to the ground as though struck by lightning. They foam at the mouth and groan; their limbs are convulsed; they lose their reason; 490 their muscles grow rigid; they writhe, gasp fitfully, and weary their limbs with spasmic movements. The fact is that the spirit in every part of their frame is so distracted by the violence of the seizure that it surges and foams, just as the waves of the salt sea seethe beneath the furious force of the winds. The groaning is wrung from them, because their limbs are suffering pain, and in general because vocal particles are ejected and swept in a body from the mouth, using their habitual egress and what one might call their highway. Loss of reason comes about, because the mind and spirit with their powers are confounded and, as I have shown, are 500 disparted, dispersed, and distracted by that same poison. Afterward, when the cause of the fit has withdrawn and the acrid humor of the distempered body has retired to its lairs, then and only then the patient totteringly rises, gradually recovers all the senses, and regains possession of the spirit.

Since the mind and spirit, even while encased in the body, are shaken by such serious maladies and are wretchedly distracted and distressed, how can you believe that they can continue to live outside the body in the open air, exposed to the whirling winds?

Moreover, the fact that the mind, like the body, manifestly can be 510 cured of sickness and can respond to the influence of medicine is another intimation of its mortality. For it is fair to assume that every endeavor to transform the mind, and indeed every attempt to alter any other substance, entails the addition of parts or the transposition of the existing parts or the subtraction of at least some tittle from the sum. But an immortal substance does not allow its parts to be transposed, nor does it permit one jot to be added or to steal away. For every change that involves a thing outstepping its own limits means the instantaneous 520 death of what previously existed.[41] Therefore, as I have shown, whether the mind falls sick or responds to the influence of medicine, it betrays its mortal nature. So firmly is true fact seen to confront false reasoning and cut off its retreat, proving the falsehood by a two-pronged refutation.

Again, we often watch a person pass away by slow degrees, and limb by limb lose the vital sensibility; first the toes and toenails grow livid; then the feet and legs mortify; and then with stealing steps chill death 530

41. **519–520:** Identical to 1.670–671, 792–793, 2.753–754.

creeps over the rest of the frame. And seeing that in this case the substance of the spirit is split up and does not issue from the body all at one
time in its integrity, it must be reckoned mortal. You may perhaps imagine that it could retreat inward throughout the frame, concentrate its parts
into one place, and so drain the sensibility from every limb. But in that
case the place where such a large quantity of spirit is collected ought to
show itself to be endowed with acuter sensibility; and since no such
place is to be found, doubtless the position is as I have already stated it:
540   the spirit is divided piecemeal and dispersed and therefore perishes. In
fact, even if I were prepared to concede the untrue and grant that the soul
can mass itself together in the bodies of those who leave the light of life
limb by limb, you would still have to acknowledge that it is mortal. It
makes no difference whether it perishes through being dispersed into the
air, or whether its sensibility is deadened by the contraction of its constituent parts, since in either case the whole person more and more loses
sensation on every side, and on every side less and less of life remains.

Moreover, the mind is a distinct part of a person and is firmly fixed in a
550   definite place, just like the ears and eyes and all the other organs of sense
that pilot our lives; and just as the hand or eye or nose, once detached
from us, cannot experience sensation or truly exist, but quickly decom-
poses, so the mind cannot exist independently of the body and the actual
person; for the body may be regarded as a vessel[42] for the mind, or as
anything else you care to imagine that implies a more intimate relationship with it, since the two are closely interlinked.

Furthermore, the body and mind as vital forces owe their energy and
560   enjoyment of life to their interconnection: divorced from the body, the
substance of the mind cannot by itself produce vital motions; and the
body, once abandoned by the spirit, cannot live on and experience sensation. The fact is that, just as an eye, ripped from its roots and detached
from the rest of the body, is unable to see anything, so the spirit and mind
evidently have no power by themselves. Doubtless the reason is that, in
their interpenetration of the veins and flesh and sinews and bones, their
elements are confined by the whole body and are unable to spring apart
freely to considerable distances; and because they are thus pent in, they
570   perform sensory motions—motions that, after death and their expulsion
from the body into the breezy air, they cannot perform, since they are not
then confined in the same manner. Indeed air would be an animate body,
if the spirit could maintain its cohesion and restrict itself to those motions

---

42. **555:** See note on 440.

that it performed previously in the sinews and in the body itself. So I insist that, when the whole bodily encasement has disintegrated and the vital breath has been expelled, you must acknowledge that the mind and the spirit with their powers of sensation suffer dissolution, since body and soul are interdependent.

Again, since the body cannot endure divorce from the spirit, but pu- 580 trefies with a foul stench, how can you doubt that the spirit, issuing from deep down within, has seeped out and dispersed like smoke, and that the reason why the body is transformed, crumbling away and collapsing in utter ruin, is that its deepest foundations have been displaced by the spirit as it seeps out right through the limbs, through all the body's sinuous channels, and through all its pores? So you have ample evidence that the substance of the spirit is already split up when it passes out through the limbs, and that it is torn apart actually within the body before it glides out 590 into the breezy air and floats away.

In fact, even before it outsteps the confines of life, the spirit is often so shaken by some force that it seems to wish to depart and to be released from the whole body; and we see that, as in life's final hour, the face grows flaccid and all the limbs droop limply from the bloodless body. This is what happens to a person who, as we say, has had a turn or fainted: instantly the scene is one of trepidation, as everyone strives to prevent life's last link from snapping. In such a case the mind and the 600 entire spirit receive a violent shock, and both collapse with the body itself; consequently a slightly stronger force could cause them to disintegrate. How then can you continue to doubt that the spirit, once weakened by its expulsion from the body into the open air, once stripped of its encasement, could not survive for the briefest moment of time, let alone subsist throughout eternity?

Moreover, it is evident that the dying never feel their spirit issuing in its entirety from their whole body or mounting, before its departure, to their throat and gullet; rather they feel it failing in the particular spot 610 where it is located, just as they are aware that each of their other senses is being snuffed out in its own domain. The truth is that, if our mind were immortal, at the moment of death, far from bemoaning its dissolution, it would rejoice that it was passing out and shedding its vesture, like a snake.

Again, why is the intelligence and reasoning of the mind never born in the head or feet or hands? Why does it always reside in one fixed place, in one particular spot, if it is not because a particular place is assigned to each thing where it can be born and where it can survive after its creation,

620 and because the manifold members of each being are so disposed that their order is never inverted? Effect invariably follows cause: flame does not spring from streams, nor is cold born in fire.

Moreover, if the substance of the spirit is immortal and retains sentient power when separated from our body, presumably we must assume that it is provided with the five senses. In no other way can we visualize spirits roaming in the infernal realms of Acheron. That is why painters 630 and writers[43] of generations past have represented spirits as endowed with senses. But, divorced from the body, the soul cannot have either eyes or nose or hands or tongue or ears and therefore cannot possess either sentience or life.

And since we feel that vital sensibility is present in the whole body, and that every part is animate, it is obvious that if some force suddenly cuts the body in two with a swift blow and separates the two halves, the 640 spirit too will be disparted, divided, and dissevered with the body. But what is severable or in any way divisible evidently disclaims an immortal nature.

Stories are told of how scythed chariots,[44] steaming with promiscuous slaughter, often shear off limbs so suddenly that the fallen member lopped from the trunk is seen to quiver on the ground; and yet the warrior's mind can feel no pain on account of the swiftness of the stroke, and also because the mind is wholly absorbed in the ardor of the battle; with the remainder of his body he seeks blood and battle, 650 often not realizing that his left arm, buckler and all, has been swept away among the horses by the wheels with their rapacious scythes. Another is unaware that his right arm has been lopped, while he menacingly mounts the chariot. A third endeavors to stand up on the leg he has lost, while on the ground nearby his dying foot twitches its toes. A head shorn from a warm and living trunk preserves on the ground its

---

43. **629:** "Painters": for example, Polygnotus (fifth century B.C.) at Delphi and Nicias (fourth century B.C.) at Athens. "Writers": notably Homer in *Odyssey* 11.

44. **642:** War chariots fitted with scythes were not used by the Greeks or Romans. An Eastern invention, they are first mentioned by Xenophon *Anabasis* 1.8.10. Livy 37.41.5–8 gives a detailed description of them in his account of the battle of Magnesia fought in 190 or 189 B.C. between the Romans and Antiochus III of Syria. Antiochus' scythed chariots proved useless when the Romans and their allies succeeded in frightening the horses, and he lost the battle. The war against Antiochus was narrated by Ennius, and it is possible that the present passage owes something to his account.

look of life and open eyes, until it has surrendered all the last traces of spirit.

Moreover, suppose you have a snake with darting tongue, threatening tail, and elongated body, and suppose you choose to take a hatchet and chop both parts[45] of the creature into many pieces, then, while the wound is fresh, you will see each section separately writhing and bespattering 660 the ground with gore; and you will observe the front part attempting to bite its own hinder part in order to smother the burning pain caused by the wounding blow.

Shall we then say that there is an entire spirit in each of those little parts? But on that supposition it will follow that a single living creature had many spirits in its body. So the position is this: that spirit which formed a single unity has been divided with the body; and since both alike can be severed into many parts, both must be considered mortal.

Moreover, if the substance of the spirit is immortal and stealthily 670 enters the body at the moment of birth,[46] why do we have no recollection of our earlier existence, and why do we retain no vestiges of past actions?[47] If the faculties of the mind are so totally transformed that all memory of past events has been obliterated, such a state, in my opinion, is not far removed from death. Therefore you must admit that the previous spirit has perished, and that the present spirit is a new creation.

Furthermore, if the living power of the mind is imported into our 680 already completed bodies at the moment of birth, when we are crossing the threshold of life, one would not then expect to see it grow with the

---

45. **658:** Comparison with 668–669 strongly suggests that by "both parts" Lucr. means "both the body and the spirit," though it is just possible that he is referring to the front and back parts of the snake's body.

46. **670–671:** Many of those who in the ancient world believed that the soul is immortal took the view that it must have had an eternal existence before birth, as well as be destined to have an eternal existence after death. In 670–783 Lucr. argues against this view. Part of his argument is directed against the doctrine of transmigration of souls, accepted by the Orphics, Pythagoreans, Empedocles, and Plato.

47. **672–673:** Plato in his *Meno* and *Phaedo* claims that we do have some recollection of an earlier existence: he says that the things that we see in this life remind us of the ideal forms of which we had knowledge before we were born; he asserts that "knowledge is recollection" and uses this doctrine as part of his proof of the soul's preexistence. Lucr. does not consider Plato's view, presumably because he regards it as too absurd to merit mention.

body and the limbs in the very blood; rather one would expect it to live in total isolation, as in a cage,[48] while still managing to flood the whole body with sensibility. So I insist that spirits must not be considered either uncreated or exempt from the law of death. For it must not be supposed that they could be so intimately connected with our bodies if they were
690 insinuated into them from without; and yet the existence of this intimate connection is a patent fact: indeed the spirit's interpenetration of the body through the veins, flesh, sinews, and bones is so complete that even the teeth are given a share in sensation, as is shown by toothache, or the twinge caused by icy water, or the crunching of rough grit concealed in a piece of bread. What is more, since the spirit is so closely interwoven with the tissue of the body, it is evident that it cannot depart in its integrity and disentangle itself intact from all the sinews, bones, and joints.

But if by chance you imagine that the spirit insinuates itself into the
700 body from without and then permeates our limbs, it is all the more certain that it will perish through fusion with the body, because permeation implies dissolution and therefore destruction. The spirit is diffused through all the pores in the body; and just as food, when it is channeled into all the members and limbs, disintegrates and converts itself into a new substance, so the mind and spirit, even if intact when they pass into the newly formed body, suffer dissolution in the process of permeation: their particles are channeled through all the pores into the limbs,
710 and form this new mind that is the present ruler of our body and the offspring of the original mind that perished when it was diffused through the frame. It is obvious therefore that the substance of the spirit is neither without a birthday nor exempt from death.

Here is another problem: are any seeds of spirit left in the lifeless body or not? If some are left inside it, there cannot be any justification for regarding the spirit as immortal, since it has withdrawn diminished by the loss of some of its parts. If, on the other hand, it has retired with its constituent elements intact and has escaped without leaving any part of itself in the body, what is the source of the maggots that corpses upheave
720 from their putrid flesh?[49] What is the source of this swarm of bloodless and boneless animate creatures that surge over the seething frame? But if by chance you believe that spirits insinuate themselves into the maggots from without, and that each of them can enter into a body, then, even if

---

48. **684:** The Pythagoreans and Plato believed that the soul does indeed live in a body as in a prison—a prison from which it longs to escape.

49. **719–721:** For belief in the spontaneous generation of worms, maggots, and suchlike, see note on 2.871–872.

you fail to ask yourself why many thousands of spirits should congregate in a place from which one only has withdrawn, there is a question that must be posed and resolved: do the spirits hunt out all the component seeds of the tiny maggots and construct a home for themselves, or do they steal into ready-made bodies? But no valid reason can be given why 730 they should take the trouble to build bodies for themselves: after all, so long as they flit about bodiless, they are not distressed by disease or cold or hunger; the body is much more susceptible to these afflictions, and it is through sympathy with it that the mind suffers many maladies. And even supposing it were very much to their advantage to build a body that they could enter, it would obviously be impossible for them to do so. Spirits, then, do not make bodies and limbs for themselves. Nor is there any possibility that they insinuate themselves into ready-made bodies: for in that case body and spirit could not be intricately interwoven or establish 740 mutual sympathy through mutual sensibility.

Again, why is cruel ferocity a permanent characteristic of the sullen breed of lions, and cunning of foxes? Why, in the case of deer, is the instinct of flight transmitted from generation to generation, so that their limbs are spurred by inherited timidity? Indeed, why are all other such qualities implanted in the constitution of body and mind from life's first dawn? Surely the explanation must be that a mind, whose nature is determined by its own seed and breed, develops along with the body of each individual animal. But if the mind were immortal and in the habit of transmigrating, the characters of living creatures would be topsy-turvy: often the hound of Hyrcanian stock[50] would flee before the onset of the 750 antlered stag; the hawk would flee trembling through the breezy air at the swoop of the dove; human beings would be irrational, while the species of brute beasts would be rational. The argument that an immortal soul undergoes alteration when it changes its body is advanced on false grounds. For change implies dissolution and therefore destruction. The parts of the soul are subject to transposition and rearrangement, and therefore must be liable also to suffer dissolution throughout the limbs, so that ultimately they all perish with the body. If it is claimed that human 760 souls always migrate into human bodies, I will still want to know why a wise soul can become foolish, why a child never possesses prudence, and why a foal is less well trained than a horse of powerful strength.[51] No

---

50. **750:** The Hyrcani, who lived on the southeast shore of the Caspian Sea, had an extremely fierce breed of dogs.

51. **764:** The case of the horse is added, because the theory that human souls always migrate into human bodies is meant to imply that the souls of other creatures always remain constant to the same species.

doubt my opponents will take refuge in the supposition that in a weak body the mind becomes weak. But if this supposition is true, you must admit that the soul is mortal, since it is so totally transformed throughout the body that it loses its former vitality and sensibility. Moreover, how will the mind be able to grow strong in concert with any particular body 770 and attain with it the coveted bloom of maturity, if it is not its partner from the moment of conception? And what prompts it to abandon the decrepit limbs? Is it afraid of remaining cooped up in the crumbling body, in case its home, worn out by long lapse of years, collapses and crushes it? But an immortal thing has no dangers to fear.

Again, it is palpably ridiculous to suppose that the souls are present at the matings and births of wild beasts—immortal souls numberless in 780 number waiting for mortal limbs, fiercely contesting who shall have priority and enter first. Or do the souls perhaps have an agreement stipulating that the first to come flying up shall enter first, and that there shall be no violent struggle between them?

Again, a tree cannot exist in the sky,[52] or clouds in the depths of the sea; fish cannot live in fields; blood is not found in timber, or sap in stones. The place where each thing may grow and exist is fixed and determined. Thus the substance of the mind cannot come to birth alone 790 without the body or exist separated from sinews and blood. But even if this were possible, the mind could far more easily reside in the head or the shoulders or the base of the heels, or be born in any other part of the body, and so at least remain within the same person, within the same vessel. However, since even within our body it is evident that a special place is firmly fixed and reserved for the existence and growth of the spirit and mind, it is all the more necessary for us to deny that they could survive or come to birth wholly outside the body. Therefore, when the body has died, you must acknowledge that the soul too has perished, torn to pieces all through the body.

800 Moreover, to yoke together the mortal and the everlasting, and to imagine that they can share one another's feelings and experiences, is fatuous. What notion can be more preposterous, incongruous, and inharmonious than that of a mortal thing being united with something immortal and imperishable, and of the two together weathering pitiless storms?

---

52. **784–797:** These lines are repeated, with minor alterations, at 5.128–141, as part of Lucr.'s argument that the parts of the world are not animate, let alone divine.

Furthermore, all things that subsist eternally must either be composed of solid substance, so that they repel blows and are impenetrable to anything that might destroy the close cohesion of their parts from within—like the elements of matter, whose nature I have already 810 demonstrated; or their ability to survive throughout all time must be due to their immunity from blows—as is the case with void, which is always intangible and never experiences any impact; or else the cause of their indestructibility must be the absence of any surrounding space into which their substance might disperse and dissolve—as is the case with the totality of the universe: for outside the universe there is no space into which its substance can escape, and no matter capable of striking it and shattering it with a powerful blow.[53]

If by chance the preferred supposition is that the soul is to be considered immortal because it is fortified and protected by the forces of life, 820 or because things fatal to its existence never approach it, or because those that do approach it are repulsed by some means before they can inflict any injury upon us, [it must be said that this supposition is at variance with the facts].[54] Besides sharing the diseases of the body, the soul is often visited by feelings that torment it about the future, fret it with fear, and vex it with anxious cares, while consciousness of past misdeeds afflicts it with remorse. Remember also madness and loss of memory—afflictions peculiar to the mind; remember the black waves of coma into which it sinks.

Death, then, is nothing to us[55] and does not affect us in the least, now 830 that the nature of the mind is understood to be mortal. And as in time past we felt no distress when the advancing Punic hosts were threatening Rome on every side, when the whole earth, rocked by the terrifying tumult of war, shudderingly quaked beneath the coasts of high heaven, while the entire human race was doubtful into whose possession the

---

53. **806–818:** These lines recur, with minor alterations, at 5.351–363, where Lucr. is demonstrating the mortality of the world. It is probably a sign of lack of revision that in the present context he does not state that the soul's failure to satisfy any of the three conditions of immortality shows that it must be mortal.

54. **819–823:** A line has been lost after 823. It is likely that Lucr. is alluding to the condition of immortality of the Epicurean gods, who, living in the intermundane spaces, continually gain new atoms to replace those which they lose.

55. **830:** "Death is nothing to us," a translation of the first words of Epicurus *PD* 2, might well serve as a title for the whole of the final section of this book (830–1094).

sovereignty of the land and the sea was destined to fall;[56] so, when we
are no more, when body and soul, upon whose union our being depends,
840 are divorced, you may be sure that nothing at all will have the power to
affect us or awaken sensation in us, who shall not then exist—not even if
the earth be confounded with the sea, and the sea with the sky.[57]

And even supposing that the mind and the spirit retain their power of
sensation after they have been wrenched from our body, it is nothing to
us, whose being is dependent upon the conjunction and marriage of body
and soul. Furthermore, if in course of time all our component atoms
should be reassembled after our death and restored again to their present
850 positions, so that the light of life was given to us a second time, even that
eventuality would not affect us in the least, once there had been a break
in the chain of consciousness. Similarly at the present time we are not
affected at all by any earlier existence we had, and we are not tortured
with any anguish concerning it. When you survey the whole sweep of
measureless time past and consider the multifariousness of the movements of matter, you can easily convince yourself that the same seeds
that compose us now have often before been arranged in the same order
that they occupy now. And yet we have no recollection of our earlier
860 existence; for between that life and this lies an unbridged gap—an interval during which all the motions of our atoms strayed and scattered in all
directions, far away from sensation.

If it happens that people are to suffer unhappiness and pain in the
future, they themselves must exist at that future time for harm to be able
to befall them; and since death takes away this possibility by preventing
the existence of those who might have been visited by troubles, you may
be sure that there is nothing to fear in death, that those who no longer
exist cannot become miserable, and that it makes not one speck of
difference whether or not they have ever been born once their mortal life
has been snatched away by deathless death.[58]

---

56. **832–837:** The reference is to the Punic Wars, fought between Rome and
Carthage, and especially to the Second Punic War (218–201 B.C.) during which
Hannibal invaded Italy and defeated the Romans in several battles.

57. **842:** That is to say, not even if the world comes to an end.

58. **869:** The paradoxical idea of "deathless death" goes back to the Greek comic
poet Amphis (fourth century B.C.), quoted by Athenaeus 8.336c: "Drink and have
fun! Life is mortal, and time on earth is short. Death is deathless, once one is
dead." Although Lucr. agrees with Amphis about the deathlessness of death, he
disagrees with the advice "eat and drink, for to-morrow we shall die," as he
makes clear in 912–918.

So, when you see people indignant at the thought that after death they 870
will either rot in the grave or be devoured by flames or the jaws of wild
beasts, you may be sure that, however emphatically they themselves
deny belief that they will retain any feeling in death, their words do not
ring true, and that deep in their hearts they are pricked by some secret
fear. In my judgment, they grant neither the conclusion they profess to
grant, nor the premise[59] from which it is derived; they do not completely
uproot and detach themselves from life, but unconsciously suppose that
something of themselves survives. Whenever people in life imagine that
in death their body will be torn to pieces by birds and beasts of prey, they 880
feel sorry for themselves. This is because they do not separate themselves from the body or dissociate themselves sufficiently from the out-
cast corpse; they identify themselves with it and, as they stand by,
impregnate it with their own feelings. Hence their indignation at having
been created mortal; hence their failure to see that in real death there will
be no second self alive to lament their own end, and to stand by and
grieve at the sight of them lying there, being torn to pieces or burned.
I mention being burned, because, if in death it is disastrous to be
mauled by the devouring jaws of wild beasts, I cannot see why it is not
calamitous to be laid upon a funeral pyre and consumed by scorching 890
flames, or to be embalmed in stifling honey, or to grow stiff with cold,
reclining on the smooth surface of an icy slab of stone,[60] or to be
pulverized by a crushing weight of earth above one.

"Never again," mourners say, "will your household receive you with
joy; never again will the best of wives welcome you home; never again
will your dear children race for the prize of your first kisses and touch
your heart with pleasure too profound for words.[61] Never again can you
enjoy prosperous circumstances or be a bulwark to your dependants.
Wretched man," they cry, "one wretched, damnable day has dis-
possessed you of every one of life's many precious gifts." They omit to 900

59. **876:** The premise is that the soul does not survive after death; the conclusion
is that there is no feeling after death.

60. **892:** E. J. Kenney well remarks that "the chilly discomfort of this situation,
in which the body has no covering, is ironically contrasted with that of the buried
body, which has too much."

61. **894–896:** These lines influenced Virgil (*Georgics* 2.523–524) and inspired a
famous stanza in Thomas Gray's *Elegy Written in a Country Churchyard* (21–
24): "For them no more the blazing hearth shall burn, / Or busy housewife ply her
evening care: / No children run to lisp their sire's return, / Or climb his knees the
envied kiss to share."

add: "No craving for these things remains with you any longer." If only
they fully grasped this fact and expressed their feelings accordingly, they
would relieve their minds of great anguish and fear.

I imagine another saying: "You, for your part, are wrapped in the sleep
of death and will remain so for the rest of time, exempt from all painful
sufferings. But we, as we stood near the dreadful pyre upon which you
were reduced to ashes, wept and wept for you insatiably; our sorrow is
undying: the day will never dawn that will banish it from our hearts."
910 The person who takes this attitude should be asked how a happening that
involves a return to sleep and repose can be so bitter that anyone should
pine away in undying grief.

It often happens too that people reclining at a banquet, drinking-cup in
hand and garlands shadowing their brows, earnestly declare: "All too
short-lived is the enjoyment of these things for us puny humans; soon it
will be gone, and we will never be able to recall it." As if the most
miserable misfortune awaiting them in death was to be consumed and
parched by a burning thirst or indeed to be afflicted with any other
craving! In fact, people never feel the want of themselves or their life,
920 when mind and body alike are sunk in sound sleep: as far as we are
concerned, this sleep might continue for ever without any craving for
ourselves affecting us. And yet, at the moment when people jerk themselves out of sleep and gather themselves together, the primary elements
of the spirit scattered throughout their limbs cannot be straying far from
the motions that produce sensation. It follows that death should be considered to be of much less concern to us than sleep—that is, if anything
can be less than what we perceive to be nothing. For at death a greater
disturbance and dispersion of matter takes place, and no one wakes and
930 rises once overtaken by life's cold stoppage.

Furthermore, suppose that nature suddenly burst into speech, and per-
sonally addressed the following rebuke to one of us:[62] "What distresses
you so deeply, mortal creature, that you abandon yourself to these puling
lamentations? Why do you bemoan and beweep death? If your past life
has been a boon, and if not all your blessings have flowed straight
through you and run to waste like water poured into a riddled vessel,[63]

---

62. **931–932:** The device of personifying nature and putting an address into her
mouth is dramatically effective and also enables Lucr. to say some harsh things
without giving offense. The same is true of the device, employed in 1024–1052,
of making Memmius and us address ourselves.

63. **936–937:** An allusion, as in 6.17–23, to the story of the Danaids, the fifty

why, you fool, do you not retire from the feast of life like a satisfied guest
and with equanimity resign yourself to undisturbed rest? If, however, all 940
your enjoyments have been poured away and lost, and if life is a thorn,
why do you seek to prolong your existence, when the future, just as
surely as the past, would be ruined and utterly wasted? Why not rather
put an end to life and trouble? There is nothing further that I can devise
and discover for your pleasure: all things are always the same. Though
your body is not yet shrunk with age, and your limbs are not exhausted
and enfeebled, all things remain the same—yes, even if in length of life
you should outlast all generations, or indeed even if you should be
destined never to die."[64] What can we say in reply, save that nature's 950
complaint is just, and that in her plea she sets out a true case?

And if someone older and more advanced in years should sorrowfully
bewail and bemoan the approach of death to an immoderate degree,
would she not be justified in rating that person still more roughly and
delivering an even sharper rebuke:[65] "Stop sniveling, you dolt![66] Away
with your whinings! You had full use of all the precious things of life
before you reached this senile state. But because you continually crave
what is not present and scorn what is, your life has slipped away from
you incomplete and unenjoyed, until suddenly you have found death
standing at your head before you are able to depart from the feast of life 960
filled to repletion. Quick then, discard all behavior unsuited to your age
and with equanimity yield to your years; for yield you must." In my
opinion, she would be justified in making this plea, justified in delivering
this rebuke and reproof. The old is ever ousted and superseded by the
new, and one thing must be repaired from others. No one is consigned to
the black abyss of Tartarus: everyone's component matter is needed to
enable succeeding generations to grow—generations which, when they
have completed their term of life, are all destined to follow you. The fate

---

daughters of Danaus, forty-nine of whom murdered their husbands on their
wedding night, and whose punishment in the underworld was to perform for
eternity the futile task of pouring water into leaking containers. To Lucr. the
Danaids represent those who are never satisfied with the good things of life, as he
explains in 1003–1010. On the vessel metaphor, see note on 440.

64. **944–949:** For the doctrine that pleasure is limited, and that infinite time
could not produce any greater pleasure, see Epicurus *PD* 18–20.

65. **952–954:** Cf. Diogenes of Oinoanda *fr.* 47.III.10–IV.2: "Or how can we
justly bring a complaint against nature, if someone who has lived for so many
years and so many months and so many days [arrives at life's last day]?"

66. **955:** Reading *barde* for *baratre*. See M. F. Smith, *Prometheus* 26 (2000) 35–
40.

in store for you has already befallen past generations and will befall
970 future generations no less surely. Thus one thing will never cease to rise
out of another: life is granted to no one for permanent ownership, to all
on lease.[67] Look back now and consider how the bygone ages of eternity
that elapsed before our birth were nothing to us. Here, then, is a mirror in
which nature shows us the time to come after our death. Do you see
anything fearful in it? Do you perceive anything grim? Does it not appear
more peaceful than the deepest sleep?

   Next let me assure you that all the punishments that tradition locates in
the abysm of Acheron actually exist in our life.[68]
980   No tormented Tantalus,[69] as in the story, fears the huge rock suspended over him in the air, paralyzed with vain terror; but in life mortals
are oppressed by groundless fear of the gods and dread the fall of the
blow that chance may deal to any of them.
   No Tityos[70] lying in Acheron has his insides devoured by winged
creatures. It is certain that they could not find anything for their beaks to
explore throughout eternity even in the depths of that huge breast: even if
the sprawling extent of his body were so enormous that his splayed-out
990 limbs covered not merely nine acres, but the whole orb of the earth, he
would not be able to endure eternal pain or furnish an inexhaustible

---

67. **971:** A justly famous line: life is not a permanent and absolute possession,
but something of which we only have temporary use.

68. **978–1023:** Denials of belief in the horrors of the underworld seem, not
surprisingly, to have been common in Epicurean teaching. So says Seneca *Epis-
tulae Morales* 24.18, and Diogenes of Oinoanda (*fr.* 73.I.1–8) writes: "[I follow
you (Epicurus)] when you make [these] statements about death, and you have
persuaded me to laugh at it. For I have no fear on account of the Tityoses and
Tantaluses whom some describe in Hades." It is not unlikely, though not certain,
that Lucr. has derived from Epicurus himself the idea that the punishments
alleged to exist in hell actually exist in our life.

69. **980–983:** Legendary king of Sipylus in Lydia, son of Zeus (Jupiter). He did
something (it is not agreed what) to offend the gods whose society he had been
privileged to share. According to Homer (*Odyssey* 11.582–592), his punishment
was to stand up to his chin in water, with fruit-laden branches over his head:
whenever he stooped to drink, the water receded; and whenever he tried to pick
the fruit, the wind blew it out of reach. The version of the punishment that Lucr.
adopts, because it suits his purpose better, is the one followed by the Greek lyric
and tragic poets.

70. **984–994:** A giant who attempted to rape Leto (Latona), the mother of
Apollo and Artemis (Diana). Lucr.'s description of his punishment is in imitation
of Homer *Odyssey* 11.576–581.

supply of food from his own body. However, Tityos does exist among us on earth: he is the person lying in bonds of love, who is torn by winged creatures[71] and consumed by agonizing anxiety or rent by the anguish of some other passion.

Sisyphus[72] too exists in this life before our eyes: he is the man who thirstily solicits from the people the rods and grim axes[73] of high office and always comes away disappointed and despondent. For to seek power that is illusory and never granted, and to suffer continual hardship in pursuit of it, is the same as to push up a mountain with might and main a   1000 rock that, after all this effort, rolls back from the summit and in impetuous haste races down to the level plain.[74]

Then again, to keep feeding an ungrateful mind with good things, without ever being able to fill it and satisfy its appetite—as is the case with the seasons of the year, when they come around with their fruits and manifold delights and yet never satisfy our appetite for the fruits of life—this, in my opinion, is what is meant by the story of those maidens[75] in the flower of their age pouring water into a riddled vessel that cannot possibly be filled.   1010

But what of Cerberus[76] and the Furies[77] and the realm destitute of light? What of Tartarus vomiting waves of fearful fumes from its jaws?[78] These terrors do not exist and cannot exist anywhere at all. But in life people are tortured by a fear of punishment as cruel as their crimes, and by the atonement for their offenses—the dungeon, the terrible precipita-

---

71. **993:** Cupids. But for *volucres* perhaps read *Veneres* ("sexual passions"), as suggested by S. Allen, *Classical Review* 14 (1900) 414.

72. **995–1002:** Legendary king of Corinth, notorious for his robberies, cunning, and treachery. Lucr. closely follows the description of his punishment in Homer *Odyssey* 11.593–600.

73. **996:** A bundle of rods with an axe in the middle (*fasces*) was carried before the chief magistrates at Rome.

74. **1002:** The stone races back down to the plain, just as the candidate for political office hurries back to the Plain of Mars (Campus Martius), where elections were held. For the possibility that a passage about the punishment of Ixion has dropped out after 1002, see especially H. D. Jocelyn, *Acta Classica* 29 (1986) 49–51.

75. **1008:** The Danaids. See note on 936–937.

76. **1011:** The monstrous dog that guarded the entrance to the lower world.

77. **1011:** Chthonian goddesses of vengeance.

78. **1011–1012:** It is possible that a line (or lines) has been lost after 1011 or 1012. If there is no lacuna, Marullus' *haec* for *qui* at the beginning of 1013 should probably be accepted.

tion from the Rock,[79] stripes, executioners, the execution cell, pitch, red-hot plates, torches.[80] Even though these horrors are absent, the mind, conscious of its guilt and fearfully anticipating the consequences, pricks
1020 itself with goads and sears itself with scourges. It fails to see how there can be an end to its afflictions, or a limit to its punishment; indeed it is afraid that its sufferings may increase in death. In short, fools make a veritable hell of their lives on earth.[81]

Now and again you might well address yourself in the following terms:[82] "Shame on you! Even good Ancus closed his eyes and left the light of life,[83] and he was a far, far better person than you.[84] Since then, many other kings and potentates, rulers of mighty nations, have passed away. Even that famous monarch[85] who once constructed a roadway
1030 over the great sea and opened a path for his legions across the deep, teaching his infantry to march over the briny gulfs while his cavalry pranced upon the ocean in defiance of its roars—yes, even he was deprived of the light of life and gasped out his soul from his dying body. Scipio,[86] that thunderbolt of war, the dread of Carthage, surrendered his bones to the earth as though he were the meanest of menial slaves. Remember too the inventors of sciences and arts; remember the companions of the Heliconian maidens,[87] among whom unique Homer bore the scepter and yet is wrapped in the same sound sleep as the others.

---

79. **1016:** The Tarpeian Rock on the Capitol at Rome from which criminals were thrown to their deaths.

80. **1017:** The execution cell is the Tullianum, the dungeon of the prison at Rome. Among those who met their end there were Jugurtha (104 B.C.) and the Catilinarian conspirators (63 B.C.). Pitch, red-hot plates, and torches are instruments of torture or death by burning.

81. **1023:** In contrast, the wise make a heaven of their lives on earth: see 322 and p. xxxi.

82. **1024:** See note on 931–932.

83. **1025:** A quotation from Ennius. Ancus Marcius was traditionally the fourth king of Rome (642–617 B.C.).

84. **1025–1026:** Lucr. is recalling Homer *Iliad* 21.107 (Achilles to the Trojan suppliant Lycaon, whom he is about to kill): "Even Patroclus died, and he was a far better man than you."

85. **1029:** The Persian king Xerxes, who invaded Greece in 480 B.C. and constructed a pontoon bridge across the Hellespont, to enable his troops to cross.

86. **1034:** Publius Cornelius Scipio Africanus the Elder, who in 202 B.C. defeated Hannibal at Zama.

87. **1037:** The Muses.

Democritus, warned by ripe old age that the motions of his mind's 1040
memory were failing, voluntarily went to meet death and offered him his
life.[88] Epicurus himself died, when the light of his life had accomplished
its course—he who outshone the human race in genius and obscured the
luster of all as the rising of the ethereal sun extinguishes the stars.[89] Will
you, then, be hesitant and indignant, when death calls? You, even while
you still have life and light, are as good as dead: you squander the greater
part of your time in sleep; you snore when awake; you never stop
daydreaming; you are burdened with a mind disturbed by groundless
fear; and often you cannot discover what is wrong with you, when, like 1050
some drunken wretch, you are buffeted with countless cares on every
side and drift along aimlessly in utter bewilderment of mind."

People evidently are aware that their minds are carrying a heavy load,
which wearies them with its weight; and if only they could also understand what causes it, and why such a mass of misery occupies their
breasts, they would not live in the manner in which we generally see
them living, ignorant of what they want for themselves, and continually
impatient to move somewhere else as if the change could relieve them of
their burden. Often a man leaves his spacious mansion, because he is 1060
utterly bored with being at home, and then suddenly returns on finding
that he is no better off when he is out. He races out to his country villa,
driving his Gallic ponies[90] hell-for-leather. You would think he was
dashing to save a house on fire. But the moment he has set foot on the
threshold, he gives a yawn or falls heavily asleep in search of oblivion or
even dashes back to the city. In this way people endeavor to run away
from themselves; but since they are of course unable to make good their
escape, they remain firmly attached to themselves against their will, and
hate themselves because they are sick and do not understand the cause of 1070
their malady. If only they perceived it distinctly, they would at once give
up everything else and devote themselves first to studying the nature of
things; for the issue at stake is their state not merely for one hour, but for

---

88. **1039–1041:** Democritus is said to have starved himself to death. Lucr.
appropriately uses an atomist's language to describe the atomist's mental decline.

89. **1042–1044:** This is the only place in the poem where Epicurus is named.
Lucr.'s praise of his master echoes the praise of Homer in an epigram by
Leonidas of Tarentum (*Anthologia Palatina* 9.24).

90. **1063:** Noted for their speed. Matthew Arnold is recalling this passage and
912–913 in *Obermann Once More* 97–104: "In his cool hall, with haggard eyes, /
The Roman noble lay; / He drove abroad, in furious guise, / Along the Appian
Way. / He made a feast, drank fierce and fast, / And crown'd his hair with
flowers—/ No easier nor no quicker pass'd / The impracticable hours."

eternity—the state in which mortals must pass all the time that remains after their death.

Finally, what is this perverse passion for life that condemns us to such a feverish existence amid doubt and danger? The fact is that a sure end of life is fixed for mortals: we cannot avoid our appointment with death. 1080 Moreover, our environment is always the same, and no new pleasure is procured by the prolongation of life.[91] The trouble is that, so long as the object of our desire is wanting, it seems more important than anything else; but later, when it is ours, we covet some other thing; and so an insatiable thirst for life keeps us always openmouthed. Then again, we cannot tell what fortune the future will bring us, or what chance will send us, or what end is in store for us. By prolonging life we do not deduct a single moment from the time of our death, nor can we diminish its 1090 duration by subtracting anything from it. Therefore, however many generations your life may span, the same eternal death will still await you; and one who ended life with today's light will remain dead no less long than one who perished many months and years ago.

---

91. **1080–1081:** Cf. 944–949 and see note there.

BOOK FOUR

Preface

The Existence and Nature of Filmy Images Emitted by Objects

Sensation and Thought

---

* All but the last two lines of the argument are lost.

Various Vital Functions: Nourishment, Locomotion, Sleep, Dreams, Sex

I am penetrating the remote regions of the Pierian maids, hitherto untrodden by any foot. Joyfully I visit virgin springs and draw their water;
joyfully I cull unfamiliar flowers, gathering for my head a chaplet of
fame from spots whence the Muses have never before taken a garland for
the brows of any person: first because I teach about important matters
and endeavor to disentangle the mind from the strangling knots of superstition, and also because on an obscure subject I compose such luminous
10 verses, overspreading all with the charm of the Muses. For obviously my
actual technique does not lack a motive. Doctors who try to give children
foul-tasting wormwood first coat the rim of the cup with the sweet juice
of golden honey; their intention is that the children, unwary at their
tender age, will be tricked into applying their lips to the cup and at the
same time will drain the bitter draft of wormwood—victims of beguilement, but not of betrayal, since by this means they recover strength and
health. I have a similar intention now: since this philosophy of ours often
20 appears somewhat off-putting to those who have not experienced it, and
most people recoil back from it, I have preferred to expound it to you in
harmonious Pierian poetry and, so to speak, coat it with the sweet honey
of the Muses. My hope has been that by this means I might perhaps

succeed in holding your attention concentrated on my verses, while you apprehend the nature of the universe and become conscious of the beneficial effect of my instruction.[1]

Well, now that I have demonstrated the nature of the soul, its constitution, the way in which it develops with the body, and the manner in which it is disaggregated and resolved into its component elements, I will begin to explain to you a matter that has an important bearing on these questions—namely, the existence of what we term images[2] of things. Images are sort of membranes stripped from the surfaces of objects and float this way and that through the air. It is these that visit us when we are awake or asleep, and terrify our minds each time we see the weird forms and phantoms of people bereft of the light of life—visions that often make us start from our heavy slumber and tremble with terror. We must not imagine that spirits escape from Acheron, or that shades of the dead flit among the living, or that any part of us can survive after death, when both the body and the substance of the soul have been destroyed and dissolved into their respective elements. I contend, then, that things emit filmy forms and images from their surfaces; and the proofs that follow will enable even the dullest wit to understand that I am right.

[Well, now that I have demonstrated the nature of the primary elements of all things, the diversity of their forms, the spontaneous manner in which they fly about under the impulse of incessant movement, and their ability to create everything, I will begin to explain to you a matter that has an important bearing on these questions—namely, the existence of what we term images of things. Images may be described as sort of membranes or bark, because each bears the appearance and form of the object from whose body it is shed and wanders away].[3]

In the first place, many things visibly discharge matter. Some of these discharges are rare and diffused, like the smoke emitted by wood or the heat by fire; others are of a closer and denser texture, like the sleek coats

30

40

50

---

1. **1–25:** These lines are repeated, with a few minor alterations, from 1.926–950. See notes there.

2. **30:** See pp. xxvii–xxviii.

3. **45–53:** These lines must have been written at a time when Lucr. intended Book 4 to follow Book 2. Lines 45–48, which are almost identical to 3.31–34, definitely refer to the subject matter of Books 1 and 2. When he changed his mind about the order of books, he wrote a new introductory passage (26–44), borrowing two lines (49–50) from the original version. If he had lived to complete the revision of his work, he would have struck out 45–53.

that cicadas periodically shed in summer, or the superficial membranes
60 of which newborn calves divest themselves, or again the vesture that the
slippery serpent works off on the thorns as is evidenced by the familiar
sight of brambles decorated with its fluttering slough. In view of these
visible discharges, there can be no doubt that subtle images too are
emitted from the surfaces of things. For why should those coarser substances fall away and withdraw from objects more readily than these
subtle films? It is impossible to say, especially when on the surfaces
of things there are multitudes of minute particles, which could be
70 discharged while preserving their previous order and configuration, and
which could be thrown off with much more velocity, because, being
comparatively few in number and stationed in the foremost positions,
they are less liable to be impeded. It is an observable fact that many
objects freely throw off particles emanating not only from deep within
them, as is the case with the substances I mentioned earlier,[4] but often
from their surfaces as well—particles of their own color. This commonly
happens, when the saffron, russet, and violet awnings stretched over
great theaters,[5] unfurled over masts and crossbeams, flap and undulate.
They dye all the scene below, projecting their rippling colors on to the
audience packed on the benches and the entire spectacle of the stage
80 . . . .[6] The more the theater is shut in by the surrounding hoard-
ings, and the less daylight is admitted, the more the whole enclosed area
laughs in a flood of gaiety. Now, since the canvas-canopies discharge
color from their surfaces, there can be no doubt that all things discharge
subtle images; for in both cases the emission is from the surface. There
are therefore definite traces of the forms that float about everywhere—
forms whose texture is so fine that they cannot be seen individually.
90   Again, the reason why smell, smoke, heat, and other similar things
invariably issue from objects diffusedly is that they emanate from deep
within and are divided up on their way to the surface, because the path is

---

4. **73:** The reference is to 56, where Lucr. mentions the smoke given off by
wood and the heat by fire. But only in 90–94 does he explain that smell, smoke,
and heat emanate from deep inside things.

5. **75–77:** Theater awnings were introduced in 78 B.C. They are mentioned
again—this time with reference to the noise that they make—in 6.109–110.
Rome did not have a stone theater until 55 B.C., and, since Lucr. almost certainly
died in that year, it is probable that he is referring to temporary theaters with
wooden seats and stage.

6. **79:** The text is seriously corrupt, and no convincing emendation has been
proposed.

a tortuous one and there are no straight passages to enable them to speed
out in a mass. However, when a fine, superficial film of color is discharged, there is nothing to tear it apart, since it is stationed in the front
rank, ready to depart.

Lastly, since the reflections that we see in mirrors,[7] in water, and in
every shining surface always resemble the objects themselves in appearance, they must be formed of images emitted by those objects. There are 100
therefore fine forms and semblances of things which, though no one can
perceive them individually, are constantly and rapidly repelled and rejected by the smooth reflecting surfaces and so produce a visible image.
It is evident that in no other way can they be so perfectly preserved that
forms so closely resembling the actual objects are produced.

Now then, I want you to grasp how fine is the substance of an image. 110
To begin with, its elements are far beneath the range of our senses and are
much smaller than the objects that are only just too small for our eyes to
discern. In order that I may convince you of the truth of this, let me show
you in a few words how subtle are the constituent atoms of all things.

First, there are some living creatures so minute that if they were one
third of their actual size, they would be quite invisible. What are we to
imagine that any one of their internal parts is like? What of their globular
heart or eyes? What of their members? What of their limbs? Of what size 120
are they? And what of the individual elements that must compose their
spirit and mind? Do you not conceive how subtle and how minute they
are?

Then again, consider all those plants that give off a pungent smell,
such as all-heal,[8] foul wormwood, aromatic southernwood, and styptic
centaury: if you should happen to take any one of these herbs [and hold]
it lightly between two [fingers, those fingers will be impregnated with a
strong smell; and yet the particles that must have issued from the herb
and attached themselves to your skin are so minute that they are quite
invisible].[9]

---

7. **98:** Roman mirrors were usually made of burnished metal. Mirrors feature
prominently in the arguments that follow: see 150–167, 269–323. Diogenes of
Oinoanda too mentions reflections in mirrors as evidence that images are constantly discharged from the surfaces of things (*fr.* 9.I.4–12).

8. **124:** A plant of uncertain identity, apparently not what we call all-heal,
which is valerian (*Valeriana officinalis*).

9. **126:** After 126 a passage, almost certainly of considerable length, has been
lost. The words in brackets give the likely sense of the first part of it.

. . . but that you should rather recognize that many images of things
stray about in many ways, lacking any faculty and without sensation.[10]

130   You must not imagine that the only images of things straying about are
those that withdraw from objects. There are others that are spontaneously
produced and self-created in the part of the sky that is called the air;
these, formed in countless ways, are swept along on high. Compare how
sometimes we see clouds effortlessly massing together in the lofty
heaven, marring the serene countenance of the firmament and fanning
the air with their motion. Often the faces of giants seem to glide by,
trailing a massive shadow; sometimes a procession of mighty mountains
and rocks wrenched from mountains appears to pass before the sun,
140   followed by some monstrous beast leading another string of storm
clouds. They constantly melt away and transform their appearance, assuming the contours of forms of every kind.

Now [I will explain] with what ease and speed the images are formed
and constantly flow off from things and slip away; [do you be sure to
lend attentive ears to my words].[11] The position is that the outermost
surface of things is always being discharged in a perpetual stream. When
an effluence meets certain objects, it passes through them—especially
through glass; whereas when it strikes against rough rocks or solid wood,
150   it is at once shattered and so prevented from producing any image. But
when its path is blocked by an object that is both shiny and compact,
especially by a mirror, neither of these things happens: for the effluence
cannot pass through the object, as it can through glass; nor can it be
shattered, because the smoothness of the surface never fails to secure its
safety. Consequently the images come streaming back to us. Present to
the mirror any object you like, as suddenly as you like, at any time you
like: the image always appears; and this is a clear indication for you that
filmy textures and filmy shapes flow in a perpetual stream from the
surfaces of things. Therefore countless images are produced in an in-
160   stant, and their creation can justly be described as rapid. And in precisely
the same way that the sun must emit countless particles of light instantaneously in order that the whole world may constantly be filled with
radiance, so all objects must in a moment of time throw off countless
images in countless ways in all directions on every side, since, in what-

10. **127–128:** Thanks to Diogenes of Oinoanda (*fr.* 10, 43), we can be confident
that 127–128 are the closing lines of a refutation of Democritus' belief that the
images possess the faculties of speech, reason, and sensation.
11. **144:** A lacuna must be assumed after 144. Probably only one line is lost. It
may have been similar or identical to 2.66 or 4.931.

ever direction we turn the mirror, the scene is reflected in it, similar in form and color.

Here is another point. The sky, perfectly clear a short while ago, suddenly becomes overcast and ugly. You might think that on every side 170 all the darkness had fled from Acheron and occupied the vast vault of heaven: so menacingly does a dreadful night of storm clouds gather, and black faces of fear scowl from above.[12] And yet an image is minute compared with these clouds—just how minute no one could say or explain.[13]

Now then, how swiftly do the images move? What velocity is given to them as they glide through the air, enabling them to cover a long distance in a short hour, no matter what the place may be toward which their various inclinations carry them? I will explain in verses melodious rather 180 than many: the swan's brief song is preferable to the clamoring of cranes that crowds the clouds of the southern sky.[14]

In the first place, it is an observable fact that swiftness is very often a characteristic of things that are light and made of minute particles. For example, this is true of the light and heat radiated by the sun, since they are composed of minute particles that hammer one another forward and, under the impulsion of blows from behind, unhesitatingly pass through the intervening air. Light instantly succeeds light, and flash spurs on 190 flash in a continuous stream. Therefore the images must equally be able to race through an inexpressible distance of space in a moment of time, first because, although the force that projects and propels them is a slight one[15] far behind them, they travel on their way so fleetly and lightly; and secondly because, when they are emitted, the rarity of their texture is such that they can easily penetrate anything[16] and, as it were, percolate through the intervening air.

Moreover, if particles that emanate from deep inside things, like the 200

---

12. **170–173:** Repeated, with one minor variation, at 6.251–254.

13. **174–175:** The argument is compressed. The idea is: clouds can fill the sky in a short time; an image is far, far smaller than those clouds and therefore can be formed in a far, far shorter time.

14. **180–182:** These lines, repeated at 909–911, seem to have been influenced by an epigram by Antipater of Sidon (*Anthologia Palatina* 7.713), though Antipater has jackdaws instead of cranes. On singing swans, see note on 2.505.

15. **193:** The slight force is the vibration of the atoms that compose objects.

16. **197:** Not in fact "anything," because at 147–149 Lucr. tells us that certain objects, such as rocks and wood, are impervious to the images and indeed shatter them.

particles of solar light and heat, manifestly glide and diffuse themselves
in an instant of time throughout the length and breadth of heaven, dart
over the sea and lands, and inundate the sky, what then of particles that
are stationed ready in the very front rank at the time of their discharge, so
that nothing retards their emission? Do you not see how much swifter
and farther they must travel, racing through a space many times as wide
as the expanse of the sky that the sun's rays pervade in the same time?
210   Here is another striking and manifestly trustworthy illustration of the
swift movement of the images. The moment glassy water is set beneath a
star-spangled sky, the serene shining constellations of the firmament are
reflected in it. Do you not see now that an image falls instantaneously
from the ethereal regions to the regions of the earth?

So I insist that you must acknowledge [that the images move] at an
extraordinary [speed].[17]

[. . . . .]
[In the first place, all objects that are visible to us must necessarily
discharge and scatter a continual stream][18] of particles that impinge on
the eyes and provoke vision. Moreover, from certain things odors flow in
a perpetual stream; cold emanates from rivers, heat from the sun, and
220   spray from the waves of the sea—spray that erodes the walls skirting the
shore. Various sounds are continually floating through the air. Again,
when we walk near the sea, a briny taste often makes its way into our
mouth; and when we watch wormwood being diluted and mixed, its
bitterness affects our palate. So true is it that from all objects emanations
flow away and are discharged in all directions on every side. These
effluences stream away without any delay or interruption, since we constantly experience sensation, and we may at any time see, smell, and hear
anything.
230   Here is a further point: when we handle an object of a particular shape
in the dark, we recognize it as having the same shape that we see in the
brilliant light of day. Therefore touch and sight must be effected by the
same cause. Now then, if we feel a square object in the dark and receive
the impression of a square, what in the light will be able to give us the
visual impression of a square, except the image of the object? It is

---

17. **216:** There is a lacuna of uncertain length after 216. Those editors who think
that only one line is missing must be mistaken, since at 217 Lucr. is already
discussing a new topic. It may be that a page of the archetype dropped out,
leaving a gap of fifty-two lines. It is to be noted that 217–229 are repeated, with a
few minor alterations, at 6.923–935, and I have assumed that 217 was preceded
by two lines identical to 6.921–922.

18. **217:** On the words in brackets, see previous note.

evident therefore that images are the cause of vision, and that without them nothing could be seen.

Now these images of which I have spoken come from all sides and are 240
discharged and distributed in every direction. But because our eyes alone possess the power of vision, it is only from the direction in which we turn our eyes that all objects come to impinge on them with their form and color.

It is the image that gives us the power to see and the means to determine how far each object is distant from us. For, the moment it is emitted, it thrusts and drives before it all the air that lies between it and our eyes; all this air then glides through our eyeballs, brushes through our pupils, and so passes on. This is what enables us to gauge the distance of each 250
object. The greater the quantity of air that is driven before the image, and the longer the current that brushes through our eyes, the remoter the object is seen to be. You must realize that these processes take place with extreme swiftness, so that we simultaneously identify the object and gauge its distance.

In this connection, you should not consider it strange that, although the images that impinge on our eyes are individually invisible, the objects themselves are visible. After all, when the wind whips us with fitful blasts, and when biting cold flows upon us, we do not feel the individual 260
particles of wind or cold, but rather their combined effect; and we then perceive that blows are falling upon our body, just as if some external force were whipping us and giving us the sensation of its body. Moreover, when we tap a stone with a finger, what we touch is merely the superficial layer of color on the outside of the rock; but what we feel, when we touch the rock, is not its surface color, but rather the hardness deep down within it.

Now then, I want you to grasp why it is that reflected images are seen beyond the surface of the mirror; for they certainly do appear to recede 270
into its depths. The position is the same as with those objects that we see in their reality[19] on the far side of a door, when the doorway affords an unobstructed view through it and enables us to see many things outside the house from inside. For in that case too vision is caused by a double current of air. First the air between us and the doorposts is perceived, followed by the leaves of the door itself on either side; next the light beyond the door brushes through our eyes, accompanied by a second current of air, then the objects outside that we see in their reality. Sim-

---

19. **270:** In contrast to the images in the mirror.

280 ilarly, as soon as the image of the mirror projects itself in the direction of
our pupils, it thrusts and drives before it all the air that lies between it and
our eyes, and causes us to perceive all this air before we perceive the
mirror. When we have perceived the mirror itself, at once the image that
is emitted from us travels to the mirror, is repulsed, and returns to our
eyes, driving and rolling before it another current of air, and causes us to
see this before we perceive the reflected image itself; and this is why the
reflection appears to be so far behind the mirror. So I insist that we have
no call to consider it strange [that this happens both in the case of those
290 objects that we see through doors and][20] in the case of those that send
back visible images from the surfaces of mirrors, since in each case the
result is produced by two currents of air.

The reason why the right side of our body appears in mirrors on the
left is that, when the image reaches the plane of the mirror and strikes
against it, it does not turn about and so remain unaltered, but rebounds
straight back. It is just as if someone were to dash a plaster mask, while it
is still moist, against a pillar or post, and the mask, preserving its features
undistorted in front, were to mold a copy of itself in reverse, with the
300 result that what was previously the right eye would now become the left,
and vice versa.

It is possible too for an image to be transmitted from mirror to mirror,
so that as many as five or six reflections are produced. For even when
objects are hidden away in the inner part of a house, no matter how long
and tortuous a way separates them from the outside, the use of a sequence of mirrors enables us to draw them all out through winding
passages and see that they are in the house. So unfailingly does the image
glance from mirror to mirror; and whenever the left side is passed on, it
310 becomes the right, and then changes back again, reverting to the same
position as before.

It should be added that mirrors with curved sides, whose curvature is
similar to that of our sides, always reflect images with the right on the
right.[21] There are two possible explanations for this: either the image is
transmitted from one side of the mirror to the other and is reflected twice
before darting back to us; or else, when it has reached the mirror, it
wheels around, because the curved shape guides it, causing it to turn
about and face us.

Moreover, you may imagine that reflected images move as we move,
320 tread as we tread, and mimic our gestures. The explanation of the illusion

---

20. **289:** At least one line seems to be lost after 289.

21. **311–313:** The reference is to horizontally concave mirrors that do not reverse images.

is this: the moment you retire from any part of a mirror, that part ceases to be able to return any images, since nature obliges all things to rebound and be reflected from objects at an angle equal to the angle of their incidence.[22]

Let us turn our attention to another matter. It is a fact that our eyes shrink from glaring objects and avoid looking at them. Indeed the sun blinds us if we try to gaze straight at it. This is because its own strength is great, and the images radiated by it, descending from a great height through pure air, move so impetuously that, when they impinge on our eyes, they disturb their atomic composition. Moreover, any object of glaring brightness is apt to burn the eyes, because it contains   330 numerous seeds of fire that penetrate into the eyes and cause them pain.

Again, the reason why all looks yellow to jaundiced people is that many seeds of this color stream from their bodies to meet the images emitted by objects; many too are mingled in their eyes, and these tinge everything with their contagious paleness.

When we are in the dark, we can see objects that are in the light. This is because, when the black murky air, being nearer to us, has invaded our open eyes first and occupied them, it is followed instantly by the bright   340 and luminous air that as it were purifies the eyes, dissipating the shadows of the dark air; for the bright air is far more mobile, far more subtle, and far more powerful. No sooner has it filled the ocular passages with light, and cleared those that previously had been blocked by the black air, than it is followed by the images emanating from objects situated in the light, and these provoke our vision.

On the other hand, when we are in the light, we cannot see objects that are in the dark, because the grosser, murky air arrives after the bright air; it fills all the pores and blocks up the ocular passages and so prevents any   350 of the images from giving rise to vision when they are projected on the eyes.

The square towers of a city, viewed by us from a distance, often appear round. This is because every angle surveyed from afar is seen as obtuse—or rather is not seen at all. The image loses its sharpness before it can deliver a blow to our eyes, because the images, during their long journey through the air, are constantly buffeted and so become blunted. In this way every angle eludes our vision, with the result that the stone   360 structures appear as though they were shaped on a lathe. Even so, they do

---

22. **318–323:** The illusion described and explained here is discussed in detail by K. Algra, *Elenchos* 20 (1999) 359–379.

not look like objects close at hand that really are round, but vaguely resemble them in a shadowy fashion.[23]

Our own shadows, moreover, appear to move with us in the sunlight, following our footsteps and mimicking our gestures—that is, if you believe that air deprived of light can walk, reproducing the movements and gestures of people. After all, what we call a shadow cannot be
370 anything else but air devoid of light. What undoubtedly happens is that particular parts of the ground are successively deprived of the light of the sun that we intercept wherever we move, while the spot we have quit is again overspread with light. This explains why the shadow cast by our body keeps the same appearance and seems always to follow exactly opposite us. New rays of light are constantly streaming from the sun to replace the old that perish: the process is like that of spinning wool into a fire. In this way the ground is easily robbed of light, and with equal ease is again flooded with radiance and washes off the sooty shadows.

However, in this connection we do not allow that the eyes are in any
380 way deceived. Their business is to observe the areas of light and shadow. But the question of whether the light is the same or not, and whether it is the same shadow passing from place to place, or whether the position is rather as I have stated it above—this can be decided only by the reasoning of the mind: the eyes cannot take cognizance of the real nature of things. Refrain, then, from foisting on the eyes the shortcomings of the mind.[24]

When we are on board a moving ship, the vessel appears to be stationary, while another, still moored at her berth, is thought to be going by;
390 and the hills and plains past which our ship skims with soaring sails seem to be fleeing astern.

The stars all appear motionless, inlaid in the ethereal vault; and yet all are in perpetual motion, since they rise and traverse the length of heaven with their lucent orbs before returning to the distant parts where they set. Likewise the sun and moon seemingly remain stationary, whereas simple fact proves that they are moving.

---

23. **353–363:** Another Epicurean who explains why a square tower, seen from the distance, appears roundish, is Diogenes of Oinoanda (*fr.* 69). His explanation agrees completely with that of Lucr. For the same example, see also Plutarch *Moralia* 1121a–e, Sextus Empiricus *Adversus Mathematicos* 7.208–209, Diogenes Laertius 10.34.

24. **379–386:** The point is that it is the function of the eyes only to record information—like a camera. This they faithfully do. It is the business of the mind to interpret the information they supply. The mind may make mistakes. Cf. 462–468, Epicurus *Hdt.* 50–52, *PD* 24, Diogenes Laertius 10.34, and see pp. xxiv–xxv.

Again, mountains rising up from the midst of the deep, though separated by a great channel wide enough for fleets to pass freely through, appear, when viewed from the distance, to coalesce to form a single island.

When children stop whirling themselves around, they have such a 400 realistic impression of the room rotating and the pillars racing around that they can hardly believe that the whole building is not threatening to collapse on top of them.

Again, consider what happens when nature begins to hoist up on high the sun, orange-bright with quivering fires, and raise it above the mountains: the sun appears to stand over the mountains and suffuse them with its fervid fire from close at hand; the distance between us and those mountains is no more than two thousand bowshots—often no more than five hundred casts of a javelin; and yet between the mountains and the 410 sun lie immense plains of ocean outspread beneath vast expanses of ether, and ten thousand tracts of land are interposed, occupied by many different peoples and species of animals.

In contrast, take the case of a pool of water that has collected between the paving stones of a street. Though no deeper than a finger-breadth, it affords a view down into the bowels of the earth as extensive as the gaping abyss of sky that stretches high above the earth, so that you seem to look down upon the clouds and the sky, and you see manifest objects miraculously embosomed in the earth.[25]

Again, when our mount, for all its mettle, has stuck fast in the middle 420 of a river, and we look down at the impetuous waters, it seems to us that the horse's body, which is in fact stationary, is being swept sideways by some force and hurried upstream; and wherever we turn our eyes, everything appears to be moving and flowing in the same direction as ourselves.

Although a colonnade is supported from end to end by columns of equal height ranged in parallel lines, when its whole length is viewed from one end, it seems to taper into the apex of a narrow cone, gradually 430 drawing roof to floor and right to left, until all converge into the vanishing point of the cone.

To sailors at sea it is as if the sun rises from the waves and in the waves

---

25. **414–419:** Shelley is probably recalling this passage in *To Jane: The Recollection* 53–58: "We paused beside the pools that lie / Under the forest bough, / Each seemed as 'twere a little sky / Gulfed in a world below; / A firmament of purple light / Which in the dark earth lay." In 418–419 there are textual problems of which there is no sure solution: for discussion, see M. F. Smith, *Classical Quarterly* 43 (1993) 337–338.

sets and buries its light. This is because nothing else but sea and sky
meets their view; so you must not rashly assume that the evidence of our
senses is wholly unreliable.

To people who know nothing of the sea, vessels in harbor look
disabled and seem to be resisting the waves with broken sterns. As for
the oars and rudders, all the parts raised above the dew-sparkling brine
440 are straight, while all the parts submerged under water have a refracted
and distorted appearance; indeed their apparent upward curve and backward bend are so pronounced that they seem almost to be floating on the
surface of the water.

And when the winds sweep scattered clouds across the night sky, the
shining stars seem to be gliding to meet the clouds and to be moving on
high in a direction quite different from that in which they are really
traveling.

Again, if we chance to place our hand beneath one of our eyes and
press the eyeball, it happens, by a certain sensory impression, that, wher-
450 ever we look, we appear to see everything double—double the light of
each lamp flowering with flame, double the furniture throughout the
house, double the faces of people, double their bodies.

Lastly, even when our limbs are prisoners of balmy slumber and our
whole body is sunk in sound repose, we imagine that we are awake and
moving our limbs; though enveloped by the blind blackness of night, we
have the illusion of seeing the sun and daylight; though confined within
our room, we fancy that we pass over sky and sea, rivers and mountains,
460 and traverse plains on foot; though encompassed by the solemn stillness
of night, we seem to hear sounds; and though quite silent, we imagine
that we speak.

We experience an extraordinarily large number of other illusions of
this kind. It is as though all of them are conspiring to undermine our
confidence in the senses. Their efforts, however, are unavailing, since the
majority of these errors are due to inferences added by our own minds,
which cause us to imagine that we have seen what our senses have not
seen. The truth is that nothing is more difficult than to separate patent
facts from the dubious opinions that our mind at once adds of its own
accord.[26]

Moreover, if people suppose that knowledge of anything is impossi-
470 ble, they do not even know whether knowledge of the impossibility of
knowledge is possible, since, on their own admission, they know noth-

---

26. **462–468:** Cf. 379–386 and see note there.

ing.[27] Against such people, who have planted themselves with their head in their own footprints,[28] I disdain to argue. However, if I were to concede that they do have this knowledge, I would put the following questions to them. Since they have never before encountered anything true, how do they recognize knowledge and ignorance? What has given them their conception of truth and falsehood? What proof have they that the doubtful differs from the certain?

You will find that our conception of truth is derived ultimately from the senses, and that their evidence is unimpugnable.[29] You see, what we   480
need is some specially reliable standard which by its own authority is able to ensure the victory of truth over falsehood. Well now, what standard can be regarded as more reliable than sensation? If the senses are false, will reason be competent to impeach them when it is itself entirely dependent upon the senses? If they are not true, all reason also is rendered false. Or can sight be corrected by hearing, or hearing by touch? Can the evidence of touch be challenged by taste, refuted by hearing, or invalidated by sight? Not so, in my opinion. The fact is that each sense has its own special sphere, its own separate function. Thus the discern-   490
ment of softness, cold, and heat must be the province of one particular sense, while the perception of the various colors and everything connected with colors[30] must be the business of another. Taste too has its own distinct function; smell is produced separately, and so is sound. It

---

27. **469–521:** Skepticism in Greek philosophy has a long and complicated history, and our knowledge of it is far from complete. It is hardly surprising therefore that there has been much disagreement about the identity of Lucr.'s source(s) and target(s) in this passage. Some scholars have been too dogmatic in a case where it would be wiser to be skeptical! Even if, as is likely, our writer's main source is Epicurus, this does not mean that he cannot be aiming his argument at, or partly at, contemporary skeptics. That Epicurean writers after Epicurus were quite capable of taking account of skeptics who lived later than their master is shown by Diogenes of Oinoanda *fr.* 5.III.12–14, where, just before the text unfortunately breaks off, there is mention of Lacydes of Cyrene, who belongs to the second half of the third century B.C.

28. **472:** On this picture of the skeptic as one who takes up a position that is not only upside down, but also back to front, see M. F. Burnyeat, *Philologus* 122 (1978) 197–206.

29. **478–499:** With this argument that sensation is the primary criterion of truth, and that there is nothing that can refute it, compare Diogenes Laertius 10.31–32. See also 1.422–425, 693–700.

30. **493:** By "everything connected with colors" Lucr. presumably means shape, outline, etc.

necessarily follows therefore that one sense cannot refute another. It is also impossible for any sense to correct itself, since it must always be considered equally reliable. Therefore all sensations at all times are true.
500 And even if reason fails to resolve the problem of why objects, which close at hand were square, have a round appearance when viewed from a distance,[31] it is better, if one is ignorant of the reason, to give an erroneous explanation of the difference in shape than to let manifest facts slip from one's grasp and to undermine the first principles of belief and tear up all the foundations upon which our life and safety are based. For if you were not prepared to trust the senses, not only would all reason fall in ruin, but life itself would at once collapse, since you would be unable
510 to avoid precipices and other such dangers and keep to places of safety. You may be sure, then, that the arguments that have been marshaled and arrayed against the senses are merely a multitude of empty words.

I conclude with an illustration. If, when you begin to construct a building, your rule is warped,[32] your square not truly rectilinear, and your level the slightest bit inexact in any part, the inevitable result is a structure full of faults—crooked, lopsided, leaning forward here and backward there, and all out of proportion, with some parts seemingly on the verge of collapse and others actually collapsing, all having been
520 betrayed by those erroneous calculations at the outset. In the same way, then, your reasoning about things must of necessity be distorted and false if the senses upon which it is based are themselves false.

Now it remains to explain how each of the other senses receives impressions of the objects within its own sphere—a task that certainly does not involve treading a stony path.

In the first place, whenever sounds and voices are heard, it is because particles of their substance have insinuated themselves into the ears and impinged on the sense organ. The corporeal nature of voices and sounds must be acknowledged in view of their ability to stimulate the senses.

Besides, the voice often abrades the throat, and shouting in its egress
530 roughens the windpipe. For when the vocal particles have crowded up through the narrow passage in an excessively dense throng and have begun to stream out, the crush in the windpipe causes the abrasion of the

---

31. **500–502:** See 353–363.

32. **513:** The Greek word for a builder's rule or straightedge, *kanōn,* was used metaphorically as the title of the work (not extant) in which Epicurus explained his theory of knowledge, known as the canonic. Therefore Lucr.'s illustration in 513–521 could not be more appropriate. For an account of the canonic, see pp. xxiv–xxv.

entrance to the mouth as well. Unquestionably, then, voices and words are composed of corporeal particles, seeing that they have the power to cause injury.

Moreover, you are well aware how much people's bodies are wasted and how much their energy and strength are sapped by an uninterrupted spell of talking protracted from the first gleam of dawn until the dark of dusky night, especially if their words are uttered in a loud voice. And 540 since those who talk a lot sustain corporeal loss, the voice must be corporeal.

The roughness of a sound results from the roughness of its constituent elements, and its smoothness is caused by their smoothness. When the snarling barbarous trumpet brays loud and deep with raucous reverberating boom, the elements that invade the ears are not of the same form as those that enter when swans from Helicon's mazy mountain vales uplift the mournful strains of their melting melody.[33]

Now, when we expel these vocal particles from deep down within ourselves and emit them straight through the mouth, the supple tongue, 550 the deft artificer of speech, molds them into articulate sounds, and the shaping of the lips plays its part in giving them form. When no great distance separates the source of each utterance from the hearer, the actual words are bound to be clearly audible, with every syllable distinct; for the vocal particles maintain their arrangement and configuration. But if the intervening distance is excessively great, it is inevitable that the words become indistinct and the voice distorted in the course of their lengthy flight through the breezy air. Consequently you receive an im- 560 pression of the sound without being able to distinguish the meaning of the words: so confused and hampered is the voice when it reaches you.

Again, it often happens that a single word, sped from a crier's mouth, stirs the ears of a whole multitude. Thus a single utterance must at once divide into many utterances, since it distributes itself to the ears of all, impressing upon each the form and distinct sound of the words. Some of the utterances, failing to fall upon the ears, pass by and fade away, wastefully dissipated in the air, while others rebound from solid objects 570

---

33. **547:** The text is hopelessly corrupt. I have translated *et cycni tortis convallibus ex Heliconis,* a tentative suggestion of mine that owes much to earlier editors, including Lachmann. It is a mere stopgap. Even the swans are doubtful: Lucr. may have mentioned nightingales instead, but surely not, as has been recently suggested (M. H. Koenen, *Mnemosyne* 52 [1999] 454–455), swallows as well, in view of the poet's uncomplimentary reference to the swallow's twittering in 3.6–7.

against which they strike, and so return the sound and sometimes delude us with the echo of a word.

Once you have clearly understood this, you can explain to yourself and to others how it is that, in lonely places, rocks return counterparts of our words in due order, when, as we seek companions straying stragglingly among somber mountains, we call them with a loud voice. I have known places return as many as six or seven cries, when only one was uttered: the words were repeatedly flung to and fro from hill to hill, as though trained to come back.

580 Such places are fancied by local people to be the haunts of nymphs and goat-footed satyrs,[34] and to be the homes of fauns,[35] by whose night-pervading clamor and frolicsome revelry the still silence is, they say, often broken; sounds of strings are heard, and sweet notes ripple from the plaintive pipe as the players' fingers strike the stops.[36] They relate also that rustic folk far and wide hear the sound, when Pan,[37] shaking the sprays of pine that shadow his half-bestial head, time and again runs over the hollow reeds with pursed lips, making a ceaseless stream of sylvan
590 music flow from his pipe. Country people tell other equally fantastic and amazing tales. Their motive for boasting of such miracles is perhaps fear of being regarded as inhabitants of parts so lonely that even the gods have forsaken them. But they may be prompted by some other reason, for human beings are always inordinately greedy for an audience.

To proceed, there is no need to wonder how it is that barriers, through which our eyes cannot see plain objects, allow sounds to penetrate them and impinge on our ears. The reason why we often witness a conversation taking place even through closed doors is undoubtedly that, whereas
600 sound particles can pass unharmed through tortuous passages in objects, images refuse to do so; for the latter are shattered unless they have straight passages through which to glide, like those in glass, which is permeable to all images.

Moreover, a single utterance distributes itself in all directions, since it splits up at once into a multitude of particles that in turn produce others, just as a spark of fire often flies into fiery fragments. And so voices crowd places hidden away from sight and make them all astir and alive

34. **580:** Greek woodland spirits, in form partly human, partly bestial (here goatish).

35. **581:** Native Italian spirits of the countryside, very similar to satyrs.

36. **585:** Repeated at 5.1385.

37. **586:** Greek rural deity, represented as partly human, partly goatish (goat's legs, horns, and ears). The pine was sacred to him. He was a musical god, whose instrument was the syrinx or panpipe.

with sound. Images, on the other hand, from the moment of their emission invariably proceed in straight lines. This explains why it is never 610 possible to see objects behind a wall, though it is possible to hear voices beyond it. Even so, the voice becomes dulled in passing through the walls of houses and penetrates our ears in a confused state, so that we seem to hear a sound rather than the actual words.

The organs of taste, namely the tongue and the palate, are equally easy to explain.

In the first place, we experience taste in the mouth when, by masticating our food, we squeeze out the juice. The process resembles that when someone begins to squeeze dry a sponge full of water. All that we 620 squeeze out is then channeled through the ducts of the palate and the tortuous passages of the porous tongue. When the particles of oozing juice are smooth, they soothingly touch and soothingly stroke all the moist, salivary regions around the tongue. On the other hand, the rougher they are, the more they prick the sensory organs and tear them in their onset.

Moreover, the pleasure derived from taste is confined to the palate. Once the food has plunged down through the throat and is all being channeled into the limbs, no pleasure is experienced. And it does not 630 matter at all with what kind of food your body is nourished, so long as you can digest what you take, channel it into the limbs, and keep the stomach in a constantly healthy condition.

I will now explain how it is that different creatures have different food, and why what tastes unpleasant and bitter to some can seem completely delicious to others. Differences and variations of taste are so great that what is food to one is rank poison to others: there is even a serpent that if touched by human saliva, perishes by biting itself to death;[38] and again, 640 although to us hellebore is rank poison, goats and quails thrive on it.

In order to understand the reason for this, you should in the first place call to mind what I said earlier about the component seeds of objects being combined in manifold ways.[39] Just as all living creatures that take food differ in outward appearance, and the external contour of their frame varies according to their species, so the seeds of which they are formed differ in shape. And since the seeds vary in shape, there must be corresponding differences in the shape of the interstices and passages— 650

---

38. **638–639:** The notion that human saliva has a deadly or harmful effect on snakes is also found in Aristotle and Pliny the Elder.

39. **643–644:** See 1.814–829, 895–896, 2.333–380.

the pores, as we term them—in every part of the body, including the mouth and the palate itself. Some pores will be smaller, others larger; in some creatures they will be triangular, in others square; often they will be round, sometimes multifariously multangular. The shapes of the pores and passages are invariably determined by the shapes and movements of the atoms that constitute the surrounding tissue. So when something that tastes bitter to one creature proves sweet to another, undoubtedly what

660 happens is this: if the food tastes sweet, extremely smooth particles are entering the pores of the palate with caressing touch; if, however, the same food tastes bitter, then rough and barbed particles are penetrating the orifices.

On the analogy of these examples it is easy to explain each individual case. Thus when fever has assailed someone through excess of bile, or when a violent disease has been provoked by some other cause, the whole body is at once disordered and the positions of the constituent elements are all changed. Consequently particles that previously suited the person's taste are now unsuitable to it; others prove better adapted to

670 it, and these penetrate the pores and produce a bitter sensation. Honey, as I have often indicated to you before,[40] derives its flavor from a mixture of rough and smooth particles.

Now then, I will explain how smell reaches and affects the nostrils. First of all, there must be countless objects from which waves of various odors flow in a rolling tide; and we must suppose that these effluences are discharged and scattered in all directions. But, because of differences of atomic shape, certain smells are better suited to certain creatures. And so bees are drawn any distance through the air by the fragrance of honey,

680 and vultures by the stench of carrion; powerful hounds, sent on ahead, lead the hunter along the track of the cloven-footed quarry; and the snow-white goose, the savior of the citadel of the descendants of Romulus,[41] is quick to detect human scent from afar. In this way different creatures are endowed with different powers of smell which, by guiding each to its own food and forcing it to recoil from foul poison, ensure the preservation of the species of wild beasts.

---

40. **671–672:** See 2.398–407, 3.191–195, though in neither passage does Lucr. state that honey contains rough particles as well as smooth. The inexactness of the reference and the abruptness of the mention of honey in this passage may well be due to lack of revision.

41. **683:** Tradition relates that, when the Gauls attacked Rome in 387 B.C., the warning given by the sacred geese of Juno enabled the Capitol to be saved.

Now, of the smells that impinge on our nostrils, some can be wafted through the air farther than others. None, however, travels as far as sound 690 and voice or, needless to say, as far as the images that impinge on our eyes and provoke vision. Smell meanders and moves sluggishly and fades away before it reaches its goal, readily dispersing little by little into the breezy air. There are two reasons for this: first, it has difficulty in issuing from the depths of the object that is its source. That odors emanate and withdraw from the interior of objects is indicated by the patent fact that every substance diffuses a stronger smell when broken, bruised, or burned. Secondly, it is evidently composed of grosser elements than voice, since it does not penetrate stone walls,[42] which are always per- 700 vious to voice and sound. Consequently you will notice that it is less easy to trace the source of a smell than that of a sound. The emanation grows cool as it loiters through the air, instead of speeding in hot haste to the sense with news of the object. That is why hounds often lose the scent and have to search for the trail.

It is not only with respect to smell and taste that different creatures are differently affected. Forms and colors too are not all equally suited to the senses of all; indeed certain of them are too acrid to the eyes of certain animals. Consider how ravening lions cannot endure the sight of the 710 cock,[43] whose habit it is to chase away the night with clapping wings and summon the dawn with shrill clarion. Their immediate reaction is to flee. Undoubtedly the explanation is that the cock's body contains certain seeds which, when projected into lions' eyes, stab the pupils and inflict such a stinging pain that the beasts, for all their courage, cannot bear it. And yet these particles have no power to hurt our eyes, either because they do not penetrate them or, if they do, because they find a free egress, 720 so that they cannot by lingering hurt the eyes in any part.

Now then, listen and learn while I explain briefly the nature and source of the objects that enter the mind and stir it to thought. My first point is that countless subtle images of things roam about in countless ways in all directions on every side. When these meet in the air, they easily become interlinked, like cobwebs or gold leaf. They are far finer in texture than

---

42. **700–701:** This statement is inconsistent with 6.952, where Lucr. says that smell, like sound, cold, and heat, does penetrate stone walls.

43. **710–713:** The idea that lions are afraid of cocks is also found in Pliny the Elder, Seneca, and St. Ambrose. But Cuvier, who tried the experiment of placing a cock in a lion's cage, found that the lion devoured it.

730 the images that occupy our eyes and provoke sight, since they pass
     through the interstices of the body, stir the subtle substance of the mind
     within, and so provoke its sensation.[44]

         In this way we see Centaurs,[45] the forms of Scyllas,[46] the faces of
     Cerberean hounds,[47] and the specters of people who are dead and whose
     bones are embosomed in the earth. For images of every kind are moving
     everywhere, some formed spontaneously in the air, others emanating
     from various things and compounded of their different shapes. Certainly
740 the image of a Centaur is not derived from a living being, since no such
     creature ever existed.[48] But when the images of a horse and a human
     being chance to meet, they instantly and easily cohere, as we have said
     before, on account of the subtlety of their substance and the tenuity of
     their texture. The images of all other such monsters are produced in the
     same way. And since these subtle images, as I have already shown,[49]
     move swiftly and with extreme lightness, any one of them can easily
     stimulate our mind with a single impression. For the mind itself is subtle
     and extraordinarily mobile.

         What follows will make it easy for you to recognize the correctness of
750 this theory. The fact that mental vision is similar to ocular vision means
     that the two processes must be effected by similar means. Since I have
     shown that I see a lion, for example, by means of images that impinge on
     my eyes, you may be sure that the mind is moved in just the same way as
     the eyes—that is, by means of images of lions or of whatever else it sees.
     The only difference is that the images perceived by the mind are finer.

         And if, when sleep has prostrated our limbs, our mind is awake, the
     reason is that it is stimulated by the same images as when we are wake-
760 ful. Indeed it receives such vivid impressions that we really seem to see
     persons who have departed from life and now belong to death and dust.

---

44. **722–732:** On the way in which thought and dreams are caused by the entry
of images into the mind, just as vision is caused by images entering the eyes, see
also Epicurus *Hdt.* 49–51, Cicero *Fin.* 1.21, Diogenes of Oinoanda *fr.* 9–10. It is
important to note the point, made in 728–729, that the images that penetrate the
mind are much finer than those that strike our eyes.

45. **732:** Fabulous creatures, partly human, partly horse. Cf. 5.878–891.

46. **732:** Scylla was a mythological sea monster with six heads and twelve feet,
mentioned again at 5.893. She lived in a cave opposite Charybdis (see 1.722).

47. **733:** See note on 3.1011.

48. **740:** For proof that Centaurs and suchlike can never have existed, see 5.878–
924.

49. **746:** 4.176–215.

The reason why nature gives us these illusions is that the activity of all the bodily senses is suspended: they are at rest throughout the limbs and therefore cannot separate the true from the false.[50] What is more, the memory is inert and sluggish with slumber and so does not object that the person, whom the mind believes it sees alive, long ago fell a victim to death and destruction.

It should be added that there is nothing remarkable in the fact that images walk and rhythmically move their arms and other limbs. It is   770 indeed true that images seen in sleep seem to do this, and the reason for it is this: when one image fades away and is succeeded by another in a different position, it looks as though the former image has changed its posture. Of course we must assume that this happens extremely rapidly: so immense is the velocity of the images, so immense is the store of them, and so immense is the store of particles emitted at any single perceptible point of time, to ensure that the supply of images is continuous.[51]

In connection with this subject, there are many questions to be asked and many points that need to be elucidated, if we wish to give a clear exposition of the truth.

First of all, we must ask how it is that the mind can instantly think of   780 anything it wants. Do the images wait upon our will, so that, as soon as we wish it, one presents itself to us, whether the object of our desire be the sea or the earth or the sky? Assemblies of people, processions, banquets, battles—does nature provide and prepare all these spectacles for us at our command?—and that too when in the same region and place the minds of others are thinking of all sorts of quite different things.

Again, how is it that in sleep we see images advancing with rhythmic steps and swaying their lissome limbs, swiftly swinging supple arms   790 alternately, while before our eyes[52] their feet again and again with measured movement fall? The roving images must indeed be gifted and expert performers, to be able to provide these nocturnal entertainments!

No, surely the true explanation of these problems is that in a single perceptible moment of time—that is, in the time it takes to utter a single sound—there are myriads of moments of time whose existence, though

---

50. **757–764:** Closely parallel with this passage, but in places more informative, is Diogenes of Oinoanda *fr.* 9.IV.7–VI.3.

51. **768–776:** Experience of cinematographic pictures makes it very easy for modern readers to follow Lucr.'s explanations.

52. **791:** Since Lucr. is describing a dream, "before our eyes" is, strictly speaking, inaccurate, but the inaccuracy is an entirely natural one.

imperceptible to our senses, is detected by reason.[53] That is why at any time in any place all kinds of images are ready at hand: so immense is
800 their velocity, and so immense is the store of them. Thus, when one image fades away and is succeeded by another in a different position, it looks as though the former image has changed its posture.[54] And because of the subtlety of the images, the mind cannot perceive them distinctly unless it concentrates its attention on them. Consequently all pass away unnoticed, except those for which it has prepared itself. It should be added that it expectantly prepares itself to see the consequences of each happening, and therefore does see them.[55] Similarly have you not noticed that when the eyes endeavor to perceive minute objects, they strain
810 themselves and prepare themselves, and that, unless they do this, we cannot see distinctly? And even in the case of objects within our field of vision, you may observe that, if you do not concentrate your attention on them, it is just as if they were all the time far removed and separated from you. Why then is it remarkable that the mind should miss all the images except those on which it is intent? Besides, we base sweeping opinions on slight indications and so involve ourselves in the error of self-deception.[56]

It sometimes happens that an image is succeeded by another of a
820 different kind: a woman is seemingly metamorphosed into a man before our very eyes; or a change of features and age takes place. But oblivious sleep ensures that these transformations cause us no surprise.

In this connection,[57] I am extremely anxious that you should carefully avoid the mistake of supposing that the lustrous eyes were created to

---

53. **794–796:** Just as the atom, though physically indivisible, is to be thought of as having parts (1.599–634), so the smallest perceptible point of time is to be conceived of as capable of division into a multitude of parts.

54. **799–801:** Except for the alteration of one word, these lines are identical to 744, 771–772. Probably this is a section that Lucr. had not finished revising.

55. **805–806:** In other words, when the mind sees an image, it expects to see the series of images that follows. For example, if it sees two objects heading straight for one another, it prepares itself to see the collision; and the fact that it expects to see the collision causes it to select the image of the collision, so that this is indeed what it sees.

56. **816–817:** Cf. 4.462–468, but the relevance of the two lines here is obscure.

57. **823–857:** When Epicurus attacked the teleological view that the organs of the body were created for the purposes that they serve, his main target will have been Aristotle. But, given that the Stoics, the chief opponents of the Epicureans in Lucr.'s time, also held the teleological view, our author must surely be thinking of

enable us to see; or that the tapering shins and thighs were attached to the feet as a base to enable us to walk with long strides; or again that the forearms were jointed to the brawny upper arms, with ministering hands 830 provided on either side, to enable us to perform the tasks necessary for the support of life. All such explanations are propounded preposterously with topsy-turvy reasoning. In fact, no part of our body was created to the end that we might use it, but what has been created gives rise to its own function. Sight did not exist before the birth of the eyes, nor speech before the creation of the tongue; rather the tongue came into being long before talking, and the ears were created long before a sound was heard. 840 In short, I maintain that all the organs were in being before there was any function for them to fulfill. They cannot, then, have grown for the purpose of being used.

On the other hand, participation in the strife of battle, mutilation of limbs, and disfigurement of bodies with blood took place long before shining spears sped through the air; and people instinctively avoided wounds before they learned the technique of holding a buckler in the left hand for protection. Again, it is obvious that the practice of consigning the weary body to rest is much older than the soft-spread bed, and that the 850 slaking of thirst preceded the invention of cups. Thus in the case of these instruments, which were invented to meet the needs of life, one is justified in believing that they were discovered for the purpose of being used. However, it is entirely different with all those things that were first created independently and suggested the notion of their utility afterward. And at the head of this class we see the sensory organs and the limbs. So I insist that you cannot possibly believe that they could have been created for the purpose of being useful to us.

Again, there is nothing remarkable in the fact that every living creature instinctively seeks food for its body. For, as I have shown,[58] many 860 particles flow away and withdraw from things in many ways. But animals inevitably suffer the greatest loss of substance: being always restless and on the move, they exude many particles in sweat from deep within, and exhale many through the mouth when they pant from exhaustion. As a result of these losses the body becomes rarefied and the whole constitution is undermined. Consequently nourishment is taken to support the frame and restore the strength by its diffusion throughout the limbs and veins, and to stop the gaping craving for food. Similarly fluid 870

them as well. For the Stoic belief that divine providence is manifested in the design and structure of human beings, see Cicero *DND* 2.133–150.

58. **861:** 2.1128–1143.

is channeled into all the parts of the body that require fluid. The numerous particles of heat, whose accumulation causes a burning in the stomach, are dispersed and quenched, like a fire, on the arrival of the moisture, so that the parching heat can no longer consume the frame. In this way, then, our body's panting thirst is swilled away, and the craving of hunger satisfied.

Now I will explain how it is that we can step forward when we wish, and move our limbs at will, and what the force is that propels the huge bulk of our body. I want you to take in what I say.

880

I maintain, as I have maintained before,[59] that first of all images of movement present themselves to the mind and impinge on it. Then comes the act of will: no one can begin to do anything until the mind has foreseen what it wills to do; and what it foresees is determined by the image. So, as soon as the mind stirs itself in such a way that it wishes to move forward, it acts on the spirit, whose force is disseminated through all the limbs and members of the body; and this is easily done, since mind and spirit are intimately connected. The spirit in its turn acts on the body, and so little by little a forward motion is imparted to the whole mass.

890

Moreover, once in motion, the body becomes rarefied,[60] and air, as one would expect of a substance that is always quick to move, penetrates the opened pores in an abundant stream and is thus distributed to every minute part of the body. So the body is driven forward by these two separate forces,[61] like a vessel propelled by the action of wind upon its sails.

There is nothing remarkable in the fact that such tiny particles can maneuver such a large body and turn about our whole bulk. Consider how the wind, though finely formed of subtle substance, drives before it a mighty vessel with mighty momentum, while a single hand guides the ship, no matter how swift its speed, and a single helm steers it in any direction; consider, too, how a crane, with the help of pulleys and wheels, moves massive loads, hoisting them with slight effort.

900

Now, by what means does sleep send repose flooding through our limbs, and disburden our breast of cares? I will explain in verses melodious rather than many: the swan's brief song is preferable to the clamor-

910

---

59. **882:** 4.724–731.

60. **892:** Cf. 4.862–865.

61. **896:** The two forces are the limbs and the air: the action of the latter upon the former is likened to the action of the wind upon the sails of a ship. For a similar comparison, see 6.1031–1033.

ing of cranes that crowds the clouds of the southern sky.[62] I want you to
lend me attentive ears and an alert mind. Be sure that you do not deny the
validity of my account and turn from me with a breast impervious to true
precepts, when you yourself are at fault and cannot see.

In the first place, sleep occurs when the substance of the spirit
throughout the body has been disturbed, and has partly been expelled
from the limbs and dispersed, and has partly been thrust down into the
deep recesses of the body. It is then that the limbs become relaxed and
limp. You see, there is no doubt that the sensation in our body is caused   920
by the spirit, and when this sensation is suspended by sleep, it can only
be assumed that the spirit has been disordered and expelled from the
body. Not all of it is expelled, however, for, if that were so, the body
would be sunk in the eternal chill of death. If no part of the spirit
remained concealed in the limbs, like fire lurking beneath a deep layer of
ashes, how could sensation suddenly be rekindled throughout the limbs,
as flame springs up from a smoldering fire?

I will now explain how this change of condition comes about, and
what causes the spirit to be disordered and the body to grow limp. I want   930
you to ensure that I do not scatter my words to the winds.

In the first place, the exterior of the body, as an inevitable result of its
close contact with the breezy air, is continually battered and buffeted by
its blows. And that is why almost all bodies are invested with hide or
shell or tough skin or bark. The interior of the body too is beaten by the
air that we breathe, when it is inspired and expired. Since our body is
battered both within and without, and since the blows penetrate through   940
the tiny pores to its ultimate particles and primary elements, a kind of
ruin gradually spreads through the limbs: the elements of body and
spirit[63] are disarranged; then part of the spirit is expelled from the body,
and part retires into its inner recesses, while a third part, dispersed
throughout the limbs, cannot maintain its cohesion or engage in interchange of motion because nature barricades all its paths of communica-
tion. These disturbances drive sensation deep down in the body; and, in   950
the absence of anything to support the frame, the body becomes weak
and all the limbs grow limp; the arms and eyelids droop; and even when
one is going to bed, it often happens that the knees give way and lose
their strength.

---

62. **909–911:** Repeated from 180–182. See note there.

63. **944:** Translating *animae,* tentatively suggested by Bailey for *animi.* The
reference should certainly be to the spirit, not to the mind. If Lucr. wrote *animi,*
either he made a mistake or he meant it to mean "mind and spirit," but elsewhere
in his discussion of sleep only the spirit is mentioned.

The reason why food induces sleep is that it produces precisely the same effect as air, while it is being channeled into all the veins; and the reason why you enjoy the heaviest sleep when you are replete or weary is that then the greatest number of atoms are disturbed in consequence of the strain of their heavy labor. At the same time, the part 960 of the spirit thrust downward is driven deeper, the part expelled from the body is more considerable, and there is greater internal discord and dislocation.

Now, whatever activity is the object of our closest interest and attachment, or whatever business has occupied much of our time in the past and has received our mind's special attention—this is usually the subject of our dreams. Lawyers dream that they are pleading cases and drafting contracts; generals that they are fighting battles; mariners that they are continuing to wage war with the winds; and I that I am tackling my task 970 of constantly investigating the nature of things and expounding my discoveries in my native tongue.[64] The position is usually the same when other pursuits and arts occupy people's minds with delusions in their dreams. In the case of those who have devoted all their attention to public entertainments for many days in succession, we generally find that, even when they have ceased to observe the shows with their senses, in their minds paths remain open through which images of the spectacles can pass.[65] Thus for many days the same sights keep presenting themselves 980 before their eyes, so that, even when awake, they seemingly see dancers swaying lissome limbs, and hear melting melodies struck from the strings of the eloquent lyre, and survey the same seated assembly with the varied splendor of the stage in all its brilliance.

So great is the importance of enthusiasm and inclination; so great too is the influence of habitual employment—and not only on human beings, but on all animals. Thus you will see spirited steeds, even when their limbs are stretched out in sleep, perpetually perspiring and panting, as 990 though exerting all their strength to win the palm of victory or [bursting]

---

64. **969–970:** No doubt Lucr. did dream of his work, but, as in 1.410–417 (see note there), where he tells Memmius that he will, if necessary, bombard him with arguments until old age has overtaken the pair of them, a touch of humor is evident.

65. **973–977:** Cf. Diogenes of Oinoanda *fr.* 9.III.6–IV.2: "And after the impingements of the first images, our nature is rendered porous in such a manner that, even if the objects that it first saw are no longer present, images similar to the first ones are received by the mind, [creating visions both when we are awake and in sleep]."

past the opened starting gates.[66] Often hunters' hounds, though subdued by downy slumber, abruptly twitch their legs and give sudden yelps and keep snuffing the air, as if they were following the newly discovered tracks of wild animals; and often, when awakened, they pursue illusive semblances of stags, as though they saw them in flight, until the delusion is dispelled and they recover their senses. Similarly the fawning breed of domesticated dogs suddenly start and snatch their bodies from the 999 ground, just as if they were seeing unfamiliar faces and features. The wilder the breed, the more fiercely it will behave in its dreams. Even the various kinds of birds abruptly take flight and with flapping wings disturb the nocturnal stillness of sacred groves, if, when wrapped in soothing sleep, they have dreamed of hawks swooping after them with 1010 hostile intent.

Similarly, human beings, whose minds with mighty motions effect mighty deeds, often repeat their actions and exploits in their dreams: kings capture cities, are themselves led captive, join battle, and cry out aloud as if they were being stabbed then and there. Many struggle desperately and give groans of pain and, as though they were being devoured by the jaws of a panther or savage lion, fill the whole place with loud shrieks. Many talk in their sleep about important schemes and have often divulged their own crimes.[67] Many meet their death. Many, 1020 under the illusion of plunging earthward with all their weight from precipitous heights, are terror-stricken; and when they awake like people out of their minds, they are so severely shaken by the ferment of the body that they have difficulty in returning to their senses. One who is thirsty sits down beside a river or delightful spring and all but gulps down the whole stream. When they are prisoners of sleep and fancy that they are lifting their dress beside a urinal or chamber pot, many people[68] often discharge the filtered fluid of their whole body, and Babylonian quilts get a wetting despite their sumptuous splendor. Then too a boy through 1030 whose adolescent body the seed is just beginning to surge, when the ripeness of time has created it in his limbs, is visited by images from some body or other, introducing an exquisitely fair face and a beautiful complexion. These visions excite and stimulate the parts that are

---

66. **990:** See note on 2.263–264.

67. **1018–1019:** Cf. 5.1158–1160.

68. **1026:** I translate Avancius' *multi* for *puri,* reverting to the reading I adopted in the 1982 Loeb. In the 1992 Loeb I preferred M. L. Clarke's *parvi,* "children," but R. D. Brown, *Harvard Studies in Classical Philology* 96 (1994) 191–196, has persuaded me that the correct reading is either *multi* or Merrill's *poti,* "intoxicated persons."

turgid with an abundance of seed, often causing him, as though in con-
summation of the act, to ejaculate great waves of fluid and stain his night
clothes.[69]

The stirring of the seed within us takes place, as I have said above,
when adolescence is just beginning to strengthen our limbs.[70] Different
1040 things are moved and stimulated by different causes; and human seed can
be elicited from the human body only by the influence of a human being.
As soon as the seed is ejected from its places of lodgement all over the
body, it passes through the limbs and members, concentrates in certain
parts of the groin, and at once arouses the genitals themselves. These
parts are stimulated and swell with seed, and the desire arises to emit the
seed toward the object of our dire craving. The body seeks the object that
has wounded the mind with love. For, as a general rule, all fall toward
1050 their wound: out gushes the blood in the direction from which the blow
has been dealt, and, if the assailant is at close quarters, he is stained by
the crimson jet. The same is true of the man who is wounded by the darts
of Venus: whether they are launched by a boy with effeminate limbs or
by a woman whose whole body radiates love, he moves toward the
source of the blow, yearning to copulate and ejaculate the accumulated
fluid from body to body;[71] for his speechless desire augurs the pleasure
to come.

69. **1030–1036:** The explanation of wet dreams neatly effects the transition from
dreams to sexual passion.

70. **1037–1287:** Lucr.'s chief philosophical source in his treatment of sex is
undoubtedly Epicurus. Not much of what Epicurus wrote on the subject survives,
but all the indications are that Lucr.'s views are in harmony with those of his
master. Epicurus placed sexual desire in his "natural-but-unnecessary" category
of desire, which means that those affected by it must proceed with caution. Since
its satisfaction brings physical pleasure (albeit a brief one), there is no reason to
avoid it *provided that* it does not also bring pain. But in practice it often does
bring pain, especially if an emotional entanglement has developed. So the recom-
mendation (see 1069–1076) is either to abstain from sexual intercourse or, if one
cannot do without it, to have it on a casual basis so that one gets the physical
pleasure, but avoids the mental pain. Lucr.'s literary sources in this section are
complex and varied: they include the Greek epigrammatists, the Roman drama-
tists Plautus and Terence, the Roman satirist Lucilius, and in one famous passage
(1160–1169) Plato and the Greek poet Theocritus. For full and excellent treatment of the sources and indeed of everything else to do with the closing section of
Book 4, see R. D. Brown, *Lucretius on Love and Sex.*

71. **1048–1056:** Wound imagery is common in Greek erotic poetry, and Lucr.
deploys it to devastating effect. The comparison of an ejaculation of semen,
during sexual intercourse, to a spurt of blood when someone has been wounded is

This is what we call Venus. This is also what gives us our name for love;[72] this is the source of that honeyed drop of Venus' sweetness that is first distilled into our heart, to be followed by chilling care. For even if 1060 your loved one is absent, images of her are with you and the darling name keeps ringing in your ears. It is advisable to shun such images, to abstain from all that feeds your love, and to turn your attention elsewhere: you should ejaculate the accumulated fluid into any woman's body rather than reserve it for a single lover who monopolizes you and thus involve yourself in inevitable anxiety and anguish. The fact is that feeding the ulcer increases its strength and renders it inveterate: day by day the frenzy grows and the misery is intensified, unless you obliterate the old 1070 wounds with new blows and heal them while still fresh by taking at random some random-roaming Venus, or unless you divert the motions of your mind into some other channel.

The man who avoids love does not deprive himself of the joys of Venus, but rather chooses those that involve no penalty. For it is undeniable that the pleasure of intercourse is purer for the healthy-minded than for the lovesick. Even in the hour of possession the passion of lovers fluctuates and wanders in uncertainty: they cannot decide what to enjoy first with their eyes and hands. They tightly squeeze the object of their desire and cause bodily pain, often driving their teeth into one another's 1080 lips and crushing mouth against mouth. This is because their pleasure is not pure: there are secret spurs that stimulate them to hurt the very object, whatever it may be, from which these germs of madness spring.

But during the act of love Venus mitigates the lovers' penalties, and the admixture of seductive pleasure curbs their bites. For the hope is that the same body that kindled the burning passion can also extinguish the flame. However, nature objects that quite the reverse happens. So far as this one thing is concerned, the more of it we have, the more fiercely our 1090 breast burns with dire craving. Food and drink are taken into our body and, since they are able to occupy fixed parts, easily assuage our hunger and thirst. But from the fair face and complexion of a human being nothing passes into the body for enjoyment except impalpable images, a sorry hope often snatched away by the wind. Just like thirsty people who in dreams desire to drink and, instead of obtaining water to quench the fire that consumes their limbs, with vain effort pursue images of water

---

designed to deglamorize sexual passion; so is the play in 1054 and 1056 on the similarity of the words *amorem* ("love") and *umorem* ("fluid," i.e., semen).

72. **1058:** If *nomen amoris* is correct (the conjectural *momen amoris,* "love's impulse," is quite tempting), the reference is apparently to Cupid, the Roman god of love, a personification of *cupido,* "desire."

1100 and remain thirsty, though they drink in the midst of a torrent stream, so, in love, lovers are deluded by Venus with images: no matter how intently they gaze at the beloved body, they cannot sate their eyes; nor can they remove anything from the velvety limbs that they explore with roving, uncertain hands. At last, with limbs interlocked, they enjoy the flower of youth: the body has a presentiment of ecstasy, and Venus is on the point of sowing the woman's fields; they greedily press body to body and intermingle the salivas of their mouths, drawing deep breaths and crush-
1110 ing lips with teeth. But it is all in vain, since they cannot take away anything from their lover's body or wholly penetrate it and merge into it. At times they do indeed seem to be striving and struggling to do this: so eagerly do they remain fettered in the bonds of Venus, while their limbs are slackened and liquefied by the force of the ecstasy. At length, when the accumulated desire has burst from their genitals, there is a brief respite in their raging passion. Then the same madness returns, and they have another fit of frenzy: they seek to attain what they desire, but fail to
1120 find an effective antidote to their suffering: in such deep doubt do they pine away with an invisible wound.

Remember too that the lover consumes his strength and is exhausted by the strain; remember that his life is ruled by another. His duties are neglected; his reputation totters and dwindles. Meanwhile the hard-earned family fortune melts away, transformed into Babylonian perfumes. His mistress's feet sparkle with lovely slippers from Sicyon.[73] You may be sure too that she wears huge green-gleaming emeralds enchased in gold, and that her sea-blue gown, worn out by constant use, soaks up the sweat of Venus. The honest earnings of his fathers are
1130 converted into tiaras and headdresses[74] and sometimes into a Greek cloak and stuffs of Alinda[75] and Ceos.[76] Banquets with exquisite draperies and dainties are prepared, not to mention entertainments, drinks in profusion, perfumes, garlands, and festoons of flowers. But it is all in vain, since from the heart of the fountain of bliss there wells up something sour to pain him among the very flowers. Perhaps his conscience experiences a twinge of remorse at the thought of a life spent in sloth and

---

73. **1125:** Greek city, Corinth's western neighbor.

74. **1129:** Headdresses (*mitrae*) were associated by the Romans with eastern luxury and loose morals.

75. **1130:** A town in Caria, southwest Asia Minor.

76. **1130:** If "of Ceos" is what Lucr. wrote, he made a mistake: it was not Ceos, one of the Sporades, that produced fine silk cloth, but Cos, one of the Cyclades. If he has confused the two islands, he is not the only ancient author to have done so.

squandered in debauchery; perhaps his mistress has thrown out an am-
biguous word and left it embedded in his passionate heart, where it burns
like living fire; or perhaps he fancies that her eyes are wandering too
freely, or that she is ogling some other man, while he detects in her face   1140
the trace of a smile.

These ills are experienced even in love that is steadfast and supremely
successful; but when love is frustrated and unrequited, the miseries you
can spot with your eyes shut are countless. So it is better to be wary
beforehand, as I have recommended,[77] and to take care that you are not
ensnared. For it is easier to avoid being lured into the traps of love than,
once caught, to extricate yourself from the nets and burst the strong knots
of Venus. And yet even when enmeshed and entangled you can still
escape the danger, unless you stand in your own way and at the outset   1150
overlook all the mental and physical imperfections of the woman for
whom you yearn and long. For men who are blinded by passion generally
do this and attribute to their mistresses virtues that in reality they do not
possess. Thus we find women with numerous defects of body and behavior being fondly loved and held in high esteem. One man derides
another and advises him to appease Venus because he is cursed with a
vile passion, often failing to see, poor fool, that his own plight is far
worse. To such men a swarthy skin is "honey-gold,"[78] a slovenly slut   1160
"beauty unadorned," the gray-eyed "a miniature Athena,"[79] a wiry and
woody wench "a gazelle," the dumpy and dwarfish "one of the Graces,
the quintessence of all charms," while a huge hulking giantess is "a sheer
marvel, the embodiment of majesty." The stammerer, who cannot speak
a word, "has a lisp"; the dumb is "modest," the fiery-tempered, spiteful
gossip "a sparkler." One becomes "a slender little darling," when she is a
victim of consumption; another, fighting a losing battle with bronchitis,
is "a delicate creature." The bulging and big-breasted is "Ceres suckling
Iacchus,"[80] the snub-nosed "a lady-Silenus"[81] or "a she-satyr"; the thick-

---

77. **1145:** See 1063–1073.

78. **1160–1169:** This famous list of euphemistic descriptions of imperfect
women seems to have been influenced, directly or indirectly, by Plato (*Republic*
474d–e) and Theocritus (10.24–27). It is possible that it is still more closely
modeled on a lost source. Most of the euphemisms are Greek words.

79. **1161:** Homer gives the goddess Athena the epithet "gray-green-eyed."

80. **1168:** A minor deity, often identified with Bacchus. He was associated with
the Eleusinian mysteries and was sometimes regarded as the son of Demeter
(Ceres).

81. **1169:** Silenus, the attendant of Bacchus, was represented with a snub nose.

1170 lipped was "made to be kissed." It would be a tedious task if I were to try
to run through the whole list.

But even supposing the beauty of her face is all that could be desired,
and the power of Venus radiates from all her limbs, what of it? There are
others like her; we have lived without her until now; and her behavior is,
as we know, just the same as that of an ugly woman. The wretched
creature fumigates herself with such foul perfumes that her maids give
her a wide berth and giggle behind her back. Her lover, so long as he is
shut out, often tearfully buries her threshold under a mound of flowers
and garlands, smears the disdainful doorposts with oil of marjoram, and
1180 plants lovesick kisses on the door. But if, once he is admitted, he should
get just one whiff as he enters, he would seek a plausible pretext to take
his leave; his plaintive speech, deep-drawn and long-rehearsed, would be
forgotten; and then and there he would own himself a fool, on seeing that
he had attributed to her more qualities than one ought to ascribe to a
mortal. All this is well known to our Venuses; and that is why they take
particular trouble to conceal all the behind-the-scenes activities of their
lives from those whom they wish to keep fettered in the chains of love.
But it is all in vain, since, despite their efforts, your mind can drag out all
1190 their secrets into the light and discover the reason for all the giggling; and
if the woman is good-natured and not disagreeable, you can in your turn
shut your eyes to her faults and make allowances for human weaknesses.

The woman is not always sighing with sham passion, when she joins
her body to the man's and holds him in a close embrace, sucking his lips
and moistening them with kisses. Often she is sincere and in search of
mutual joys spurs him on to run the race of love to the goal. The same
applies to female birds and beasts, cows, ewes, and mares: they could not
submit to the male, were it not that their own exuberant nature is in heat
1200 and aflame with desire and gladly draws in the penis of the mounting
male. Moreover, you must have observed how couples enchained by
mutual pleasure are often tortured in common chains: a common sight at
a crossroads is that of two dogs, longing to separate, straining eagerly
and with all their strength in opposite directions, but still remaining
fettered in the bonds of Venus. They would never get themselves into this
position, unless they experienced mutual delights strong enough to lure
them into the trap and keep them enchained. So I insist that sexual
pleasure is shared.

1210   And if at the intermingling of seed it happens that the woman with
sudden strength masters the man's might and overpowers it, children are

conceived of the maternal seed and resemble their mother;[82] if the reverse happens, children are conceived of the paternal seed and resemble their father. But what of those in whom you see resemblances to each parent, and a combination of the characteristics of both? Well, they spring equally from the father's body and the mother's blood; and this comes about when mutual passion has conspired to dash together the seeds roused throughout the limbs by the goads of Venus, and neither partner's semen has been victorious or vanquished.

Furthermore, children sometimes may resemble their grandparents and not infrequently reproduce the features of their great-grandparents. This is because their parents often keep concealed in their bodies many 1220 elements, mingled in many ways, that are derived from the ancestral stock and transmitted from father to father. From this material Venus produces a chance combination of various features, recalling the expressions, voices, and hair of forebears; for these characteristics are derived from a specific seed just as much as our faces, limbs, and bodies.

Then, too, female children may spring from the father's seed, and males may be produced from the mother's body. For every offspring is formed from the seed of both parents, but it is predominantly composed 1230 of the seed of whichever parent it more closely resembles. You may see that this is so, whether the child is male or female.

It is not the divine powers that deprive any man of procreative capacity so that he is prevented from ever being called father by sweet children and is condemned to live a life cursed with sterility. This is indeed a widespread belief, which induces men mournfully to saturate the sacrificial slabs with streams of blood and set the altars ablaze with offerings, in the hope of making their wives pregnant with a full flow of semen. They importune the gods and their oracles in vain. For the cause 1240 of their sterility is either the excessive thickness of their semen, or its undue fluidity and thinness. The thin semen, failing to attach itself firmly to the appropriate parts, trickles away at once and withdraws without causing conception. The excessively thick semen, on the other hand, being discharged in an unduly condensed state, either does not spurt forward sufficiently far or does not properly penetrate the appropriate parts or, having penetrated them, has difficulty in mixing with the woman's semen. It is a patent fact that sexual harmony varies widely: some men impregnate some women more easily than others, while some 1250

---

82. **1211:** Epicurus was one of several Greek philosophers who thought that the female, as well as the male, emits semen.

women receive the burden of pregnancy from some men more readily than from others. Often a woman, having proved infertile in several earlier marriages, has at last found a husband from whom she could conceive babies and be enriched with sweet offspring. Often too a man whose previous wives, in spite of their fertility, had been unable to have babies, has found a partner of compatible makeup who could give him children to be the prop of his old age. All this shows how very important it is that semen should be able to mix with semen in a manner suited to produce conception, thick seed blending with fluid, and fluid with thick.

1260 And here diet plays an important part; for some foods thicken the semen in our limbs, while others dilute and weaken it.

Another factor of paramount importance is the position in which the seductive pleasures of sex are enjoyed. The generally accepted view is that wives conceive most readily in the style and manner of four-footed beasts, because in this position, with the breasts below and the loins raised, the semen can occupy the appropriate parts. It should be added that wives have no need to make voluptuous movements: the woman

1270 opposes and prevents conception, if in her delight she receives the man's penis with her buttocks while making undulating movements with her body all limp; for she drives the furrow out of the direct path of the plowshare and diverts the seed from the vital parts. Whores regularly make these movements for their own ends, to minimize the risk of conception and pregnancy and at the same time to make sexual intercourse itself more pleasing to men. But obviously our wives have no need of such methods.

It is not due to divine intervention or the arrows of Venus that a woman

1280 with little pretension to beauty sometimes comes to be loved. Not infrequently the woman herself, by her behavior, by her obliging ways, and by the scrupulous neatness of her person, easily accustoms a man to spend his life with her. Furthermore, mere habit generates love. For anything that is struck by incessant blows, no matter how lightly, in long lapse of time is overpowered and made to yield. Have you not noticed that even drops of water falling upon a rock in long lapse of time hollow out that rock?

BOOK FIVE

Preface

The Nature and Formation of Our World

Astronomical Phenomena

The Beginnings of Life on Earth

Who possesses the powerful inspiration to compose a poem worthy to
match the majesty of my theme and these discoveries? Who has the
command of language needed to devise praises proportionate to the
merits of him who has bequeathed to us such rich treasures, sought and
acquired by his own intellect? No one, I think, who is of mortal birth. For
if we are to speak as the majesty of his revelations demands, a god he was,

a god,[1] illustrious Memmius, who first discovered that principle of life
which is now identified with wisdom, and who by his genius saved 10
life from such mighty waves and such deep darkness and moored it in
such calm water and so brilliant a light.[2]

Do but compare with his gifts the divine discoveries of others in
ancient times. Ceres, according to legend, introduced corn to mortals,
and Liber[3] the liquor made from the juice of the grape; and yet these
things are not essential to life: indeed it is reported that some peoples
even now live without them. But a good life could not be lived without a
pure mind,[4] and so we have the more justification for deifying the author
of the sweet consolations of life that, disseminated throughout mighty 20
nations, even now are soothing people's minds.

If you consider that his achievements are surpassed by those of Hercules,[5] you will stray still further from the path of sound judgment. What
harm could come to us now from those great gaping jaws of the Nemean
lion or from the bristly Arcadian boar? What could the Cretan bull do, or

---

1. **8:** Although Epicurus was mortal (1.66, 3.1042–1044), he deserves to be
called a god or godlike, because he himself achieved tranquillity of mind such as
the gods enjoy, and because he enabled others to achieve the same goal. See pp.
xii, xix, xxxi.

2. **11–12:** For the image of darkness and light, see also, e.g., 1.146–148 (repeated in three other places), 2.15, 3.1–2. As for the image of storm and calm, it
is relevant to note that Epicurus himself uses it in reference to the mind in turmoil
and at peace, and that *ataraxia,* the Greek word for the Epicurean moral ideal of
"freedom from disturbance," is a metaphor derived from calm water and weather.
See M. F. Smith, *Classical Review* 16 (1966) 265–266.

3. **14:** Native Italian god of fertility, especially associated with wine and frequently identified with the Greek Dionysus or Bacchus.

4. **18:** By "a pure mind" Lucr. means a mind free from unnecessary fears and
desires and from the ills that result from them. See 43–48, 6.24–25.

5. **22:** Hercules, a sort of patron saint of the Cynics, was adopted as a moral
hero by the Stoics as well. Lucr. mentions eight of the twelve Labors: (1) the
killing of the Nemean lion (Nemea is near Argos); (2) the capture of the Ery-
manthian boar (Erymanthus is a mountain in Arcadia); (3) the capture of the
Cretan bull; (4) the killing of the Hydra of Lerna (a marsh near Argos); (5) the
capture of the cattle of Geryon, a mythical king of Spain with three bodies; (6) the
destruction of the dangerous birds that inhabited lake Stymphalus in Arcadia; (7)
the capture of the horses of Diomedes, king of the Bistones, a Thracian people
who lived near Mt. Ismarus; (8) the plucking of the golden apples from the
serpent-guarded tree in the garden of the Hesperides (note the parallelism between this myth and the story of the Garden of Eden).

the scourge of Lerna, the hydra with its palisade of poisonous snakes, or
mighty triple-breasted, triple-bodied Geryon? How could our safety be
30 threatened by the [birds] haunting the Stymphalian [lake][6] or Thracian
Diomedes' horses breathing fire from their nostrils near the Bistonian
plains and Ismarus? As for the guardian of the gold-gleaming apples of
the Hesperides, the fierce, cruel-eyed serpent, with its huge body coiled
around the tree trunk, what possible harm could it do beside the Atlantic
shore and those stern tracts of ocean that none of us visits, and where
not even barbarians venture? And all other such monsters that were
destroyed—if they had not been vanquished, but were still alive, what
harm could they possibly do? None at all, in my judgment; for the earth
40 even now swarms to repletion with wild beasts: the woods and mighty
mountains and deep forests all teem with trembling terror; for the most
part, however, we have the power to avoid these places. But unless our
minds are purified, what strife and what dangers find their way into us
against our will! What poignant pangs of passion disturb and distract us,
and equally what fears! And pride, impurity, and petulance—what havoc
do they not make? What of luxury and laziness? And will not the man
who, using words instead of weapons, subdued all these monsters and
50 banished them from the mind rightly be considered worthy of a place
among the gods? Especially since it was his wont to present many
precepts in a good and godlike manner about the immortal gods themselves and to reveal the whole nature of things in his discourse.

Treading in his footsteps, I have been following his doctrines and
explaining in my verses the necessity for each thing to abide by the law
that governs its creation, and its impotence to rescind the strong statutes
60 of time. Most important of all, we have discovered that the soul is
fashioned and formed of substance that is subject to birth; and we have
found that it cannot endure unscathed through vast eternity, but that the
mind is deceived by images in sleep when we have a vision of one whom
life has deserted.

To proceed, I have now reached the point in my argument where I
must demonstrate that the world is composed of substance subject to
birth and death. I must also explain how that great confluence of matter
established earth, sky, stars, sun, and the globe of the moon; what living
70 things sprang from the earth, and what creatures have never been born;[7]
how human beings began to converse with one another, using various
sounds to denote various things; and how their minds were infiltrated by

---

6. **28:** It must be assumed that a line has been lost after 28.

7. **70:** Creatures like Centaurs, Scylla, and Chimaera. See 878–924.

that fear of the gods which all over the earth maintains the sanctity of the shrines, lakes, groves, altars, and images of deities. Furthermore, I will show by what force piloting nature steers the courses of the sun and the motions of the moon, in order to preclude the possibility of our thinking that these bodies freely and spontaneously pursue their perennial courses between heaven and earth out of kindly consideration for the growth of 80 crops and living creatures, or that they roll on by some divine design. For even those who have rightly learned that the gods lead lives free from care may wonder how all things can be carried on, especially the phenomena above their heads in the ethereal regions; and then they relapse into the old superstitions and subject themselves to cruel tyrants whom they believe, poor fools, to be omnipotent, in their ignorance of what can be and what cannot, and again by what law each thing has its scope restricted and its deeply implanted boundary stone.[8]   90

To proceed, and to delay you no longer with promises, first of all, Memmius, consider the sea, the earth, and the sky: their triple nature, their three bodies, their three different forms, their three huge fabrics, a single day will consign to destruction; and the massive structure of the world, sustained for countless years, will collapse. I am well aware how strange and stupendous to the mind is the notion that heaven and earth are destined to be destroyed, and how difficult it is for me to win belief by words alone. This is always the case when one brings to people's ears 100 something hitherto unfamiliar, without being able to set it before their eyes or place it in their hands—the two highways that give belief easiest access to the human breast and the precincts of the mind. Nevertheless I will speak out. Perhaps the actual event will confirm my words, and you will see the whole world shattered in a brief space of time by violent earthquakes. But may piloting fortune steer this catastrophe far from us, and may reasoning rather than reality convince you that the whole world may give way and collapse with a horrendous crash.

But before I begin to utter oracles on this subject[9]—oracles more holy 110

8. **82–90:** Repeated at 6.58–66. Lines 89–90 are also identical to 1.76–77 and 595–596.

9. **110–234:** Although this passage is a digression in that it separates the introduction to the argument that the world is mortal (91–109) from the argument itself (235–415), it is fully relevant to the main purpose of Book 5 and indeed to one of the main purposes of the whole work, which is to show that the world is not divinely made and governed, and that the gods are not to be feared. There has been much disagreement about Lucr.'s source(s) and target(s) in the

and much more reliable than those that the Pythia pronounces from the tripod and bay of Phoebus[10]—I will expound to you many consolations in words of wisdom, lest, restrained by superstition's curb, you should suppose that earth and sun and sky, sea, stars, and moon, by virtue of their divine body, must endure eternally, and therefore should think it right that, as with the Giants,[11] punishment appropriate to their monstrous crime should be inflicted on all who by their reasoning destroy the
120 ramparts of the world and seek to extinguish the celestial radiance of the sun, degrading immortal things with mortal speech. The fact is that the phenomena that I have mentioned are so far from being divine, and are so unworthy to be enrolled among the gods, that they may rather be regarded as outstanding examples of the inanimate and insensible.

It cannot be supposed that mind and intelligence can exist in company with any and every kind of body. A tree cannot exist in the sky,[12] or
130 clouds in the salt sea; fish cannot live in fields; blood is not found in timber, or sap in stones. The place where each thing may grow and exist is fixed and determined. Thus the substance of the mind cannot come to birth alone without the body or exist separated from sinews and blood. But even if this were possible, the mind could far more easily reside in the head or the shoulders or the base of the heels, or be born in any other part of the body, and so at least remain within the same person, within the same vessel. However, since even within our own body it is evident that a
140 special place is firmly fixed and reserved for the existence and growth of the spirit and mind, it is all the more necessary for us to deny that they could survive wholly outside the body and the living frame in crumbling clods of earth or in solar fire or in water or in the coasts of high heaven. Such things, then, are not endowed with divinity, since they cannot even be animated with life.

---

passage. Undoubtedly his main source is, as usual, Epicurus, whose main targets will have been Plato in some places and Aristotle in other places, but (see notes on 1.638, 4.823–857) one should not assume that Lucr.'s targets are always the same as those of his master, even if he is deploying the same arguments. Most of the beliefs attacked in this passage, including the beliefs that the world and the heavenly bodies are divine, and that the world was created by the gods for the benefit of human beings, were held by the Stoics (see, for example, Cicero *DND* 2) and, as my notes on 156–173 and 200–203 show, it is the Stoics whom Diogenes of Oinoanda names as his opponents in passages that present identical arguments to those put forward by Lucr.

10. **111–112**: Repeated from 1.738–739. See note on 1.737–739.

11. **117**: The Giants stormed heaven and were destroyed by thunderbolts.

12. **128–141**: Repeated, with slight alterations, from 3.784–797.

Another notion that you cannot possibly accept is that the holy habitations of the gods are located in any part of the world.[13] In fact, the nature of the gods is so tenuous, and so far removed from our senses, that it is scarcely perceptible even to the mind; and since it eludes the touch and 150 impact of our hands, it cannot touch anything that is tangible to us; for what is itself intangible cannot touch. Therefore the gods' habitations also must be dissimilar to our habitations and as tenuous as their bodies. This I will subsequently prove to you with ample argument.[14]

To assert, moreover, that the gods purposely prepared the world and its wonders for the sake of human beings; that we should therefore praise their admirable handiwork and regard it as eternal and immortal; that it is 160 sinful to use any means at any time to displace what was established by the ancient design of the gods for the perpetual use of the human race, or to assail it by argument and turn it topsy-turvy; to invent these and all other such conceits, Memmius, is preposterous. For what benefit could immortal and blessed beings derive from our gratitude, that they should undertake to do anything for our sake? What new occurrence could induce them, after such ages of tranquillity, to desire to change their former mode of life? Obviously a new state of things is bound to please 170 one who is discontented with the old; but when one has suffered no distress in time past, but has led a life of happiness, what could kindle in one a passion for novelty?[15] Again, how could it have harmed us never to have been created? Are we to believe that our life lay groveling in murk and misery until the first day of creation dawned for us? All people, once born, must certainly wish to remain in life, so long as seductive pleasure detains them; but if one has never tasted the love of life or been num- 180 bered among the living, how does it harm one not to have been created?

---

13. **146–147:** The Epicureans located the homes of the gods in the spaces between the worlds (*intermundia*).

14. **155:** The apparent failure to fulfill this promise is to be attributed to lack of revision. See p. xi.

15. **156–173:** Cf. Diogenes of Oinoanda *NF* 126–127.VI–IX, *fr.* 20. Attacking the Stoics for believing that the gods created the world either for human beings or for their own benefit, and that they take providential care of their creations, he pours scorn on the idea that they wanted the world as their city and human beings as their fellow citizens. Like Lucr., he wants to know what could have induced them to do what they did: "For god [is] . . . a living being who is indestructible [and] blessed from [age to] age, having complete [self-sufficiency]. Moreover, what [god, if] he had existed for infinite [time] and enjoyed tranquillity [for thousands of years, would have got] this idea that he needed a city and fellow citizens?"

Furthermore, how was a model for the creation of things implanted in the gods? How did they obtain the conception of human beings, so that they might know and perceive in their minds what they wished to produce? And how did they ever recognize the capacity of the primary particles and the potential effect of their different arrangements, if nature herself did not furnish them with a pattern for creation?[16] The fact is that from time everlasting countless elements, impelled by blows and by their
190   own weight, have never ceased to move in manifold ways, making all kinds of unions and experimenting with everything they could combine to create.[17] It is not surprising therefore that they have at last fallen into such arrangements, and acquired such movements, as those whereby this aggregate of things is maintained and constantly renewed.

Even if I had no knowledge of the primary elements of things, I would venture to deduce from the actual behavior of the sky, and from many other facts, evidence and proof that the world was by no means created for us by divine agency: it is marked by such serious flaws.[18]
200   In the first place, of the whole space pavilioned by the sweeping expanse of heaven, mountains and forests, the haunts of wild beasts, have seized a greedy portion, while part is occupied by rocks and waste marshes and the wide sea that separates the coasts of continents.[19] Mortals are deprived of almost two thirds of the remaining land by torrid heat

16. **181–186:** The same argument is used in 1046–1049, where Lucr. is maintaining that language cannot have been an artificial invention. The point is that neither the gods nor the inventors of language can have had a conception of what they wanted to create, if nature had not already created a world or language that they could use as a model. The argument depends on an important principle of Epicurean epistemology, which is that repeated reception of sense impressions creates in the mind a general conception of each class of things, and that without these conceptions, to which further sense impressions are referred, scientific knowledge would be impossible. On (pre)conceptions as a criterion of truth, see p. xxv.

17. **187–191:** Repeated (except the beginning of 187) at 422–426.

18. **195–199:** Repeated, with minor alterations, from 2.177–181.

19. **200–203:** Diogenes of Oinoanda, arguing against the view, which he assigns to the Stoics, that the gods created the world for the sake of human beings, draws attention, as Lucr. does, to its imperfections. He too mentions the sea, but gives more prominence to it than Lucr. does. He says that the sea occupies so much space that "it makes a peninsula of the inhabited world"; he adds that it has many other drawbacks and, "to cap all, has water that is not even drinkable, but briny and bitter, as if it had been purposely made like this by the god to prevent human beings from drinking" (*fr.* 21.I.13–II.10).

and the perpetual fall of frost; and as for the rest, nature would cover it with briars, if her strength were not resisted by the strength of human beings who, in order to gain a livelihood, persistently groan over the stout mattock and furrow the earth with the deep-driven plow. Unless, by 210 turning up the fertile clods with the plowshare and trenching the soil, we rouse seeds from dormancy, plants cannot spontaneously emerge into the limpid air. And even then, just when our heavy labor is being rewarded, and all over the countryside things are bursting into leaf and flower, they are often scorched by the excessive heat of the ethereal sun or destroyed by sudden rainstorms or battered by the blasts of tearing tornadoes.

Furthermore, why does nature nurture and multiply the terrible tribes of wild beasts, so harmful to the human race by land and sea? Why do the 220 seasons of the year bring diseases? Why does premature death prowl about?

Consider too how a baby, like a shipwrecked sailor tossed ashore by the savage waves, lies on the ground naked, speechless, and utterly helpless, as soon as nature has cast it forth with pangs of labor from its mother's womb into the shores of light; and how it fills the place with its woeful wailings—as well it may, seeing that life holds so much sorrow in store for it.[20] On the other hand, the various domestic animals and wild beasts grow up without ever needing rattles or the soothing and broken 230 baby-talk of a fostering nurse; they do not require different clothing according to the season of the year; and they need no weapons or lofty walls for the defense of their property, since for every one of them everything is produced in abundance by the earth herself, and by nature the deft artificer of things.

---

20. **222–227:** Imitated by Wordsworth in *To —, Upon the Birth of Her First-Born Child* 1–12: "Like a shipwrecked Sailor tost / By rough waves on a perilous coast, / Lies the Babe, in helplessness, / And in tenderest nakedness, / Flung by labouring Nature forth / Upon the mercies of the earth. / Can its eyes beseech? no more / Than the hands are free to implore: / Voice but serves for one brief cry; / Plaint was it? or prophesy / Of sorrow that will surely come? / Omen of man's grievous doom!" Lucr.'s comment on the appropriateness of the newborn baby's crying has been interpreted as pessimistic, but, although it cannot be dismissed as nothing more than a joke (both the crying of newborn babies and the unhappiness of most human beings are facts), account should be taken not only of the polemical nature of the whole passage, but also of an element of playfulness seen also in the remark, which immediately follows the comment about what awaits the baby, that the young of animals do not need rattles or a nurse's prattle to keep them contented. Lucr. was certainly no pessimist, believing as he did that, thanks to Epicurus, we can achieve a happiness comparable to that of the gods.

In the first place,[21] since the substance of earth and the water and the light breezes of air and the fiery heat that manifestly constitute this aggregate of things all consist of a substance subject to birth and death, 240 we must consider the whole world to be of the same nature. It is an observable fact that all objects whose parts and members manifestly consist of substance subject to birth and death are themselves invariably subject to birth and death. Therefore when I witness the wasting and recreation of the massive members and components of the world, I may be sure that the sky and the earth as well had a beginning and will suffer destruction.

In this connection, do not imagine that I have begged the question in assuming that earth and fire are mortal, in affirming that water and air are 250 perishable, and in asserting that the same elements are reborn and grow again. In the first place, part of the earth, when baked by the sun's incessant rays and trampled by the tread of many feet, sometimes gives off smoky clouds of flying dust, which strong winds disperse throughout the air. Again, part of the soil is washed away by the rains, and rivers abrade and erode their banks. Moreover, whatever the earth sustains and strengthens is duly returned to the earth; and since it is undoubtedly a 260 patent fact that the universal parent is also the universal tomb, you may be sure that the earth is diminished and then is recruited and grows again.

Furthermore, there is no need of words to show that the sea, rivers, and springs are constantly being replenished with a perennial flow of water: the vast downrush of streams on every side is proof enough. But the foremost parts of the water are continually being removed, so that on balance there is no superabundance of liquid. The volume of water is diminished partly by the strong winds that sweep the surface of the sea, partly by the ethereal sun's unraveling rays, and partly by distribution in all directions under the ground. The brine is filtered off, while the fluid 270 streams back and all collects at the riverheads, from which it flows overland in a fresh current, following the channel that once was carved for it to roll down in its liquid course.[22]

I turn now to air, whose whole substance undergoes countless changes each passing hour. For all the emanations from objects are constantly flowing into the vast ocean of air; and unless the air in its turn restored particles to objects and replaced the substance that flows away, everything would by now have been resolved and converted into air. Air, then, 280 is continually being generated from objects and returning to them, since

---

21. **235:** Lucr. abruptly resumes the argument interrupted at 109.

22. **269–272:** Repeated, with two minor alterations, at 6.635–638.

it is certain that all things are in constant flux.

Likewise the free-flowing fount of limpid light, the ethereal sun, ceaselessly inundates the sky with fresh radiance, instantly supplying new light to replace light. For the foremost part of each bright beam perishes on whatever spot it impinges, as you may learn from what follows. The moment that clouds begin to pass beneath the sun and, as it were, interrupt the rays of light, all the lower part of those rays at once disappears, and, wherever the clouds are carried, the earth is cast into shadow. Here you have proof that objects always need new radiance, that 290 the foremost part of each shining shaft perishes, and that it would be impossible for things to be seen in the sunlight if the source of light itself did not furnish a perpetual supply.

Moreover, you may observe that the lights that we use at night on earth—pendant lamps, and torches with flashing flames flickering through thick, rich smoke—hasten in the same manner, with the help of their burning, to supply new light; their tremulous fires press on and on, so that the light is never interrupted and never leaves the spots that it illuminates: with such rapidity is the extinction of the old flame con- 300 cealed by the swift birth of the new from all the fires. In the same way, then, we must suppose that the sun, moon, and stars owe their radiance to successive generations of light, and that the foremost parts of their beams perpetually perish. Therefore you cannot possibly believe that these celestial bodies have an unviolable vigor.

Again, do you not see even stones being overpowered by time, tall towers tumbling down, and rocks crumbling away? Do you not see the shrines and statues of the gods succumbing to the stress and strain of age, their sanctity being powerless to extend the limits of destiny or defy the 310 laws of nature? Do we not also observe the monuments of the great moldering, while continuing to inquire whether we believe that they grow old?[23] Do we not see flinty rocks ripped from the heights of mountains crashing down, unable to endure the fierce force of even finite time? The truth is that they would not suddenly be wrenched away and fall, if from time everlasting they had successfully withstood all the assault and battery of time and remained unscathed.

Further, consider this expanse that around and above enfolds the entire

---

23. **312:** The reading of the manuscripts is manifestly corrupt. I have translated Munro's suggestion *quaerere proporro sibi sene senescere credas,* which, though probably not exactly what Lucr. wrote, gives the likely sense of the line. The idea seems to be that even monuments that, as their inscriptions show, are intended to make the memory of the dead eternal, crumble away.

320 earth in its embrace: if, as some[24] say, it produces all things from its own substance and takes them back again when they perish, it must itself consist of matter subject to birth and death. For whatever sustains and strengthens other things from itself must be diminished, and then must be recruited when it takes them back.

Moreover, if heaven and earth never had a beginning or birth, but have existed from everlasting, why have there not been other poets to sing of other events prior to the Theban war and the tragedy of Troy?[25] Why have so many heroic deeds so often been buried in oblivion, instead of
330 flowering somewhere, implanted in eternal memorials of fame? The true explanation, in my judgment, is that our world is in its youth:[26] it was not created long ago, but is of comparatively recent origin. That is why at the present time some arts are still being refined, still being developed. This age has seen many improvements in shipbuilding; it is not long since musicians first molded melodious tunes; our system of philosophy too is a recent invention, and I myself am found to be the very first with the ability to expound it in the language of my country.[27]

If by chance you believe that all these same things happened before,
340 but that the races of human beings perished in a great conflagration, or that their cities were razed by a mighty convulsion of the world, or that rivers, rapacious after unremitting rains, inundated the earth and submerged towns, there is all the more necessity for you to admit defeat and acknowledge that heaven and earth are destined to be destroyed. For the fact that the world was assailed by such serious disorders and dangers indicates that, if it had been attacked by a fiercer force, it would have collapsed in vast ruins. Indeed the one certain indication of our own

---

24. **320:** It is not clear who are in Lucr.'s mind. Lines 318–323 are based on lines of Ennius' nephew Pacuvius (220–c.130 B.C.), a tragedian.

25. **326:** A lost epic poem, the *Thebaïs,* described the struggle of Eteocles and Polynices, sons of Oedipus, for the throne of Thebes. "The tragedy of Troy" is the subject of Homer's *Iliad.*

26. **330:** On the face of it, the opinion that the world is still young looks to be inconsistent with the view, expressed elsewhere (826–836, 2.1150–1174), that the earth is already in decline.

27. **335–337:** Certainly Lucr. was the first to expound Epicureanism in Latin verse, but it is usually thought that Gaius Amafinius, who popularized the philosophy in Latin prose and, according to Cicero (*Tusc. Disp.* 4.6–7), achieved considerable success, wrote before him. If the usual view is correct (and it probably is), the justification for Lucr.'s claim may be that he was the first Latin writer to give a systematic account of Epicurean physics.

mortality is our susceptibility to the same maladies that affected those 350
whom nature has removed from life.[28]

Furthermore, all things that subsist eternally must either be composed
of solid substance, so that they repel blows and are impenetrable to
anything that might destroy the close cohesion of their parts from
within—like the elements of matter, whose nature I have already
demonstrated; or their ability to survive throughout all time must be due
to their immunity from blows—as is the case with void, which is always
intangible and never experiences any impact; or else the cause of their
indestructibility must be the absence of any surrounding space into 360
which their substance might disperse and dissolve—as is the case with
the totality of the universe: for outside the universe there is no space into
which its substance can fly apart, and no matter capable of striking it and
shattering it with a powerful blow.[29]

But, as I have shown,[30] the world is not formed of solid substance,
since there is an admixture of void in things; nor is it like void; nor is
there any lack of particles that could fortuitously gather together out of
infinite space and overthrow this aggregate of things in a tearing tornado
or inflict on it some other kind of dangerous disaster; nor again is there 370
any shortage of unfathomable space into which the ramparts of the world
could be dispersed; or else they may be destroyed by the impact of some
other force. Therefore the door of death, far from being closed against
the sky or the sun or the earth or the deep waters of the ocean, stands
wide open and confronts them with vast gaping jaws. And so you must
acknowledge that the world had a birth; for, being of mortal substance, it
could not from time everlasting up to the present have succeeded in
defying the strong assaults of measureless ages.

Again, since the massive members of the world fight so furiously with 380
one another, engaging in an unrighteous war,[31] do you not see that some
end may be assigned to their long struggle? It may be that the sun and
every kind of fire will gain victory by drinking up all the waters. But in
spite of their strenuous efforts to do this, they are not yet achieving their

---

28. **348–350:** So, we are meant to understand, the disorders that affected the
world are indications of its mortality.

29. **351–363:** These lines also occur (with minor variations) at 3.806–818.

30. **364:** 1.329–369.

31. **380–381:** "The massive members of the world" are the four elements—fire,
water, air, earth. The war between them is called "unrighteous," because it is a
civil war, the elements being members of a single "state."

aim; for the rivers make up the supply of water and moreover threaten to inundate the whole world with a deluge from the unfathomable abyss of ocean. The threat is vain, however, since the winds that sweep the surface of the sea, and the ethereal sun with its unraveling rays, diminish the
390 volume of fluid and are confident of their ability to dry up the whole world before the water can attain its goal. Such is the warlike spirit of these elements, as in equal contest they strive and struggle with one another for the control of a mighty empire. But once, according to legend, fire triumphed, and once water held sway on the plains.

Fire was victorious and went around burning up much of the world, when the strong steeds of the sun went astray and wildly whirled Phaëthon[32] through the whole heaven and over every land. But then the
400 omnipotent father, deeply incensed, with a sudden stroke of his thunderbolt struck the presumptuous Phaëthon from his chariot to the earth; and Phoebus, meeting him as he fell, caught the eternal lamp of the world,[33] retrieved the scattered steeds, reyoked the trembling creatures, and then, guiding them along their proper path, restored everything to order. At least so sang the ancient poets of Greece.[34] But the story is very far removed from the truth. In reality, fire can triumph only when an excessive number of igneous particles have gathered together out of infinite space; and then unless its strength is subdued in turn by some other force
410 and subsides, it destroys and consumes everything with scorching blasts.

Once too, so legend relates, water gathered together and began to triumph, when its waves overwhelmed much of the human race.[35] Then, when the great mass of particles, which had gathered together out of infinite space, was by some means diverted and repelled, the rains stopped and the rivers diminished their violence.

---

32. **397:** Phaëthon, whose Greek name means "Shiner," was the son of the sun (Phoebus in our passage). He obtained his father's permission to drive the chariot of the sun for a day, but lost control and would have set the earth on fire if Jupiter ("the omnipotent father") had not killed him with a thunderbolt. Ovid tells the story in detail in *Metamorphoses* 1.750–2.400. (Appropriately, in recent years an asteroid that orbits the sun on a wildly eccentric course has been named Phaëthon. In 1988 astronomers calculated that this body will eventually pass very close to the earth, and that a collision around A.D. 2250, though unlikely, is not impossible. So perhaps Jupiter will have to intervene a second time.)

33. **402:** Needless to say, Lucr. does not believe in an eternal sun any more than he believes in Jupiter's omnipotence or indeed in the existence of Phaëthon. He is parodying the language of "the ancient poets of Greece" mentioned at 405.

34. **405:** One poet of whom Lucr. is thinking may be Euripides, of whose tragedy *Phaëthon* fragments survive.

35. **411–412:** An allusion to the flood in the time of Deucalion, the Greek Noah.

I will now explain in order how that great concourse of matter established the earth and the sky and the unfathomable ocean and the sun and the moon and their courses.

Certainly the primary elements did not intentionally and with acute 420 intelligence dispose themselves in their respective positions, nor did they covenant to produce their respective motions. In reality, from time everlasting countless elements of things, impelled by blows and by their own weight, have never ceased to move in manifold ways, making all kinds of unions and experimenting with everything they could combine to create; and that is why, after wandering far and wide during mighty ages of eternity and experiencing every kind of movement and combination, at last those atoms have met which, when suddenly dashed together, often 430 form the foundations of mighty fabrics—earth, sea, and sky, and the family of living creatures.

At first it was not possible to see the wheel of the sun soaring aloft with free-flowing light, nor the stars of the spacious firmament, nor sea nor sky nor earth nor air nor indeed anything resembling the things we know. There was only a newly formed, turbulent mass of primary elements of every kind; and these were discordantly waging a war that involved constant confusion of interspaces, courses, interlacements, weights, impacts, concurrences, and motions, because, owing to the 440 diversity of their shapes and the variety of their forms, they could not all form lasting unions or intercommunicate appropriate motions. Then the different parts began to separate, and like elements began to unite with like, thus starting the evolution of the world, the distribution of its members, and the disposition of its vast components—that is, the division of the high heaven from the earth, the allocation of a separate place to the sea for its expanse of water, and the isolation of the ethereal fires so that they should be pure and unmixed.

In the first place, all the particles of earth, by reason of their weight 450 and intertanglement, congregated in the middle and occupied the lowest positions; and the more closely they became united and intertangled, the more they squeezed out the elements that were to form the sea, the stars, the sun, the moon, and the ramparts of the mighty world. For the component particles of all these bodies are smoother, rounder, and much smaller than the elements of earth. And so first the fire-laden ether immediately[36] burst out through the interstices of the porous earth and raised itself on high and, being light, carried with it many fires. The 460 process was not dissimilar to one which we often witness, as soon as the

---

36. **458:** I follow W. S. Watt, *Philologus* 140 (1996) 252, in adopting Bentley's *protinus* for *partibus*.

morning light of the radiant sun begins to glow golden over the dew-pearled grass: the ponds and perennial streams exhale a mist, and the earth itself is sometimes seen to steam; and when all these exhalations rise and mass together high above us, their substance condenses to form a cloudy tissue that veils the sky. Similarly, then, at that time the light and elastic ether condensed to form the vault that overarches the world on
470 every side and, spreading out widely in all directions on all sides, enclosed all other things in a greedy embrace.

The formation of the ether was followed by the birth of the sun and moon, whose spheres revolve in the air midway between the earth and the vast ether: they were not appropriated by either of these elements, because they were neither so heavy as to sink and settle, nor so light that they could glide through the loftiest regions. And yet, despite their intermediate position, they revolve like living bodies and are component parts of the world as a whole. Compare how, with our own bodies, some members may remain still, while others are moving.
480   After the withdrawal of these elements, the earth suddenly subsided in those parts where the vast, dark-blue expanse of ocean now extends, and flooded the depressions with salt surge. And day by day, the more the surrounding ether's seething tides and the sun's rays compressed the earth by constantly beating on its outer surface from every side, so that it condensed and contracted to its center, the more salt sweat was exuded from its body to swell with its flow the floating plains of the sea, and the
490 more, too, the numerous particles of fire and air slipped out and flew far away to reinforce the lofty, lambent precincts of the sky. The plains subsided, while the mountains grew in height; for the rocks could not sink down, and not all parts of the ground were able to settle to the same level.

Thus, then, the earth, because of the heaviness and compactness of its substance, stood firm, and all the world's sludge (as it were) by virtue of its weight sank down to the bottom and settled there like dregs. Then the sea, then the air, then the fire-laden ether were all left limpid and pure.
500 Each of these elements is lighter than the last, and ether, the most limpid and light of all, floats above the breezy air without mingling its limpidity with the turbulence of the atmosphere: it leaves all the parts below to be tossed by tearing tornadoes, leaves them to be disturbed by capricious squalls, while it bears its own fires along, gliding forward at a steady pace. The ether's ability to flow at an even speed and with uniform effort is indicated by the Pontus,[37] which flows with an unchanging current, constantly preserving the equability of its gliding motion.

---

37. **507:** The Pontus is the Black Sea. In antiquity it was thought that it constantly flows into the Propontis (Sea of Marmara), toward the Aegean. The same

Let us now consider what causes the motions of the heavenly bodies.[38] In the first place, if the vast sphere of sky rotates, we must assume that its 510 axis is stabilized and enclosed at both ends by the pressure of extramundane air on each pole. Then we must suppose either that another current of air flows above, moving in the same direction in which the sparkling stars of the everlasting[39] firmament revolve, or that another current of air flows below in the opposite direction and drives along the sphere from beneath in the same way that we see streams turning the scoops on a water wheel.

Alternatively it is possible that the sky as a whole remains stationary, while the glittering constellations move onward. A possible explanation for this is that impetuous currents of ether are imprisoned in the sky and, 520 as they whirl around and around in search of an egress, roll with them the fires scattered all over the night-thundering precincts of heaven; or perhaps a current of air from some other outside quarter impels and wheels the fiery stars; or it may be that they can creep forward spontaneously, moving wherever their sustenance attracts and invites them as they feed their flaming bodies all over the celestial field.[40]

Which of these causes operates in our world it is difficult to determine with certainty. I am teaching what can and does happen throughout the universe in the various worlds variously formed; and I am striving to set out several causes that may account for the motions of stars throughout 530 the universe as a whole. One of these causes must impart motion to the heavenly bodies in our world; but to assert dogmatically which of them it is, certainly does not befit one proceeding with cautious steps.[41]

---

idea is found in Shakespeare's *Othello* 3.3.453–456: ". . . like to the Pontick Sea, / Whose icy current and compulsive course / Ne'er feels retiring ebb, but keeps due on / To the Propontick and the Hellespont."

38. **509–770:** On Epicurean astronomy, and on the proper way to investigate astronomical phenomena, see especially Epicurus *Pyth.* and *Hdt.* 78–80. See also p. xxiv. Epicurean astronomy may not be very inspired, but it did inspire Lucr. to write some splendid poetry: see, for example, 731–750.

39. **514:** If the Latin text is correct here, the epithet "everlasting" is very unfortunate, seeing that Lucr. has recently devoted several hundred lines to demonstration that the world, including the sky, is not everlasting. Merrill's tentative suggestion *nocturni* for *aeterni* is tempting: "in which the sparkling stars of the night-sky revolve."

40. **523–525:** The stars are pictured as a flock of grazing sheep moving slowly over a field, as comparison with 2.317–319 confirms.

41. **526–533:** On the doctrine of plurality of causes, cf. 6.703–711 and see pp. xxiv–xxv.

Now, seeing that the earth is able to remain at rest in the middle of the world, it must be assumed that its mass gradually diminishes and disappears, and that it has another substance beneath, which from the beginning of its existence has been conjoined and united with the world's aerial regions in which it is implanted and lives. Consequently the earth
540 is no burden to the air and does not depress it, just as a person's limbs are no burden to their owner: the head is no burden to the neck, and we do not feel that the whole weight of the body is resting on the feet, whereas all weights of external origin that are laid upon us cause us discomfort, though they are often far less heavy than our limbs. So much depends on the properties of each object. The earth, then, far from being an extraneous, alien body suddenly intruded and thrown on an alien air, was conceived simultaneously with the air at the beginning of the world and forms a definite part of the world, just as our limbs manifestly form part of ourselves.
550 Furthermore, when a violent thunder-stroke suddenly shakes the earth, the earth in its turn shakes all the atmosphere above it; and it could not possibly do this, unless it were closely bound to the aerial and celestial regions of the world. The fact is that earth and air cohere together by common roots[42] and have been conjoined and united from the beginning of their existence. Do you not see too that the soul, despite the extreme subtlety of its substance, is able to sustain the big bulk of our body, because it is so closely conjoined and united with it? And what is the
560 force that can make the body give a nimble leap, if it is not the soul, the helmsman of the limbs? Do you see now how powerful a subtle substance can be when it is conjoined with a heavy substance, as air is conjoined with earth, and the mind with our body?

The wheel of the sun and the heat that it emits cannot be much greater or less than they seem to our senses. For, no matter how distant a fire is, as long as it can project its light on us and breathe a hot blast on our limbs, its size is not diminished at all by the intervening distance: there is
570 no perceptible contraction. Therefore, since the sun's heat and lavish light reach our senses and irradiate the terrestrial regions, it must be assumed that the form and contour of the sun are seen from the earth in their true dimensions with absolutely no enlargement or diminution.[43]

---

42. **554:** Repeated from 3.325, where the close connection between the body and the soul is emphasized. In 556–563 Lucr. uses that connection to illustrate the connection between the earth and the air.

43. **564–573:** For a sympathetic and interesting discussion of Epicurus' strange conclusion about the size of the sun, see D. Sedley, *Cronache Ercolanesi* 6 (1976) 48–53.

The moon too, whether it illuminates the earth with bastard beams as it moves across the sky, or whether it radiates its own light from its own body, in any case has a magnitude no greater than it appears to have when we perceive it with our eyes. For all objects that we view from a considerable distance through a large tract of air become blurred in 580 appearance before their outline is diminished. Consequently, since the moon displays a distinct form and a clearly defined outline, it must appear to us on earth just as it really is on high—with its true contour and in its true dimensions.

Lastly, what of all the ethereal fires that are visible from the earth? Since, in the case of all our terrestrial fires, the outline seems to vary only occasionally and only a very little one way or the other according to the distance, it is evident that the ethereal fires cannot be more than a minute 590 degree smaller or larger than they appear to be.

It need occasion no surprise that so small a sun can emit so great a light, sufficient to inundate all seas and lands and sky and deluge the whole world with blazing heat. It is possible that this one free-flowing fountain for the whole world has been opened to pour out light in a gushing stream because particles of heat, converging from all parts of the world, congregate and flow together in such a way that they form a single 600 source from which all this heat issues. Have you not noticed how widely a small spring of water sometimes irrigates the meadows and floods the fields?

Another possibility is that, though the sun's fire is not large, its heat affects the air and sets it alight, if there happens to be air ready to hand that is easily ignited by the impact of weak rays of heat. Compare how we sometimes see corn and stubble set ablaze over a wide area by a single spark.

Or perhaps the sun, whose rose-red lamp shines on high, is surrounded 610 by a great deal of invisible fire which, though not distinguished by any radiance, is charged with heat and so greatly strengthens the stroke of the solar rays.

There is no single and simple explanation available of how the sun passes from his summer quarters to the winter tropic of Capricorn and then turns around and returns to his goal, the solstitial point of Cancer, or of how the moon seemingly traverses in a month the course that the sun spends a whole year traveling. As I say, no single cause can be assigned 620 for these phenomena.

Seemingly one of the most plausible possibilities is the revered hy-

pothesis of the great Democritus.[44] According to this, the nearer a heavenly body is to the earth, the less rapidly it is whirled around by the revolution of the sky; for the swiftness and impetuosity of the vortex decreases and diminishes in its lower parts, and so the sun, being much lower in the sky than the blazing signs of the zodiac, gradually falls back among the rearward signs. And the moon falls behind even more: the
630 lower her course, the farther it is from the sky and the nearer to the earth, the less able is she to keep pace with the constellations; and the more languid the vortex that carries her along at a lower level than the sun, the more do all the constellations round about catch up and overtake her. So the reason why the moon apparently returns to each sign more swiftly than the sun is that the signs are returning to her more rapidly than to the sun.

A further possibility[45] is that at fixed times two currents of air blow across the sun's path alternately from opposite regions of the world, and
640 that one is able to push him from the summer constellations right down to the winter tropic with its stiffening frosts, while the other drives him all the way back from the realms of icy darkness to the sultry regions of the blazing signs. Similarly we may suppose that the moon, and the stars that revolve for great years in great orbits, can be propelled by alternating currents of air blowing from opposite directions. Have you not observed that clouds, driven by different winds, move in different directions, the lower contrary to the upper? Why then is it not equally possible for the heavenly bodies to be carried by contrary currents through their vast circuits of the ether?

650   Night covers the earth with its vast pall of darkness, either because the sun, on reaching the farthest verge of the sky at the end of his long course, in exhaustion breathes out his fires, which have been impaired and weakened by the journey through so much air; or because the same force that carried the solar disk above the earth impels it to change course and pass beneath the earth.

Similarly, the reason why Matuta[46] at a definite hour diffuses the rose-red dawn through the ethereal regions and outspreads her light may be that the selfsame sun, returning from beneath the earth, projects his rays

---

44. **622:** Repeated from 3.371. See note there.

45. **637–649:** This passage, which is introduced as if it were an alternative to the explanation, offered in 621–636, of varying orbital speeds, actually offers a possible explanation of a different phenomenon, the sun's ecliptic. For full discussion of Lucr.'s confusion, see Bailey's commentary.

46. **656:** Roman goddess of dawn.

into the sky before he appears, striving to set it ablaze. Alternatively 660
it may be that at that particular time particles of fire congregate and
numerous seeds of heat regularly stream together, thus causing new
sunlight to be created every day. Compare the story of how from the
mountain heights of Ida[47] at daybreak one sees scattered fires, which
then gather together into a single globe and form a complete disk.

In this connection, it should not be considered strange that these seeds
of fire can stream together at so fixed a time to renew the radiance of the
sun, seeing that in all departments of nature we observe numerous phenomena occurring at fixed times. Trees blossom at a fixed time, and at a 670
fixed time shed their blooms. At times no less surely fixed, age com-
mands teeth to be shed and a youth to clothe himself in soft pubescent
down and have a silky beard flowing down from either cheek. Again,
lightning, snow, rains, clouds, and winds occur at more or less fixed
seasons of the year. For since causes have operated thus from the beginning, and things have happened in this way from the birthday of the
world, they still continue to recur in a fixed order and sequence.

The reason why days wax as nights wane, and daylight diminishes as 680
the nights increase, may be that the selfsame sun, as he runs his course
below and above the earth, describes unequal curves in the ethereal
regions, dividing his daily circuit into uneven parts; and what he sub-
tracts from one part he adds, as he revolves, to the opposite part, until he
reaches the celestial sign[48] where the node of the year[49] makes the
nocturnal darkness equal in length to the light of the day. For when the
sun has been blown halfway by the north wind or by the south wind,[50]
the point that he occupies in the sky is equidistant from the tropics. This 690
is due to the position of the entire zodiacal zone, through which the slow-
moving sun takes a whole year to pass, irradiating earth and sky with
slanting light, as is clearly shown by the charts of those who have
mapped out all the celestial regions and marked the array of constellations with which they are adorned.

Alternatively it may be that the air is denser in certain parts, with the
result that the quivering brilliance of the solar fire is retarded beneath the

---

47. **663:** Mount Ida in Phrygia. The phenomenon to which Lucr. refers is
described or alluded to by several other ancient writers.

48. **687:** Aries at the vernal equinox, Libra at the autumnal.

49. **687–688:** The "node of the year" is one of the two points at which the
ecliptic and equator intersect (at the equinoxes).

50. **689:** That is, at the vernal or autumnal equinox. For the theory that winds,
blowing across the sun's path, push it alternately north and south, see 637–645.

earth and cannot easily penetrate the air and emerge above the horizon.
700 This would explain why in winter nights drag on for a long time, before
the dazzling diadem of day appears.

A further possibility is that particles of fire, whose confluence causes
the sun to rise at a particular point, regularly stream together more slowly
or more swiftly at alternate seasons of the year. Therefore it is evident
that those persons speak the truth . . . .[51]

As for the moon, it may be that she owes her brilliance to the impingement of solar rays,[52] and that day by day, as she recedes farther from the
sun's disk, she turns her light more fully toward our view, until, when
exactly opposite him, she shines with her fullest splendor and, as she
710 soars high above the horizon, sees his setting. Then she must hide her
light little by little behind her, as she glides nearer to the sun's fire,
moving through the zone of the zodiac from the opposite side. This is the
view of those who suppose the moon to be a spherical body, whose
course is lower than that of the sun.

It is also possible that as she revolves she may shine with her own
light and present various phases of brightness. For she may be accompanied by another body, which glides along with her, continually
occulting and obstructing her, but which is invisible because it moves
720 devoid of light; or she may possibly rotate like a ball, one half of whose
surface is tinged with gleaming light, and by rotating her sphere present her various phases, until she turns to our wakeful eyes the half
that is illuminated before gradually twisting back and withdrawing the
luminous part of her sphere. This is the theory that the Babylonian teaching of the Chaldaeans[53] attempts to prove in opposition to the hypothesis of the Greek astronomers—as though the view championed by
730 either party might not be correct, or as though there were any reason why you should venture to embrace the one opinion less than the
other.

Lastly, it is difficult to give any convincing reason why a new moon
should not be created every day, with a fixed succession of phases and
forms, each new-created moon being extinguished each day and replaced

---

51. **704:** A lacuna must be assumed here. The sense of the missing line or lines is
disputed.

52. **705:** The discovery that the moon's light is derived from the sun was probably made by Anaxagoras (on whom see note on 1.830).

53. **727:** Lucr. must be referring especially to the theory of Berosus, who belongs
to the late fourth and early third centuries B.C.

by another: one sees many things created in so[54] fixed an order. Spring[55] comes and Venus, preceded by Venus' winged harbinger,[56] and mother Flora,[57] following hard on the heels of Zephyr, prepares the way for them, strewing all their path with a profusion of exquisite hues and 740 scents. Next in the procession comes the parching heat of summer, accompanied by dusty Ceres and blasts of etesian[58] winds. Then autumn advances, and with her walks Bacchus acclaimed with cries of joy. Then follow other seasons and other winds—Volturnus thundering on high and Auster[59] mighty with lightning. At length the solstice brings snow, and winter returns with numbing frost, followed by cold with teeth chattering.[60] Seeing that many things can occur at so fixed a time, it is 750 not surprising if the moon is created at a fixed time and again at a fixed time is destroyed.

In the same way you must suppose that eclipses of the sun and occultations of the moon may be produced by several causes. For why should it be thought that the moon alone is able to cut off the earth from the sunlight and high in the sky interpose her head between the earth and the sun, obstructing his blazing rays with her opaque disk? Why should it not be considered equally possible that some other body, gliding along ever devoid of light, produces the same effect? And again why should not the sun at fixed times grow languid and lose his fires, and then renew his radiance when he has passed through tracts of air so hostile to his flames 760 that his fires are temporarily extinguished and destroyed? And why should the earth alone be able, in her turn, to deprive the moon of light and, as she passes above the sun, herself keep him suppressed while the

---

54. **736:** Both here and in 750 *tam* is often taken with *multa* rather than with *certo.* However, the word order is against this, and so is 667 where *tam* certainly belongs with *certo.*

55. **737–740:** These lines may have indirectly (through Politian) influenced Botticelli's *Allegory of Spring,* but Lucr. was certainly not the painter's only source of inspiration (see my note in the Loeb).

56. **737–738:** Cupid.

57. **739:** Italian goddess of flowers.

58. **742:** The Greek *etēsios* means "annual," and the epithet was applied to northwesterly winds blowing in the Mediterranean for about forty days annually in the summer. These winds are mentioned again at 6.716, 730.

59. **745:** Volturnus and Auster: east-southeast wind and south wind respectively.

60. **747:** Imitated by Spenser in *The Faerie Queene* 7.7.31.1–2: "Lastly, came Winter cloathed all in frize, / Chattering his teeth for cold that did him chill."

moon in her monthly course glides through the clear-cut cone-shaped
shadow? Why should it not be equally possible that some other body
passes beneath the moon or glides over the sun's disk so as to interrupt
the free flow of radiant light? Furthermore, if the moon shines with a
splendor of her own, why should she not grow languid in a certain part of
770 the world while she is passing through regions unfriendly to her own
beams?

I have shown how each phenomenon can occur in the azure expanse of
the vast firmament, in order that we might understand what force causes
the varied courses of the sun and the motions of the moon, and how it is
possible for them to suffer eclipse through the interception of their light
and shroud the unexpecting earth in shadow, as though they blinked and
then with reopened eyes again surveyed all places resplendent with
780 radiant light. And now that I have explained these phenomena, I return to
the time when the world was young and the fields were soft, to show
what in her first fecundity the earth resolved to raise into the shores of
light and entrust to the capricious winds.

First of all the earth produced the various sorts of grasses and invested
the hills and all the plains with lustrous verdure, so that the flowery
meadows gleamed with green; and then the different kinds of trees were
started on a great race of unbridled growth through the air. As feathers,
hair, and bristles are the first growths on the limbs of four-footed crea-
790 tures and the bodies of birds strong of wing, so at that time the newborn
earth threw up grasses and saplings first, and then created animals—
many species variously produced in many ways.
Certainly living creatures cannot have dropped from heaven,[61] nor can
terrestrial animals have emerged from the briny gulfs of the sea.[62] So it
follows that the earth has deservedly gained the name of mother, since
from the earth all things have been created. Indeed even now multitudes
of living creatures spring from the earth under the influence of rains and
the heat of the sun.[63] So it is not surprising if at that time more and larger
800 animals were produced, since they grew up when earth and air were
young. First of all the various kinds of winged birds were hatched out of
their eggs in the springtime, just as now in the summer cicadas spontaneously leave their smooth chrysalises in search of a living and life.
The earth, you see, first produced animals at that time because there was

---

61. **793:** Cf. 2.1153–1154 and see note there.

62. **794:** Cf. 2.1155 and see note there.

63. **797–798:** See note on 2.871–872.

a great abundance of warmth and moisture in the ground. So, wherever a suitable spot offered, wombs grew up, adhering to the earth by roots; and when at the time of maturing these had been burst open by the young 810 ones in their eagerness to escape from the moisture and obtain air, then nature directed to them the ducts of the earth and made her exude from her opened veins a milklike juice, just as now every woman after childbirth is filled with sweet milk because the entire urgent flow of nutriment is directed into her breasts. The earth provided her children with food, the warmth served as clothing, and the grass formed a couch thickly spread with soft down. Moreover, the youth of the world did not produce severe cold or excessive heat or winds of great violence; for all 820 things grow and gain strength together.[64] So I insist that the earth has deservedly gained and deservedly retains the name of mother, since she herself created the human race, and almost at a fixed time[65] produced every species of animal that ranges wildly and widely over the mighty mountains, as well as the various birds of the air.

But because there must be some limit to her fecundity, she stopped bearing, like a woman worn out by lapse of years. For time transforms the nature of the entire world, and everything inevitably passes on from one stage to another. Nothing remains constant: everything is in flux; 830 everything is altered by nature and compelled to change. As one thing decays and declines and droops with age, another arises and emerges from obscurity. In this way, then, time alters the nature of the entire world, and the earth passes on from one stage to another, so that what she once bore she can bear no longer, while she can bear what she did not bear before.[66]

And at that time the earth experimented with the creation of many prodigious things, which were born with bodies of grotesque appearance. There were androgynes—beings halfway between the two sexes, belonging to neither, differing from both; there were some creatures devoid 840 of feet or deprived of hands; there were others dumb for want of a mouth, or blind for want of eyes, or fettered by the adhesion of all the limbs of the body so that they were powerless to do anything or move anywhere or avoid danger or take what they needed. Other equally monstrous and

---

64. **818–820:** Even climatic phenomena were weak because, like everything else, they were young.

65. **823:** "Almost at a fixed time," i.e., after an almost fixed period of gestation.

66. **836:** D. A. West, *Classical Quarterly* 14 (1964) 102, may be right in taking the meaning to be "so that what bore cannot (namely Earth), and what could not bear can (namely the parents of each species)."

prodigious beings were produced by the earth. But they were created in vain, since nature denied them growth and they were unable to attain the coveted bloom of maturity or find food or be united in the acts of Venus.
850 For we see that the ability of creatures to propagate and perpetuate their species is contingent upon the conjunction of many circumstances: first there must be a supply of food; then there must be a channel by which the generative seeds throughout the body may issue from the slackened limbs; and for the female to be united with the male, both must have organs for the interchange of mutual delights.

At that time, too, many species of animals must have perished and failed to propagate and perpetuate their race. For every species that you see breathing the breath of life has been protected and preserved from the beginning of its existence either by cunning or by courage or by speed.
860 There are also many that survive because their utility has commended them to our care and committed them to our guardianship. In the first place, the fierce breed of savage lions owes its preservation to its courage, the fox to its cunning, and the deer to its speed in flight. On the other hand, the light-slumbering and loyal-hearted dog and every kind of beast of burden, as well as the fleecy flocks and horned herds, are all committed, Memmius, to the guardianship of human beings. They were glad to escape from the wild beasts and seek peace and the plentiful provisions,
870 procured by no exertion of theirs, which we give them as a reward for their utility. But those animals that nature endowed with none of these qualities, so that they were unable either to be self-supporting or to render us any useful service, in return for which we might allow their kind to have sustenance and security under our protection, were of course an easy prey and prize for others, shackled as they all were by the bonds of their own destiny, until nature brought their species to extinction.

But Centaurs never existed,[67] and at no time can there be creatures
880 with a dual nature and double body, so composed of heterogeneous limbs that the powers derived from the two parts can be sufficiently harmonious.[68] The proofs that follow will enable the dullest wit to understand that this is so. In the first place, when three full years have passed round, a horse is in its prime, whereas a boy is by no means so; for often at this age he will still seek in his sleep the milky nipples of his mother's

---

67. **878:** On the impossibility of such creatures existing, see also 2.700–709. See also 4.732–748, where it is explained how it is that the mind receives images of them.

68. **881:** The text and exact sense are uncertain.

breasts. Later, when the steed's sturdy strength is failing in old age and its limbs are growing languid as life recedes, then and only then the boy's youthful prime is beginning and is clothing his cheeks with silk-soft down. So you cannot possibly believe that Centaurs, compounded of 890 human being and burden-bearing horse, can exist, or Scyllas[69] with half-fish bodies and girdles of ravening dogs, or any other such monsters whose limbs are manifestly incongruous. The parts of such creatures do not simultaneously attain their prime or gain physical strength or decline in old age; they are not enflamed with the same sexual desires; they do not agree in their habits; and they do not find the same foods agreeable: thus one may often see flocks of bearded goats growing fat on hemlock, which 900 is rank poison to human beings. Moreover, seeing that flame will scorch and burn the tawny bodies of lions just as much as any other kind of flesh and blood that exists on earth, how could there be a Chimaera, a single monster compounded of three bodies—lion in front, dragon behind, and she-goat in the middle—belching out fierce flame from its body?[70]

Those who imagine that such animals could have been produced when the earth was young and the sky newly formed, basing their belief only on this empty word "young," may as well babble countless other such 910 absurdities: they may as well say that in that age rivers of gold flowed all over the earth, and that trees regularly bore jewels instead of blooms, or that a man was born with limbs of such prodigious size and strength that he could stride over the deep seas and with his hands make the whole heaven revolve around him.[71] The fact is that, although there were manifold seeds of things in the ground at the time when the earth first produced animal life, this is no proof that beasts of mixed breed, combining limbs of different animals, could have been created. For the things that 920 even now shoot in profusion from the earth—the various kinds of grasses and crops and exuberant trees—cannot, despite their abundance, be created intermixed: each proceeds in its own manner, and all preserve their distinguishing characteristics in conformity with an immutable law of nature.

The human beings who lived on earth in those early days[72] were far tougher than we are, as one would expect, seeing that they were children

---

69. **893:** See note on 4.732.

70. **904–906:** Cf. 2.705. The description of the Chimaera in 905–906 closely follows that in Homer *Iliad* 6.181–182.

71. **913–915:** Presumably Lucr. is thinking chiefly of the Titan Atlas, who supported the sky.

72. **925–1010:** This justly famous account of the life of primitive human beings

of the tough earth:[73] larger and more solid bones formed the inner framework of their bodies, while their flesh was knit with strong sinews,
930 and they were not easily affected by heat or cold or unaccustomed food or any physical malady. During many lusters of the sun revolving through the sky they lived random-roving lives like wild beasts. No sturdy farmer guided the curved plow; no one knew how to work the fields with iron implements or plant young saplings in the earth or cut the old boughs from tall trees with pruning hooks. What the sun and rains had given them, what the earth had spontaneously produced, were gifts rich enough to content their hearts. For the most part they nourished their
940 bodies among the acorn-bearing oaks; and arbute berries, which you now see turning crimson as they ripen in winter, were then produced by the earth in great abundance and of a larger size. And many other foods were then produced by the world in her youthful prime—coarse foods, but amply sufficient for miserable mortals.

Streams and springs called them to allay their thirst, just as nowadays torrents of water cascading down from mighty mountains with sonorous sound summon far and wide the thirsty troops of wild beasts. Moreover, they occupied sylvan sanctuaries of the nymphs, familiar to them in their
950 wanderings, from which they knew that sliding streams of water slipped to lave with lavish flow the rocks, the wet, wet rocks all green with moss and dripping with moisture; they knew too of places where welling springs gushed out over the open plain.

As yet they had no knowledge of how to utilize fire or clothe their bodies in skins stripped from wild beasts. They lived in woods and mountain caves and forests and, when compelled to escape from the lashing of wind and rain, sheltered their shaggy limbs among the thickets.

They were unable to look to the common interest, and had no knowl-
960 edge of the mutual benefits of any customs or laws. Individuals in-

is no doubt based chiefly on an account that Epicurus gave in *On Nature*. Epicurus' account, which does not survive, will have been heavily indebted to the speculations of the sophists and Democritus. Although Lucr. does not believe that primitive humans lived in a Golden Age (he is well aware of the dangers they faced, especially from wild animals), he considers their simple way of life to have been in many ways more wholesome and happy than the life of "civilized" humans, whose moral progress has not kept pace with their progress in other fields.

73. **926:** The first human beings were literally earth's children: see 805–815 and Diogenes of Oinoanda *fr.* 11 and *fr.* 12.III.2–3. In 962–965 Lucr. refers to primitive men and women having sexual intercourse but does not say whether they had it at the stage when the earth was producing human offspring.

stinctively seized whatever prize fortune had offered to them, trained as they were to live and use their strength for themselves alone.

Venus united the bodies of lovers in the woods. The woman either yielded from mutual desire, or was mastered by the man's impetuous might and inordinate lust, or sold her favors for acorns or arbute berries or choice pears.[74]

And trusting in the extraordinary strength of their hands and feet, they pursued the wild beasts of the forests with sling-stones and ponderous clubs. Many of them they overcame; a few they avoided in hiding places.

When overtaken by night, they laid their shaggy limbs naked on the ground like bristly boars and blanketed themselves with leaves and branches. They did not roam panic-stricken through the countryside in the shadows of the night, seeking the day and the sunlight with loud lamentations, but waited silent and buried in sleep for the sun's rose-red torch to spread its radiance over the heavens. Having always been accustomed from their infancy to see darkness and light born alternately, they could not possibly have ever wondered at the departure of day, or feared that the sunlight might withdraw forever, leaving the earth in the possession of perpetual night. A much greater cause of concern was the way in which the tribes of wild beasts often made rest perilous and wretched for them. Driven from their homes by the arrival of a foaming boar or powerful lion, they would flee panic-stricken from their rocky shelters and at dead of night surrender their leaf-strewn beds to their ruthless guests.

Mortal beings did not leave with lamentations the sweet light of life in greater numbers then than now. Then it more often happened that individuals were caught by wild beasts and provided them with living food for their teeth to tear, and filled the woods and mountains and forests with their shrieks as they saw their living flesh being buried in a living tomb.[75] Others, who had escaped with their bodies part devoured, afterward pressed the palms of their quivering hands over hideous sores and called on Orcus[76] with dreadful cries until they were robbed of life by agonizing pains, destitute of help and ignorant of what treatment their wounds wanted. But never in those times did a single day consign to

970

980

990

---

74. **965:** Notice "*choice* pears." As W. E. Leonard and S. B. Smith well remark, "even the wild woodland wench had some discrimination and her wooer some technique."

75. **993:** The idea that the devouring beast is its victim's tomb has a long history. In my Loeb note I list sixteen authors, from Aeschylus to Alexander Pope, in whom it is found.

76. **996:** Death.

destruction many thousands of men marching beneath military stan-
1000 dards; never did the boisterous billows of the ocean dash ships and
sailors upon the rocks. Then, although the waves often rose and raged,
they did so idly, vainly, and ineffectually, and lightly laid aside their
empty threats. The seductive serenity of the sea was unable to ensnare
anyone with the treacherous laughter of its waves: the presumptuous art
of navigation was as yet undiscovered.[77] Moreover, whereas in those
times it was lack of food that consigned people's languid limbs to death,
nowadays it is surfeit to which they succumb; and whereas in those times
1010 they often served poison to themselves unwittingly, nowadays they make
away with themselves more expertly.

Next they provided themselves with huts and skins and fire,[78] and
woman, united to man, went to live in one [place with him. The advan-
tages (?) of cohabitation][79] were learned, and they saw the birth of their
own offspring. It was then that human beings first began to lose their
toughness: the use of fire rendered their shivering bodies less able to
endure the cold beneath the pavilion of the sky; Venus sapped their
strength; and the children with their charming ways easily broke down
the stern disposition of their parents. It was then, too, that neighbors, in
1020 their eagerness neither to harm nor be harmed, began to form mutual
pacts of friendship,[80] and claimed protection for their children and wom-
enfolk, indicating by means of inarticulate cries and gestures that everyone ought to have compassion on the weak. Although it was not possible
for concord to be achieved universally, the great majority kept their
compacts loyally. Otherwise the human race would have been entirely
extinguished at that early stage and could not have propagated and preserved itself to the present day.

As for the various sounds of speech, it was nature that prompted
human beings to utter them, and it was utility that coined the names of
1030 things.[81] The process was not greatly dissimilar to that when infants, in

---

77. **1002–1006:** Cf. 2.552–559 and see note there.

78. **1011:** On the discovery of fire, see 1091–1104.

79. **1012:** A line is lost after this line.

80. **1019–1020:** On Epicurus' conception of justice as a social contract, see *PD*
31–38. In *PD* 33 he says, "Justice was never an independent entity, but in the
relations of people with one another at any place and at any time it is a kind of
agreement not to harm or to be harmed." On the Epicurean theory of justice, see
also note on 1144.

81. **1028–1090:** On the Epicurean theory of language, of which this passage is

consequence of their inability to speak, are seen to have recourse to gesture, and point with the finger at objects around them. The fact is that every creature is instinctively conscious of the purpose for which it can use its peculiar powers: a calf, when enraged, will butt and thrust aggressively with its forehead, even before its sprouting horns appear; cubs of leopards and lions will fight with claws and paws and snapping jaws, even when their teeth and claws are scarcely formed; and as for birds of every species, we see them, when first fledged, trusting to their wings and seeking fluttering support from their pinions.   1040

Therefore the hypothesis that in those early times someone assigned names to things, and that people learned their first words from him, is preposterous. Why should it be supposed that this man had the ability to designate everything by a name and to utter the various sounds of speech, while others could not do it? Moreover, if others had not also used words among themselves, how was the conception of their utility implanted in him, and how did he obtain the original power to know and perceive in his mind what he wished to produce?[82] Again, it would have been   1050 impossible for one individual to assemble[83] many people and exercise mastery and control over them, so that they would consent to learn the

---

the longest statement to survive, see also Epicurus *Hdt.* 75–76 and Diogenes of Oinoanda *fr.* 12.II.11–V.14. The view that language was artificially invented and imposed by an individual, divine or human, is emphatically rejected. Rather it is held to have had a natural origin in the instinctive use which primitive human beings made of their vocal organs in reaction to different sensations and emotions. Later, when the practical convenience of using the same sounds to express the same things was understood, a gradual process of inventing words was started. This theory is typical of Epicurean views on advances in civilization: it is always a case, as Lucr. keeps emphasizing in his account, of nature showing the way and of developments taking place gradually by a process of trial and error.

82. **1046–1049:** Cf. 181–186 and see note there.

83. **1050:** I follow A. Verlinsky, *Hyperboreus* 4 (1998) 302–339, in taking *cogere* to mean "assemble" rather than "compel." As he points out, this interpretation is strongly supported by the parallel passage of Diogenes of Oinoanda: "It is the height of absurdity, as well as quite impossible, that any one individual should have assembled such vast multitudes (at that time there were as yet no kings, and indeed . . . no writing; and with regard to these multitudes, it would have been quite impossible, except by means of a decree, for their assembly to have taken place) and, having assembled them, should have taken hold of a rod and proceeded to teach them like an elementary schoolmaster, touching each object and saying 'let this be called "stone," this "wood," this "human being" or "ox" or "ass" . . . ' " (*fr.* 12.IV.3–V.14).

names of things; and it is by no means easy to tell and teach the deaf what needs to be done: the truth is that they would not tolerate it or under any circumstances endure for long to have their ears dinned to no purpose by unintelligible vocal sounds.

Lastly, why is it so very remarkable that human beings, with their power of voice and tongue, should designate things by different sounds according to their different feelings? Even domestic animals and the 1060 species of wild beasts, despite their dumbness, regularly utter distinct and different sounds according to whether they are afraid or in pain or full of joy—a fact that may be proved by familiar examples.

When Molossian mastiffs,[84] roused to anger, start to snarl and fiercely draw back their great pendulous lips to bare their cruel teeth, the menacing noise they make is very different from that when they bark and fill the whole neighborhood with their clamor. And when they begin to lick their pups tenderly with their tongue, or when they cuff them with their paws and, snapping at them with checked teeth, pretend gently to swallow 1070 them, the whining they make as they fondle them is a very different sound from the howls they give when left alone to guard the house, or the whimpering they make as they slink away from a beating with cringing body. Again, it is surely evident that the neighing of a stallion in his youthful prime when, goaded by the spurs of winged love, he rampages among the mares and from dilated nostrils snorts for the fray,[85] is a different sound from his whinnying when on some other occasion his limbs are shaking with fear. Lastly, consider the various kinds of winged 1080 birds—hawks and lammergeyers, and the gulls that seek a living and life in the waves of the briny sea: the cries they utter when they are fighting for food and their prey is offering resistance are very different from their usual cries. And there are some birds that change their raucous notes with the weather: thus the ancient crows[86] and gregarious rooks are said to change their notes according to whether they are calling for water and rain or summoning winds and breezes.

So if animals, despite their dumbness, are impelled to utter various sounds expressive of various feelings, how much more natural is it that 1090 mortals in those early times should have been able to designate different things by different sounds!

---

84. **1063:** These dogs, highly prized as watchdogs and for hunting, were so called because they were bred by the Molossi, a people of Epirus (northwest Greece).

85. **1076:** By "the fray" Lucr. means the sexual encounter with the mare.

86. **1084:** Crows were proverbially long-lived.

At this point, to preclude the possibility of your putting the question to yourself, let me tell you that it was lightning that brought the first fire down to earth for the use of mortals, and that this is the ultimate source of all fiery flames. For we often see things set ablaze by the implantation of celestial flames when a stroke from the sky has charged them with its heat. However, we also observe that when a branchy tree, buffeted by blasts of wind, sways and tosses to and fro, so that it presses against the branches of another tree, the strong stress of friction forces out fire and sometimes makes a fervid flash of flame flare forth, as boughs and trunks 1100 are rubbed together.[87] So either of these happenings may have given fire to mortals. Afterward it was the sun that taught them to cook their food and soften it with the heat of flame, since they saw many things mellowing throughout the countryside, subdued by the strokes of its fiery rays.

And more and more every day those endowed with exceptional talents and mental power showed the others how to exchange their former way of life for new practices and, in particular, for the use of fire. Kings began to build cities, and to choose sites for citadels to be strongholds and places of refuge for themselves; and they distributed gifts of flocks and 1110 fields to individuals according to their beauty, strength, and intellect; for beauty was highly esteemed, and strength was held in honor. Later wealth was invented and gold discovered, and this easily robbed the strong and handsome of their prestige; for as a general rule, no matter how much physical strength and beauty people possess, they follow in the train of the rich.

And yet if human beings would guide their lives by true principles, great wealth consists in living on a little with a contented mind; for of a little there is never a lack.[88] But people wanted to win fame and power 1120 for themselves, in order that their fortune might be based on a firm foundation and their wealth might enable them to lead a peaceful life. But all in vain; for as they strove to climb to the summit of success, they made their path perilous. And even when they reach the summit, envy, like lightning, sometimes strikes them and hurls them down into a hideous hell of ignominy; for envy, like lightning, usually blasts the highest places and all that are elevated above others. So it is far better to live peacefully as a subject than to desire the dominion of states and the 1130

---

87. **1094–1100:** Cf. 1.897–903.

88. **1117–1119:** Cf. Epicurus *VS* 25: "Poverty, when measured by the natural end of life, is great wealth, and unlimited wealth is great poverty." See also Us. *fr.* 135 quoted on p. xxxi.

control of kingdoms.[89] Let them, then, sweat out their blood and weary themselves in vain, struggling along the narrow[90] path of ambition, since their wisdom is derived from the mouths of others and their aims are determined by hearsay rather than by their own sensations; and such folly does not succeed today and will not succeed tomorrow any more than it succeeded yesterday.

So the kings were slain, the time-honored majesty of thrones and proud scepters tumbled down in the dust, and the glorious crown that adorned the sovereign head, now blood-bespattered beneath the feet of
1140 the rabble, mourned the loss of its high prerogative; for people eagerly trample on what once they intensely feared. Thus the situation sank to the lowest dregs of anarchy, with all seeking sovereignty and supremacy for themselves. At length some of them taught the others to create magistracies and established laws, to induce them to obey ordinances. The human race, utterly weary as it was of leading a life of violence and worn out with feuds, was the more ready to submit voluntarily to the restraint of ordinances and stringent laws.[91] The reason why people were sick and tired of a life of violence was that each individual was prompted by anger to exact vengeance more cruelly than is now allowed by equitable laws.
1151 Ever since that time fear of punishment has poisoned the blessings of life. Violence and injustice enmesh all who practice them: they generally recoil on the wrong doers, and it is not easy for those who by their actions violate the mutual pacts of peace to pass a placid and peaceful life; for even if their crime goes undetected in heaven and on earth,[92] they are bound to fear that it will not remain hidden for ever. And indeed many people, so it is said, by talking in their sleep or in the delirium of disease,
1160 have betrayed their own guilt and disclosed deeply hidden matters and their misdeeds.

---

89. **1129–1130:** Epicurus advised his followers to "live unnoticed" (Us. *fr.* 551).

90. **1132:** The path of ambition is described as "narrow" because there is not room for many to negotiate it at once.

91. **1144:** It is to be noted that, in the Epicurean view, justice—true justice—is independent of the law. Laws exist not to prevent the wise from doing wrong, but only to protect them from being wronged (Epicurus Us. *fr.* 530), and in an ideal society there would be no need of laws. See J. M. Armstrong, *Phronesis* 42 (1997) 324–334. See also my presentation, in *Anatolian Studies* 48 (1998) 131–143, of an important new passage of Diogenes of Oinoanda (*NF* 126–127.V).

92. **1156:** The expression translated "in heaven and on earth" is a conventional one and is not to be taken as inconsistent with the Epicurean belief that the gods do not interest themselves in human affairs. All Lucr. means is "even if their crime goes completely undetected."

Now what cause has made belief in the gods universal throughout mighty nations and filled cities with altars and prompted the institution of solemn religious rites—rites that now flourish in great states and places? What is it that even now implants in mortals this shuddering fear that all over the earth raises new shrines to the gods and crowds them with congregations on festal days? The explanation is quite easy to supply.[93]

The truth is that even in remote antiquity the minds of mortals were 1170 visited in waking life, and still more in sleep, by visions of divine figures of matchless beauty and stupendous stature. To these beings they attributed sensation, because they saw them move their limbs and speak in a majestic manner appropriate to their splendid appearance and ample strength. They gave them immortal life, because their images presented themselves in constant succession and their forms remained unchanged, but above all because they thought that beings endowed with such mighty strength could not easily be overcome by any force. And they regarded them as consummately happy, because fear of death did not 1180 trouble any of them and also because in sleep they saw them perform many marvelous feats without experiencing any fatigue.

Furthermore,[94] they observed the orderly movements of the heavenly bodies and the regular return of the seasons of the year without being able to account for these phenomena. Therefore they took refuge in ascribing everything to the gods and in supposing that everything happens in obedience to their will. And they located the habitations and sacred quarters of the gods in the sky, because it is through the sky that night and the revolving moon are seen to pass, yes the moon, day and 1190 night, and night's austere constellations, and the night-roving torches and flying flames of heaven,[95] clouds, sunlight, rains, snow, winds, lightning, hail, and the rapid roars and mighty menacing rumbles of thunder.

O hapless humanity, to have attributed such happenings to the gods and to have ascribed cruel wrath to them as well! What sorrows did they then prepare for themselves, what wounds for us, what tears for generations to come! Piety does not consist in veiling one's head and turning with ostentatious frequency to a stone, or in visiting every altar, or in 1200 prostrating oneself on the ground with outstretched palms before the

---

93. **1161–1193:** On the gods as conceived by the Epicureans, on the cause of our visions of them, and on the importance of worshipping them, see p. xxviii–xxix.

94. **1183–1193:** This second cause of belief in the gods is regarded by Lucr. as false. The Epicureans denied that the gods have any control over celestial phenomena.

95. **1191:** Comets and meteors.

shrines of the gods, or in saturating the sacrificial slabs with the blood of four-footed beasts, or in linking vows to vows, but rather in possessing the ability to contemplate all things with a tranquil mind.

When we look up and survey the celestial precincts of the mighty firmament, and the ether above studded with sparkling stars, and reflect upon the courses of the sun and moon, then in our breasts already burdened with other cares a new fear begins to awaken and lift its head— a fear that there may possibly be some immeasurable divine power above
1210   us that wheels the dazzling heavenly bodies on their various courses. Our minds, disturbed by their inadequate knowledge of the truth, are uncertain whether the world had a beginning and birth, and equally whether there is a limit to the ability of the world's walls to endure the strain of restless motion, or whether they are not divinely endowed with everlasting life and so can glide on through an eternal tract of time, defying the strong assaults of measureless ages.

Moreover, whose heart does not contract with dread of the gods, and
1220   who does not cower in fear, when the scorched earth shudders beneath the terrible stroke of the thunderbolt, and rumbles of thunder run across the vast heaven? Do not nations and peoples tremble, and do not proud kings shrink in every limb, stricken with terror of the gods, in case the dreadful moment of reckoning has come for some heinous deed or arrogant word?

Again, when the full violence of vehement winds raging at sea sweeps the admiral of a fleet over the ocean plains along with his powerful legions and elephants, does he not attempt to appease the gods with
1230   vows? Does he not in his panic pray that the winds may be calmed and succeeded by propitious breezes? But all in vain; for often, despite his prayers, he is seized by the tearing tornado and hurled to his death on the shoals. It all goes to show that there is some invisible force that tramples on human ambitions and seemingly treads underfoot the glorious rods and grim axes of high office,[96] and treats them as its playthings.

Lastly, when the whole earth rocks underfoot, and shaken cities fall or totteringly threaten to fall, is it surprising if mortal beings feel humbled and admit the existence of gods with such vast powers and such stupen-
1240   dous strength that they can govern all things?

Next I must explain that copper,[97] gold, and iron, as well as weighty silver and serviceable lead, were discovered when on the mighty moun-

---

96. **1234:** See note on 3.996.

97. **1241:** I have translated *aes* "copper" here and in 1257, where mention is made of the discovery of the metal, but "bronze" in 1270–1294, where its use is

tains a fire had consumed vast forests with its flames. The conflagration may have been started by a thunderbolt from the sky, or when, while waging war in the woods, people had set fire to them to strike terror into the enemy, or when, tempted by the richness of the soil, they wished to open up fertile fields and make the countryside fit for pasture, or else when they wanted to kill wild beasts and enrich themselves with game; for the use of pit and fire for hunting preceded the enclosing of covers 1250 with nets and driving with dogs. Anyhow, whatever the cause of the conflagration, when the raging flames had devoured the forests to their deepest roots with a terrible crackling noise, and the fire had thoroughly baked the earth, streams of silver and gold and also of copper and lead trickled out of the earth's glowing veins and collected in cavities on the surface. Afterward, when these metals had solidified and people saw them glittering brightly on the ground, they picked them up, captivated by their lovely luster and polish, and observed that in each case their 1260 shape corresponded exactly to the outline of the cavities in which they lay. Then it struck them that these metals, when melted, could be made to run into the shape and form of any object they pleased, and furthermore could be hammered out into points and edges of any degree of sharpness and fineness, thus giving them weapons, and enabling them to fell forests and hew timber and plane planks smooth, as well as to drill, punch, and bore holes. And initially they attempted to do these things with silver and gold as much as with the sturdy strength of stubborn bronze. But without 1270 success; for these metals, despite their apparent firmness, failed and gave way, lacking bronze's ability to withstand severe strain. At that time bronze was the more highly esteemed, while gold was scorned as useless because it was easily dulled and blunted. Now it is bronze that is scorned, and gold has risen to the highest place of honor. Thus fashions change with the rolling years: what was once esteemed becomes utterly despised; while something else emerges from obscurity to take its place, is more and more sought after day by day, and, once discovered, blossoms into fame and enjoys extraordinary honor among mortals. ·   1280

Now, Memmius, you yourself can easily deduce how the discovery of iron and its properties came about. Weapons in primitive times were hands, nails, and feet, as well as stones, branches broken from forest trees, and flaming fire as soon as it was known. Later strong iron and bronze were discovered; and the use of bronze preceded that of iron, for it is more malleable and more abundant. With bronze they tilled the soil,

---

described. Only bronze, an alloy of copper and tin, would make effective tools and weapons.

1290 and with bronze they embroiled the billows of war, broadcast[98] wide-gaping wounds, and plundered flocks and fields; for everything unarmed and defenseless readily yielded to the armed. Then by degrees the iron sword came into prominence and the bronze sickle became an object of scorn: with iron they began to furrow the soil, and the chances of unpredictable war were equalized.

Mounting armed on horseback and guiding one's steed with reins while fighting with one's right hand is an earlier practice than braving the 1300 perils of war in a two-horsed chariot. And yoking a pair of horses is an earlier practice than yoking two pairs or mounting armed on scythed chariots.[99] Later Lucanian oxen,[100] dreadful snake-handed creatures with turreted backs, were trained by the Carthaginians to endure the wounds of war and make havoc among mighty martial hosts. Thus grim discord produced a succession of new inventions to strike terror into peoples involved in fighting and day by day heightened the horrors of war.

They also tried to use bulls in the work of war and made the experi-
1310 ment of sending savage boars against the enemy.[101] Sometimes too they sent powerful lions ahead of them with armed trainers and cruel masters to restrain them and hold them in leash. But without success; for the savage beasts, maddened by the promiscuous slaughter and tossing their

---

98. **1290:** The metaphor "broadcast" or "sowed" may well have been prompted by the agricultural reference in the preceding line. For similar thought-links, see notes on 1436, 2.276.

99. **1301:** On scythed chariots, see note on 3.642.

100. **1302:** Elephants, which the Romans first encountered in the army of Pyrrhus, king of Epirus, who invaded Lucania (a region of southern Italy) in 280 B.C. and won the original Pyrrhic victory. For the epithet "snake-handed," see note on 2.537.

101. **1308–1349:** The information (which, as is clear from 1341–1349, is not Lucr.'s own invention) that experiments in battle were made not only with elephants, but also with bulls, boars, and lions, is to be compared with the information that, when metals had been discovered and people wanted to make tools, experiments were made not only with bronze, but also with gold and silver (1269–1272). But surely Lucr. is also making a moral point: whereas in primitive times people ran away from fierce animals, including boars and lions (969, 982–987), and occasionally individuals were eaten alive by them (990–993), in more recent times people deliberately used the same animals in battle. The vivid description of the rampaging beasts probably owes much to observation of scenes in the arena, where killing of and by fierce animals was a favorite Roman entertainment.

terrible manes on every side, confounded the cavalry squadrons, making
no distinction between friend and foe; and the horsemen were unable to
soothe the spirits of their steeds terror-stricken by the roaring, or to turn
them around with the reins to face the enemy. The lionesses launched
their frames in furious springs on every side: they flew at the faces of
oncoming riders, and surprised others from behind and tore them down   1320
from their mounts and, twining around them, hurled them to the ground
mortally wounded, gripping them with powerful jaws and hooked claws.
The bulls tossed their masters and trampled them underfoot, gored the
flanks and underbellies of the horses with their horns, and plowed up the
ground in a menacing manner. And the boars killed their allies with their
powerful tusks, savagely dyeing with their own blood the darts broken in
their bodies, and massacred cavalry and infantry indiscriminately. In at-   1330
tempting to evade the fierce thrust of the tusk, steeds would shy or rear up
and paw the air. But all in vain; for you would see them crash down ham-
strung and cover the ground in a heavy fall. Even those animals that were
thought to have been sufficiently tamed at home beforehand were seen
amid the heat of battle to foam in fury, maddened by wounds, shouts,
flight, terror, and tumult. And it proved impossible to regain control of
any of them; for the various kinds of beasts all scattered this way and that,
just as nowadays Lucanian oxen, horribly hacked by the sword, often
scatter in all directions after savaging many of their human allies.   1340

But did people really make this experiment?[102] I must confess that I
find it almost incredible that they were unable to anticipate and imagine
the consequences of their action, before the dreadful common disaster
occurred; and it would be easier to maintain that it happened somewhere
in the universe of various worlds variously formed than to assign it to any
one specific earth. Certainly the experiment must have been inspired not
so much by a hope of victory as by a desire to give the enemy cause for
sorrow even at the cost of self-destruction, in a situation involving people who distrusted their numbers and were short of arms.

Plaited clothing preceded woven garments.[103] Woven cloth came after   1350
iron, which is used for the making of the loom: without iron it is impos-

---

102. **1341–1349:** Lucr. sensibly finds it hard to believe that people could have
been so foolish as to fail to foresee the disastrous consequences of their experiment. In an infinite universe containing an infinite number of worlds there are an
infinite number of chances, and such an event might have occurred sometime
somewhere, but, if so, only in a situation where people were desperate and
wanted to sell their lives as dearly as possible.

103. **1350:** Cf. Diogenes of Oinoanda *fr.* 12.I.10–II.3.

sible to produce instruments of such smoothness as treadles, spindles, shuttles, and noisy leash rods.

And nature obliged men to work wool before women; for the male sex is, generally speaking, far superior in skill and ingenuity. But eventually the sturdy farming folk came to regard the occupation with such con-tempt that the men willingly left it to women's hands, took their share in 1360 enduring tough toil, and with this tough labor toughened their limbs and hands.

As for planting and grafting, the original pattern for these opera-tions was provided by creative nature herself, since fallen berries and acorns in due time produced swarms of seedlings beneath the trees; and this gave people the idea of entrusting slips to branches and of plant-ing young saplings in the earth all over the countryside. Then they kept on experimenting with new methods of cultivating the little plot of land they loved, and saw wild fruits improve in the ground in response 1370 to their kindly care and coaxing. And day by day they forced the the forests to retreat farther and farther up the mountains and sur-render the parts below to cultivation, so that on hills and plains they might have meadows, ponds, streams, crops, and exuberant vines, and so that the distinctive gray-green zone of olives might run be-tween, spreading over down and dale and plain. They created land-scapes such as we see today—landscapes rich in delightful variety, attractively dotted with sweet fruit trees and enclosed with luxuriant plantations.

1380   People imitated with their mouths the liquid warblings of birds long before they were able to join together in singing melodious songs with pleasure to the ear. And it was the whistling of the zephyr in the cavities of reeds that first taught country folk to blow into hollow stalks. Then little by little they learned the sweet notes that ripple from the plaintive pipe as the player's fingers strike the stops[104]—the pipe invented in pathless woods and forests and forest glades, in the solitary spots where 1390 shepherds rest in the open air. With this music they would soothe and charm their hearts after they had eaten their fill; for that is the time when everything affords pleasure. So they would often lie in friendly company on velvety turf near a running brook beneath the branches of a tall tree and provide their bodies with simple but agreeable refreshment, especially when the weather smiled and the season of the year embroi-

---

104. **1385:** Repeated from 4.585.

dered the green grass with flowers.[105] Then there would be jokes, talk,
and peals of pleasant laughter; for then the rustic muse was at its best.
Then, prompted by playful gaiety, they would deck their heads and   1400
shoulders with garlands of interwoven flowers and foliage and move
their limbs clumsily in an unrhythmical dance, striking mother earth with
clumsy feet. These performances would provoke smiles and peals of
pleasant laughter, because all such pastimes, being new and wonderful, had a greater effect at that time. And the wakeful would find
ready consolations for sleeplessness in guiding their voices through the
many modulations of a song and in running over the reeds with pursed
lips. This old tradition is still kept up by watchmen today; and although they have learned to keep time, they do not derive any more   1410
pleasure from their music than did those woodland folk, the children of
earth.

The fact is that our present possessions, so long as we have not
experienced anything more agreeable in the past, please us preeminently
and are considered to be the best; but when something superior is subsequently discovered, the new invention usually ousts all the old things and
alters our feelings toward them. Thus acorns came to be disliked; thus
those beds strewn with grass and heaped high with leaves were abandoned. Thus too the clothing of wild beasts' skins fell into contempt; and
yet I suppose that, at the time of its discovery, it excited such envy that its   1420
first wearer was waylaid and slain, even though, after all that, the mur-
derers, in squabbling over the garment, ripped it to pieces and besmeared
it with blood so that it was ruined and rendered valueless. Then it was
skins, now it is gold and purple that plague human lives with cares and
weary them with war. And here, I think, the greater blame rests with us
today. For whereas the children of earth were tormented by cold when
they had no skins to cover their naked bodies, it is no hardship for us to
go without robes of purple patterned with great gold-embroidered figures, provided that we have the protection of some common garment.[106]
And so human beings never cease to labor vainly and fruitlessly, con-   1430
suming their lives in groundless cares, evidently because they have not
learned the proper limit to possession, and the extent to which real
pleasure can increase.[107] And it is this ignorance that has gradually

---

105. **1392–1396:** Repeated, with minor variations, from 2.29–33. See note there.

106. **1427–1429:** Cf. 2.34–36.

107. **1430–1433:** See pp. xxix–xxx.

carried life out into the deep sea and has stirred up from the depths the mighty boiling billows of war.

It was the watchmen of the sky,[108] the sun and moon, who, as they traveled with their light all round the vast revolving vault, taught people that the seasons of the year roll around, and that everything happens by a fixed law and in a fixed order.

1440   By now people were living their lives surrounded by sturdy fortifications, and the land was divided up and marked out for cultivation. The deep sea was aflower[109] with the flying sails of ships, and already they had confederates and allies under formal treaties, at the time when poets began to record human exploits in song. But the letters of the alphabet were invented only a short time before. Consequently our age cannot look back to earlier events, except insofar as reason reveals their traces.

Navigation, agriculture, city walls, laws, arms, roads, clothing, and all
1450   other practical inventions as well as every one of life's rewards and refinements, poems, pictures, and polished statues of exquisite workmanship, all without exception were gradually taught by experience and the inventiveness of the energetic mind, as humanity progressed step by step. Thus by slow degrees time evolves every discovery, and reason raises it up into the regions of light. People saw one thing after another become clear in their minds until each art reached the peak of perfection.

---

108. **1436:** The metaphorical use of "watchmen" here was probably prompted by the reference to human watchmen in 1408. See 1290 and 2.276 for metaphors generated in a similar way.

109. **1442:** "Aflower" no doubt refers primarily to the colorful and petal-like appearance of the ships' sails, but also suggests large numbers of vessels sailing the seas in prosperous circumstances.

BOOK SIX

It was Athens[1] of glorious name that in former days first imparted the knowledge of corn-producing crops to suffering mortals[2] and remodeled their lives and established laws; and it was Athens that first bestowed soothing solaces when she gave birth to a man[3] endowed with such great genius, whose lips once gave utterance to true pronouncements on every subject. And even now, though his life's light is extinguished, the godlike nature of his discoveries ensures that his fame, spread far and wide long ago, is raised to the skies.

He saw that almost everything that necessity demands for subsistence
10 had been already provided for mortals, and that their life was, so far as possible, established in security; he saw too that they possessed power, with wealth, honor, and glory, and took pride in the good reputation of their children; and yet he found that, notwithstanding this prosperity, all of them privately had hearts racked with anxiety which, contrary to their wish, tormented their lives without a pause, causing them to chafe and fret. Then he realized that the cause of the flaw was the vessel itself,[4] which by its own flaw corrupted within it all things, even good things,
20 that entered it from without. He became convinced of this, partly because he saw that the vessel was leaky and riddled, so that it could never possibly be filled,[5] and partly because he observed that it contaminated with a foul flavor everything it had taken in. Therefore with words of truth he purged people's minds by laying down limits to desire and fear; he explained the nature of the supreme good[6] that is our universal goal, and indicated the way, the short and straight path, by which we might reach it; he pointed out what evil there is everywhere in human af-
30 fairs, and how the various forms of it arise and fly about[7] from natural

---

1. **1–42:** On this passage and how it is related to the closing section of Book 5 and to that of Book 6, see note on 30 and p. xxxiii.

2. **1–2:** An allusion to the legend that Demeter (Ceres) sent Triptolemus, son of King Celeus of Eleusis, to teach agriculture to humanity. Eleusis is near Athens.

3. **5:** Epicurus.

4. **17:** The mind. See notes on 20–21, 3.440.

5. **20–21:** For the leaky vessel as a metaphor for the mind that cannot be satisfied, cf. 3.936–937 (see note there), 1003–1010.

6. **26:** Pleasure.

7. **30:** "Fly about" strongly suggests that Lucr. is thinking here above all of diseases and plagues. Compare his introduction to that topic: "there must be many [elements] *flying about* that produce disease and death" (1095–1096). This is by no means the only verbal repetition linking the preface and the closing passage on plagues (see my note in the Loeb edition pp. 492–493). The plague of Athens is a prime example of the sort of disaster which, before Epicurus showed

causes—either from chance or from necessity, according as nature has
ordained; he showed from what gates one should sally out to encounter
each of these ills; and he proved that human beings have no reason for
the most part to arouse within their breasts the rolling billows of bitter
care. For, just as children tremble and fear everything in blinding darkness, so we even in daylight sometimes dread things that are no more
terrible than the imaginary dangers that cause children to quake in the
dark. This terrifying darkness that enshrouds the mind must be dispelled   40
not by the sun's rays and the dazzling darts of day, but by study of the
superficial aspect and underlying principle of nature.[8] Therefore I will
continue the more zealously to weave the web of my argument.

Well, now that I have demonstrated[9] that the precincts of the world are
mortal, and that the heaven is composed of substance subject to birth,
and have explained most of the celestial phenomena that occur and must
necessarily occur,[10] attend carefully to what remains to be said. Seeing
that [I have ventured] to mount the splendid chariot [of the Muses,[11]
I will now describe how raging storms] of winds arise, and how they
are appeased so that, once their fury is allayed, everything returns to
normality. I will also explain all the other terrestrial and celestial phe-   50
nomena that, when observed by mortals, make them perplexed and panic-
stricken and abase their minds with dread of the gods and crush them
right down in the dust, because their ignorance of the causes obliges

them the way, people did not know how to confront. On the Epicurean attitude to
chance, see especially Epicurus *Men.* 133–135, *PD* 16, Us. *fr.* 489, Diogenes of
Oinoanda *fr.* 71–72 and *NF* 132.

  8. **35–41:** Repeated from 2.55–61, 3.87–93. Lines 39–41 are also identical to
1.146–148.

  9. **43:** The demonstration occupies 5.91–770.

  10. **45:** As Lucr. here indicates, most of the phenomena discussed in Book 5 are
regular ones. Book 6, however, focuses most attention on irregularly occurring
phenomena—the sort of happenings that people were particularly liable to attribute to the gods. The conviction that extraordinary phenomena are indications
of divine will was a very important part of Roman religion, and it is hardly
surprising that Lucr. is so concerned to show that thunder and lightning (for
example) have purely natural causes.

  11. **47:** After this line there is a lacuna of uncertain length and, to make matters
still more difficult, there are textual problems in 48–49. In 92–95, in his invocation to the Muse Calliope, Lucr. again pictures himself as riding in a chariot. The
first philosopher-poet to put himself in a chariot, in his case the chariot driven by
the daughters of the sun, was Parmenides (*fr.* 1). Empedocles prays for the Muse
to come to him in her chariot (*fr.* 3.2–5).

them to attribute everything to the government of the gods and to admit
their sovereignty. For even those who have rightly learned that the gods
60 lead lives free from care may wonder how all things can be carried
on, especially the phenomena above their heads in the ethereal regions;
and then they relapse into the old superstitions and subject themselves
to cruel tyrants whom they believe, poor fools, to be omnipotent, in
their ignorance of what can be and what cannot, and again by what
law each thing has its scope restricted and its deeply implanted boundary stone.[12] So they are led further and further astray by their blind
reasoning.

Unless you expel such notions from your mind and put far from you all
70 thoughts unworthy of the gods and incompatible with their peace, their
sacred persons, thus disparaged by you, will often do you harm. I do not
mean that the supreme might of the gods can be offended and angrily
seek to exact cruel vengeance; rather I mean this: you will fancy that
those calm beings blessed with placid peace set in commotion mighty
waves of wrath; you will be unable to approach their shrines with an
untroubled breast; and you will be impotent to receive in peace and
tranquillity the images that emanate from their sacred bodies and enter
human minds with news of divine beauty.[13] So you can see what kind of
a life must result from such misconceptions.
80   In order to repel such a life far from us by truest reasoning, many
arguments have already left my lips; many, however, still remain to be
embellished in polished verses. We must grasp the law and aspect of the
sky; and we must sing of storms and dazzling lightning flashes, their
effects, and the causes that set them in motion; for we must ensure that
you do not divide the sky into parts and, distracted with terror, observe
from which quarter the flying fire has come, into which part it has
passed, how it has penetrated the walls of buildings, and how, after acting
the tyrant, it has darted out again.[14]

---

12. **58–66:** Repeated from 5.82–90. Lines 65–66 are also identical to 1.76–77
and 595–596.

13. **68–78:** See pp. xxviii–xxix.

14. **86–89:** The reference is to the augural practice, derived from the Etruscans,
of dividing the sky into sixteen parts, and of observing from which part the
lightning comes and into which it disappears. One of Memmius' praetor-
colleagues in 58 B.C. was the scholar and mystic Publius Nigidius Figulus, among
whose many writings were works on augury. No wonder Lucr. gives Memmius
this warning! He returns to the subject again in 381–386, and in fact 383–385 are
identical to 87–89.

And as I race toward the white line that marks the end of my course,[15]   91
do you, clever Muse Calliope, repose of human beings and delight of the
gods,[16] point out the track to me, that under your guidance I may win the
garland of victory with glorious praise.[17]

In the first place, the reason why the azure regions of the sky are
convulsed with thunder is that clouds soaring high in the heavens collide,
when driven together by warring winds. For no sound comes from a clear
quarter of the sky; but the more densely the ranks of clouds are massed   100
together in any part, the more frequently do reverberating roars and
rumbles burst from that quarter.

The substance of clouds cannot be as dense as that of stones or wood,
nor yet as thin as that of drifting mists and smoke. Otherwise, either they
would be bound to fall, like stones, pulled down by their sheer weight; or,
like smoke, they would be unable to maintain their cohesion or retain
within them frozen snow and showers of hail.

Sometimes the clouds give out over the expanses of the spacious
firmament a sound that resembles the cracking noise made at times by
canvas awnings stretched above great theaters, as they billow between   110
the masts and crossbeams.[18] At other times, when rent in pieces by
wanton winds, they imitate in their rage the noise of papyrus sheets being
torn; for this kind of sound too can be recognized in thunder. Or the noise
they make is similar to that when hanging clothes or flying sheets of
papyrus are beaten and buffeted by blasts of wind and slapped through
the air. It sometimes happens too that the clouds, instead of meeting in
head-on collision, pass alongside each other as they move in opposite

---

15. **92:** The finishing line of a racecourse was marked with chalk. Lucr. makes
clear that he is now working on the final book. For the poet chariot-riding, see
also 47 and the note there.

16. **93–94:** Calliope, mother of Orpheus, as well as being the Muse of epic
poetry, was favored by philosophers (see, for example, Plato *Phaedrus* 259d,
Maximus of Tyre 1.2.28–30 [ed. Trapp]). It is therefore entirely appropriate that
she should be invoked by the writer of a philosophical epic. Moreover, the
invocation is a compliment to Empedocles, whose address to her (*fr.* 131) Lucr. is
recalling. The words "repose of human beings and delight of the gods" echo
"delight of human beings and the gods" in 1.1. There the addressee is Venus,
whom Lucr. invokes not only as the power of physical creation, but also as the
one who can inspire the creation of his philosophical poem. Calliope is therefore
identified with Venus in that second role.

17. **95:** Cf. 1.922–930.

18. **109–110:** Cf. 4.75–77 and see note there.

directions, slowly and painfully grazing body against body; and this
120 causes that protracted rasping sound to grate on our ears until the clouds
have escaped from close quarters.

Often too, when everything appears to shudder with the shock of
violent thunder, and the mighty ramparts of the capacious world seem in
an instant to have been breached and shattered, it is because a suddenly
gathered storm of wild wind has whirled its way into a cloud. Once
imprisoned there, it swirls around and around and with its eddy makes a
larger and larger hollow and an envelope of thicker and thicker substance; and then, when the cloud has been weakened by the wind's force
130 and fierce impetuosity, it splits and bursts with an appalling crash. And
no wonder, seeing that even a tiny bladder full of air makes a loud noise,
if suddenly exploded.

Clouds may also make a noise of thunder when the wind blows
through them. For we often see clouds with numerous branches and
jagged edges swept across the sky; and I can assure you that the wind has
much the same effect on them as a blustery northwester has on a dense
forest when it blows through it, making the leaves rustle and the branches
creak.

It sometimes happens too that the wild wind, when its force is aroused,
tears through a cloud, bursting it with a frontal attack. The power of
blasts of wind up in the sky is clearly indicated to us by our experience
140 here on earth, where, even though they are less violent, they topple tall
trees and pluck them up by their deepest roots.

Also the clouds contain waves that in breaking give a sort of low roar
similar to the noise made by deep rivers or by the mighty sea when the
surf is breaking.

Thunder occurs too when the blazing violence of lightning streaks
from cloud to cloud. If the cloud that receives the fire happens to contain
much moisture, the fire's life is at once extinguished with a loud clamor,
in much the same way that iron white-hot from a fiery furnace hisses
150 when we have plunged it into cold water nearby. If, however, the cloud
that receives the lightning is comparatively dry, it is immediately ignited
and burned up with a tumultuous roar, just as when flames driven by
whirling winds range over a mountain, consuming its fleece of bay trees
with irresistible fury; for there is nothing that burns with a more terrible
crackling sound than Phoebus' Delphic bay.[19]

Lastly, a great cracking of ice and falling of hail frequently produces a
din in the vast clouds on high. For when mountainous masses of cloud,

---

19. **154:** Delphi was famous for its oracle of Apollo (Phoebus), to whom the bay
was sacred. See note on 1.739.

closely condensed and mingled with hail, are crammed together by the
wind, they break up.

As for lightning, it occurs when clouds have collided and struck out   160
numerous seeds of fire. The process is similar to that when stone strikes
stone or iron; for in that case, too, light leaps out, scattering glowing
sparks of fire.

The reason why our ears hear the thunder after our eyes see the
lightning is that sounds invariably travel to us more slowly than the
images that provoke vision, as you may perceive from the following illustration: if you observe someone at a distance chopping down a
huge tree with a two-edged axe, you will see the stroke before the sound
of the blow enters your ears. Similarly we see the lightning before we   170
hear the thunder, even though the latter is emitted at the same time as the
flash and from the same cause, having been produced by the same
collision.

There is a second way in which the clouds illuminate places below
with swift flashes, and the storm lights up with rapid coruscations. When
the wind has invaded a cloud and by whirling around inside has, as I
explained before,[20] hollowed its center and condensed its crust, it becomes hot by reason of its own velocity. Thus you see all things heated
through and through and ignited by motion: indeed a leaden missile
actually liquefies when it is whirled a long distance.[21] So when this   180
burning wind has burst the black cloud, it suddenly scatters these seeds
of fire that form the winking flashes of flame. Then follows the sound,
which is slower to strike our ears than the visible image is to impinge on
our eyes. All this happens of course when the clouds are dense and at the
same time heaped up on high one above the other in a prodigious pile.
You must not be deceived by the fact that from below we perceive the
breadth of the clouds more easily than the height to which they are
banked up. Observe carefully when the winds carry mountainous clouds   190
across the sky, or when you see them accumulated heap upon heap along
a chain of mighty mountains, weighing one another down and remaining
motionless with all the winds buried in sleep: you will then be able to
appreciate the massiveness of their bulk and see what look like caverns
formed of hanging rocks. When, at the gathering of a storm, the winds
have filled these caverns, they express their indignation at being imprisoned in the clouds by roaring as loudly and menacingly as wild beasts

---

20. **176:** 124–129.

21. **178–179:** The incorrect idea that leaden missiles are melted in flight recurs
in 306–307. It goes back to Aristotle (*De Caelo* 289a).

confined in cages. Now this way, now that, they send their growling[22]
200 through the clouds; and as they pace around and around in search of an
egress,[23] they roll together numerous seeds of fire collected from the
clouds and send this flame spinning round in hollow furnaces until they
burst the cloud and streak out in a flickering flash.

Another reason why that swift-streaming, gold-gleaming fire darts
down to earth is that the clouds themselves must contain multitudes of
igneous seeds; for when they are devoid of moisture, they generally have
the brilliant color of flame. They must necessarily absorb numerous
210 igneous seeds from the light of the sun; so it is natural that they should be
ruddy and discharge fire. When therefore the wind has driven these
clouds together, condensing, compressing, and concentrating them into
one place, they squeeze out and discharge the seeds that cause the lightning's flaming flashes.

Lightning is also produced by the rarefaction of the clouds in the sky.
For when the wind gently divides and dissolves them as they move, the
seeds that form the flashes must inevitably fall out of their own accord. And then no appalling din, no terrifying tumult accompanies the
lightning.

220   As for the nature of thunderbolts, it is made manifest by their strokes,
by the marks branded by their heat, and by the dents exhaling oppressive
fumes of sulfur. These are signs not of wind or rain, but of fire.

Moreover, they often set ablaze the roofs of houses and with streaking
flame act the tyrant even within the buildings. Their fire, you see, is the
most subtle of all fires: nature has formed it of such minute and mobile
particles that absolutely nothing can resist it. The powerful thunderbolt
penetrates the walls of houses, like cries and sounds;[24] it penetrates rocks
230 and brazen objects and in a moment of time liquefies bronze and gold. It
causes wine to evaporate in an instant, while leaving the vessels intact;
this is doubtless because its heat, when it arrives, easily loosens and
rarefies all the earthenware material of the vessel, makes its way into the
vessel itself, and swiftly separates and disperses the primary elements of
wine. This is something that the sun's heat evidently could not effect in

22. **199:** Wakefield's *fremitum* is preferable to *fremitus,* the reading adopted by
most editors, for reasons given by me in *Prometheus* 26 (2000) 238–240.

23. **197–200:** The vivid image of the caged wild animals is appropriate not only
because of the noise they make, but also because of their movements. No doubt
the animals whose behavior Lucr. has observed were to be used in the arena (see
note on 5.1308–1349).

24. **228–229:** Cf. 1.489–490.

an age, despite all the power of its glittering blaze. So much more rapid
and overwhelming is the force of the thunderbolt.

How are thunderbolts produced? How do they acquire such irresistible
speed and strength that with their stroke they can split towers in two, ruin 240
houses, tear away beams and rafters, displace and demolish the monuments of the great, kill human beings, and slaughter flocks and herds
wholesale? What is the force that enables them to do these and all other
such things? I will now explain, without delaying you any longer with
promises.

We must assume that thunderbolts are produced from clouds that are
dense and heaped up high; for they are never launched from a cloudless
sky[25] or from clouds of slight density. This is proved beyond all doubt by
experience: at times when thunderbolts are hurled, the clouds are massed 250
together throughout the atmosphere; indeed we might think that on
every side all the darkness had fled from Acheron and occupied the vast
vault of heaven: so menacingly does a dreadful night of storm clouds
gather and black faces of fear scowl from above[26] when the tempest
begins to discharge its thunderbolts. Moreover, it frequently happens that
far out at sea a black storm cloud descends upon the waves, like a stream
of pitch poured down from the sky; it is so crammed with darkness, and
draws with it a dusky tempest so pregnant with thunderbolts and squalls,
and is itself especially so charged with fire and wind, that even on shore 260
people shudder and seek shelter.[27] In this way, then, we must suppose
that the storm extends high above our heads. For the clouds would not
shroud the earth in such deep darkness, unless they were built up high,
massive layer upon layer, so as to blot out the sun; nor could such
torrential rains come to overwhelm us, making rivers overflow and in-
undating the plains, if clouds were not high-heaped in the ether.

In such conditions, then, everything is full of wind and fire; and that is 270
why there is thunder and lightning on all sides. For, as I have shown
above,[28] hollow clouds contain multitudinous seeds of heat; and they
must inevitably absorb many from the blazing rays of the sun. So when
the same wind that happens to collect the clouds into any one place has

---

25. **247–248:** Cf. 400–401. Later, Horace was to write an ode (1.34) in which he
claims that he abandoned Epicureanism after witnessing a bolt from the blue in
the literal sense.

26. **251–254:** Repeated, with one minor alteration, from 4.170–173.

27. **256–261:** This passage, including the comparison of the cloud to pitch,
echoes Homer *Iliad* 4.275–279.

28. **271:** See 206–210.

forced out numerous seeds of heat and simultaneously has mingled itself
with that fire, a vortex makes its way into the cloud and whirls around in
the confined space, sharpening the thunderbolt within the fiery furnace.
280 The vortex is ignited in two ways, since it is heated by its own velocity
and by contact with the fire. Then, when the vehement wind has become
exceedingly hot and the fierce force of the fire has entered it, the fully
formed thunderbolt suddenly bursts the cloud and streaks away, illuminating all places with the flickering flashes of its flame. It is followed by such a violent crash that the precincts of the sky above seem
suddenly to be bursting apart and overwhelming us. Then a terrible
trembling pervades the earth, and rumblings run across the heights of
heaven; for almost the entire tempest trembles with the shock, and uproar
290 is aroused. This convulsion is followed by such a violent downpour that
the whole sky seems to be converted into rain and to be tumbling down in
an attempt to cause a second Flood: so vast a volume of rainwater is
released by the rending of the cloud and by the tumultuous wind, when
the thunder bursts forth with blazing stroke.

Sometimes too the impetuous force of the wind strikes the exterior of a
cloud pregnant with a fully formed thunderbolt. As soon as it has burst
the cloud, out falls that fiery vortex which in our native speech we call a
thunderbolt. This same phenomenon occurs in different directions, according to the direction of the wind.

300 Again, it sometimes happens that a vehement wind, though starting
without fire, ignites in the course of its long journey: it loses on the way
certain gross particles that cannot penetrate the air as easily as the rest;
and at the same time it collects from the air itself and sweeps along other
tiny particles that combine with it and produce fire by the speed of their
flight. The process is very similar to the way in which a leaden missile
often grows glowing hot in its transit through the air,[29] when it sheds
numerous particles of cold and takes up fire.

310 It may happen too that when a cold blast of wind containing no
igneous particles has struck a cloud, the very violence of the impact
forces out fire. This is evidently because, when the wind has delivered a
violent blow, particles of heat from the wind itself and from the cloud
that receives the blow can stream together. Similarly, when we strike iron
on a stone, fire flies out and the coldness of the metal does not make the
seeds of gleaming heat less swift to meet at the point of impact. In the
same way, then, an object is bound to be ignited by the thunderbolt,
provided that it happens to be susceptible of combustion. Moreover, it is
hardly possible for a vehement wind to be absolutely and utterly cold

---

29. **306–307:** Cf. 178–179 and see note there.

when it has been sped with such force from above: even if it does not   320
actually catch fire before completing its course, it arrives at least warm
and mingled with heat.

The velocity of the thunderbolt, the violence of its stroke, and the
swiftness with which it invariably makes its descent have the following
cause: before it is discharged from the cloud, it collects all its force and
acquires mighty momentum; and then, when the cloud can no longer
contain its increasing impetuosity, it bursts out violently and so flies with
extraordinary impetus, like a projectile discharged from a powerful
catapult.

It should be remembered too that the thunderbolt is composed of small   330
and smooth elements, and that it is not easy for anything to resist such a
substance. It darts through objects, penetrating their porous passages.
Thus it is not often impeded and delayed by collisions; and that is why it
flies on smoothly with such swift impetus.

Again, all things, owing to their weight, always have a natural downward tendency and, when an impulse is given as well, their velocity is
doubled and their momentum increased. Consequently the thunderbolt,
with added impetuosity and swiftness, strikes and shatters all obstacles in
its path and continues on its way.

Furthermore, because the thunderbolt travels with rapid motion from a   340
long distance, it must continually gather more and more speed, which
grows as it goes, thus increasing the vehemence of its impetus and
strengthening its stroke. For this velocity causes all the component seeds
of the thunderbolt to move in a straight line toward one spot, driving
them all together, as they roll along, into the same course.

Perhaps too the thunderbolt in transit attracts from the air itself certain
particles that, by their impact, accelerate its velocity.

It passes through many objects, leaving them unharmed and intact,
because the elasticity of its fire enables it to glide through the interstices.
It bores its way through many others, when its own component particles   350
have struck against the particles that constitute the fabric of the objects. It
dissolves bronze with ease and melts gold in a moment, because its
substance is finely formed of small particles and smooth elements that
easily penetrate the metals and, having penetrated them, at once untie all
the knots and loosen all the joints of their fabric.

It is in autumn, and also when flowery springtime unfolds, that thunderbolts most often convulse the whole pavilion of heaven, spangled
with sparkling stars, and the entire earth too. In the cold of winter there is   360
a lack of fire, while in the heat of summer winds fail and the clouds are

not sufficiently dense. So it is during the intermediate seasons of the year that the various causes of the thunderbolt all concur. For the surging channels of the year combine cold and heat (both of which are indispensable to the clouds for forging thunderbolts), so that the air billows furiously with fire and wind in a mighty tumult. In springtime, which is
370 both the first period of heat and the last period of cold, it is inevitable that the opposites should fight and make a commotion as they mingle. And when the last days of heat come around to mingle with the first days of cold in the season called autumn, then too there is a conflict between summer and biting winter. Therefore these seasons are rightly termed the surging channels of the year. And it need occasion no surprise if at these times thunderbolts occur most frequently and tumultuous tempests are stirred up in the sky, since all is turmoil, with a wavering war being waged between flames on the one side and a combination of wind and water on the other.

This is the way to grasp the true nature of the fire-fraught thunderbolt
380 and to understand by what force it produces each of its effects; yes, this is the way, and not by unrolling the Etruscan scrolls[30] in a vain search for indications of the mysterious purpose of the gods, nor by observing from which quarter the flying fire has come, into which part it has passed, how it has penetrated the walls of buildings, and how after acting the tyrant it has darted out again,[31] or what harm[32] the stroke of the celestial thunderbolt can do.

If it is Jupiter and the other gods who shake the lambent precincts of heaven with terrifying crashes,[33] and if they hurl the fire wherever they
390 please, why do they not ensure that those who have recklessly committed some execrable crime are struck and exhale the lightning's flames from transfixed breasts, as a severe lesson to mortals? Why, instead, are those who are guiltless of any heinous offense enveloped and trapped, despite their innocence, in the flames, seized suddenly by the fiery whirlwind from heaven?

Why also do the gods aim at deserts and waste their labor? Or are they

30. **381:** The Etruscan books, probably written in verse, contained the rules of divination from lightning.

31. **383–385:** Repeated from 87–89. See note on 86–89.

32. **386:** By "harm" Lucr. means not physical damage, but religious pollution.

33. **387–422:** A highly rhetorical passage in which Lucr. argues against the view that thunderbolts are instruments of the gods. His points, several of which have already made a brief appearance in 2.1099–1104, are for the most part traditional ones: see Aristophanes *Clouds* 398–402, Cicero *Div.* 2.44–45.

then exercising their arms and strengthening their muscles? Why do they allow the Father's missile to be blunted in the ground? Why does Jupiter himself permit this and not reserve the weapon for his enemies? Again, 400 why does he never hurl a bolt upon the earth and sound his thunder from a sky that is completely clear?[34] Does he wait for the clouds to roll up beneath him and then hurry down into them, so that he can aim his blows from near at hand? And why does he hurl his bolt into the sea? What does he have against its waves, its watery mass, and its floating plains?

Furthermore, if he wants us to beware of the stroke of his bolt, why is he unwilling to let us see it being discharged? If, however, he wants to overwhelm us unawares with his fire, why does he thunder in the quarter from which he aims and so enable us to avoid it? Why does he first fill 410 the sky with darkness and roarings and rumblings?

And how can you believe that he hurls his bolts in many directions at once? Or would you venture to maintain that it never happens that several strokes are made simultaneously? In fact, it has often happened and must often happen that, just as showers of rain fall in many places at once, so numerous thunderbolts are launched at the same moment.

Lastly, why does he shatter the sacred shrines of deities and his own splendid seats with destructive thunderbolts? Why does he smash finely fashioned statues of the gods and deface his own images with violent 420 wounds? Why does he usually aim at lofty places, so that we most often see traces of his fire on mountaintops?

Now, from the preceding explanations it is easy to understand how the phenomenon, which, because of its character, the Greeks have termed "prester,"[35] is dispatched from above into the sea. It sometimes happens that a kind of column is lowered from the sky and descends into the sea; around it the surging waters seethe, whipped up by violent blasts of wind, and all ships caught in that turbulence are buffeted about and brought 430 into extreme peril. This occurs when, as sometimes happens, a wind fails, despite its vehemence, to burst a cloud from which it is endeavoring to escape; it then depresses it, so that a kind of column is let down gradually from sky to sea: it is as though something were being forced down by the thrust of a fist and arm from above and so stretched out into the waves. And when the impetuous wind has torn open the cloud, it bursts out into the sea and causes an extraordinary ferment among the

---

34. **400–401:** Cf. 247–248 and see note there.

35. **424:** The Greek word *prēstēr,* which literally means "burner," denotes a fiery whirlwind or waterspout. However, the fiery element is not mentioned either by Lucr. or by Epicurus *Pyth.* 104–105.

waves; for it descends as a whirling eddy, drawing down with it the
440   ductile body of the cloud; and as soon as it has thrust this pregnant cloud
down to the surface of the ocean, it suddenly hurls itself wholly into the
water and embroils all the sea, making it seethe with a tumultuous roar.
It may happen too that a vortex of wind envelops itself in clouds by
collecting particles of cloud from the air and thus imitates a "prester"
lowered from the sky. When the vortex has dropped on land and burst, it
spews out a whirlwind and tempest of prodigious violence. But because
this phenomenon very seldom occurs, and mountains inevitably obstruct
450   our view of it on land, it is observed more often on the sea with its wide
prospect and open sky.

As for the formation of clouds, this results from the sudden coales-
cence of numerous particles flying about in the spacious sky above us—
particles whose rather rough shape enables them to maintain their cohesion even though they are only loosely interlocked. These first form
small clouds; then the small clouds coalesce and combine and by combination grow, and are carried along by the winds until at length a savage
storm gathers.
460   It is a fact too that the nearer a mountain's summit soars to the sky, the
more its heights constantly smoke with a mist of tawny cloud. This is
because, when the clouds begin to form and are still too tenuous to be
visible to the eye, the winds carry them along and collect them on the
highest mountain peaks. It is then and only then, when they are assembled in a larger and denser throng, that they can become visible; and so
they appear to be rising from the mountaintop itself into the bright sky.
That lofty places are windswept is a plain fact, proved by the evidence of
our senses when we climb high mountains.
470   Moreover, multitudinous particles are raised by nature from the whole
surface of the sea, as is shown by the way in which garments, hung up on
the shore, absorb clinging moisture. This makes it all the more evident
that many particles can also rise from the swell of the briny ocean to
augment the clouds; for the two kinds of moisture[36] are wholly akin.
Furthermore, we see rivers and the earth itself exhale mists and vapors. These exhalations, which are expelled like breath, are carried up-
480   ward and overspread the sky with a veil of darkness, gradually uniting to
form the clouds on high. For pressure is also exerted on them from above
by the star-studded ether's heat that, by condensing them, weaves a web
of cloud beneath the azure spaces of the sky.

---

36. **475:** The moisture of the sea and the moisture contained in the clouds.

It may be too that constituent particles of clouds and scudding storm rack enter our sky from outside this world. For I have proved[37] that the number of atoms is numberless, and that the sum of the unfathomable void is infinite; and I have shown[38] at what a prodigious speed the ultimate particles fly, and how in a moment of time they can traverse an inexpressible distance of space. Therefore it need occasion no surprise if it often takes only a short time for tempest and darkness, scowling from   490 above, to shroud lands and seas with such huge storm clouds, since on every side, through all the pores of the ether, through all the vents of the vast world around us, the elements can pass freely in and out.

Now then, let me explain how rainwater collects in the clouds on high, and how showers are precipitated and fall to the earth.

In the first place, you will grant me that numerous particles of water rise from all things at the same time as the clouds themselves, and that both the clouds and the water contained in them grow together, just as   500 our body grows together with the blood and the sweat and indeed all the moisture that is in our limbs. Often too the clouds absorb much moisture from the sea when, like hanging fleeces of wool, they are wafted by the winds over the mighty main. Similarly moisture is raised to the clouds from every river. And when multitudinous particles of water have come together in many ways and have been augmented from all sides, the crammed clouds hasten to discharge their moisture for two reasons: the   510 force of the wind thrusts them together, and the very mass of storm clouds, when they have been driven together in a dense throng, causes intense downward pressure and so makes showers stream out. Moreover, when the clouds are rarefied by the winds or dissolved by the sun's heat striking them from above, they discharge rainwater in drops, just as wax drips fast as it melts over a hot flame.

A violent shower is caused when the clouds are subjected to the violent pressure of both forces—their own accumulation and the impetuosity of the wind. As for persistent and prolonged rains, these oc-   520 cur when numerous particles of water are collected, and clouds heaped upon clouds and streaming storm rack are swept on from every quarter, and the whole earth smokes, returning the moisture in the form of exhalations.

When in such conditions the sun's rays pierce the gloom of the tempest and strike straight on the rain sprayed from the storm clouds, then the colors of the rainbow shine out amid the blackness of the clouds.

---

37. **485–486:** See 1.984–1051.
38. **486–488:** See 2.142–164.

What of the other phenomena that grow and are produced up in the sky, and that collect in the clouds? I mean all, absolutely all, of them—
530   snow, winds, hail, icy rime, and the mighty force of frost, that great solidifier of waters, which everywhere checks and curbs rushing rivers. Despite their great number, you can easily explain every one of them and see with your mind's eye how they are formed and why they are created, once you have gained a firm grasp of the properties of primary particles.

Now then, I want you to learn the causes of earthquakes. And first of all you must imagine that the earth, in its depths as well as on its surface, is everywhere full of windy caverns, and that it holds in its bosom many
540   lakes and many chasms, also cliffs and precipitous crags; and you must suppose that there are many rivers hidden under its crust, impetuously rolling submerged boulders beneath their waves. For plain fact demands that the earth should have the same character throughout.

So, having these things attached to it beneath, the earth quakes on its surface with the shock of mighty subsidences when huge subterranean caverns, undermined by time, collapse. Entire mountains tumble down, and the mighty convulsion instantly causes tremors to spread far and wide. And no wonder, seeing that whole houses by a roadside tremble
550   and shake when wagons of no great weight pass by, and [axles] jump no less [when the surface of the road]³⁹ jolts the iron rims of the wheels on either side.

It happens too, when a huge mass of soil, loosened by lapse of time, rolls down into vast wide watery gulfs, that the agitation of the water makes the earth rock and reel in the same way that a vessel sometimes cannot stand still until the liquid within it has stopped undulating and oscillating.

Moreover, when the wind pent up in the subterranean caverns gathers together and rushes forward from one quarter, battering and buffeting the
560   deep caves with great violence, the earth tilts in the direction in which the vehement force of the wind presses it. Then the houses that are built upon the earth's surface lean over threateningly, inclining in the same direction, while their beams protrude and hang in readiness to fall; and the more the buildings tower skyward, the more pronounced are these effects. And yet people shrink from believing that a day of doom and

---

39. **550:** The text is seriously corrupt, and no satisfactory emendation has been proposed. I have translated *nec minus exultant axes ubi summa viai,* suggested by me as a stopgap. The reading, which owes much to suggestions of earlier scholars, is very unlikely to be exactly what Lucr. wrote.

disaster awaits the fabric of the vast world, even when they witness the
subsidence of such a mighty mass of earth! If the winds did not abate, no
force could curb things or hold them back from rushing to destruction.
As it is, because winds alternately abate and increase, now rallying and   570
returning to the attack, now retiring repulsed, the earth more often
threatens to collapse than actually does so. It leans over and then sways
back again and, after slipping forward, recovers its proper position in
equilibrium. This is why all the buildings rock, the tallest more than
those of medium height, those of medium height more than the lowest,
and the lowest scarcely at all.

Here is another cause of the same great quaking. When a mighty blast
of violent wind, either coming from without or arising within the earth
itself, has suddenly hurled itself into the hollows of the earth, it first roars   580
there tumultuously among the vast caverns, whirling around and around;
then its impetuous force, lashed to fury, bursts out and, in so doing,
cleaves the earth to its depths and opens a yawning chasm. This is what
happened at Sidon in Syria and at Aegium[40] in the Peloponnese, where
the cities were destroyed by such an eruption of wind and the ensuing
earthquake. Many other walled towns have been razed to the ground by
mighty movements of the earth, and many cities, citizens and all, have   590
sunk to the bottom of the sea.

Even if the wind fails to burst out, its impetuosity and fierce force
spread, like an ague, through the numerous pores of the earth and so cause
a tremor, just as, when cold penetrates deep within our limbs, it shakes
them and makes them tremble and shiver involuntarily. Thus the panic-
stricken inhabitants of the cities have a twofold terror: they fear the collapse of the roofs above them, and they are afraid that beneath them the
earth may suddenly break up its caverns and, rent asunder, open its wide-
gaping jaws and in complete confusion seek to fill them with its own ruins.   600

So let people imagine that heaven and earth will remain imperishable,
entrusted to eternal safety. And yet from time to time the influence of
immediate danger applies on some side or other a goad of fear that the
earth may suddenly be snatched away from under their feet and swept
into the bottomless abyss, that the aggregate of things, utterly deprived of
its foundation, may follow, and that the world may be reduced to a
chaotic ruin.

---

40. **585:** The date of the Sidonian earthquake is uncertain. Probably it occurred
in the second half of the fifth century B.C. The earthquake that destroyed the
towns of Helice and Buris near Aegium, on the Peloponnesian side of the Gulf of
Corinth, occurred in 373–372 B.C.

In the first place,[41] people marvel that nature does not increase the size
610 of the sea, considering how such a vast volume of water is poured into it
by all the rivers running from every side. Add to these the straying
showers and scudding storms that sprinkle and saturate all lands and
seas; add the ocean's own springs. And yet, in comparison with the sum
of the sea, all these waters combined represent an increase scarcely
equivalent to a single drop. This makes it less marvelous that the mighty
main does not grow mightier still.

Moreover, a large quantity of water is evaporated by solar heat. For we
observe how soaking-wet garments are dried by the sun's blazing rays.
We see that the oceans are many and spread out far and wide beneath the
620 sky; and so, although at a particular spot the sun takes only a small sip
from the surface, yet over such a vast expanse it will take a considerable
amount of water from the waves.

Then again, the winds too are able to remove a large quantity of
moisture as they sweep the surface of the seas, since we frequently
observe that they dry a road and encrust its soft mud in a single night.

Furthermore, I have shown[42] that the clouds too absorb much moisture
taken from the surface of the vast ocean, and sprinkle it everywhere over
630 the whole round of the earth when it rains on land and the winds carry the
clouds across the sky.

Lastly, since the earth is of a porous consistency and is in close contact
with the sea whose shores it girdles on every side, it is inevitable that,
just as water passes from the land into the sea, so it should also ooze from
the salt sea into the land. The brine is filtered off, while the fluid streams
back and all flows together at the riverheads, from which it returns
overland in a fresh current, following the channel that once was carved
for it to roll down in its liquid course.[43]

640   I will now explain why it is that from time to time fiery blasts burst
with such tornadic fury from the jaws of Mount Etna.[44] For no ordinary

---

41. **608–638:** This explanation of why the sea's volume remains constant comes
in unexpectedly here between the explanations of earthquakes and volcanoes. It
comes in abruptly too, for it lacks an introduction. It is difficult to believe that
Lucr. intended to leave things as they are: the passage would come in more
naturally before the explanation of why the Nile floods in summer (712–737).
However, it is not our business to revise the poet's work for him.

42. **627:** See 470–475, 503–505.

43. **635–638:** Repeated, with two minor alterations, from 5.269–272.

44. **639–702:** Vesuvius was not active in Lucr.'s time (the great eruption that
buried Pompeii and Herculaneum occurred in A.D. 79), and so naturally he

disaster was caused by the flaming tempest that arose and tyrannized the territory of the Sicilians, and attracted the gaze of neighboring peoples who, at the sight of the precincts of heaven all full of smoke and flakes of flame, were filled in their hearts with panic and apprehension that nature might be preparing some catastrophic upheaval.

In considering this subject, it is essential to take a wide and deep view and look far in every direction; for you must remember that the aggregate of things is unfathomable, and realize that a single sky is so very small, 650 so infinitesimally small a part of the whole universe, that it is not even so considerable a fraction of it as one person is of the whole earth. If you place these principles firmly before your mind, contemplate them clearly, and clearly comprehend them, you will cease to marvel at many things.

Who among us is astonished if someone contracts a fever whose onset affects the frame with burning heat, or develops any other disease that pains the whole body? A foot will suddenly swell; often a sharp pain tortures the teeth or penetrates right into the eyes; the holy fire[45] breaks 660 out and creeps over the body, inflaming every part it attacks as it crawls across the frame. Evidently the reason why these maladies occur is that multitudinous seeds of things exist, and our earth and sky contain enough harmful germs to allow a measureless amount of disease to be produced. In the same way, then, we must suppose that the whole heaven and earth receive from the infinite a sufficient supply of all kinds of elements to enable the earth suddenly to be convulsed and moved, and tearing tornadoes to sweep over sea and lands, and Etna's fire to burst forth and inflame the skies. For it does happen too that the celestial precincts are 670 set ablaze, just as exceptionally violent rainstorms occur when particles of water have in the same way chanced to accumulate.

"But," you may object, "the turbulent blaze of Etna's fire is prodigiously vast." Quite true; but it is also true that a river seems enormous to someone who has never before seen a larger one; so does a tree or a human being; indeed, with all things of all kinds, the largest that a person has seen is considered by the viewer to be enormous. And yet all these objects, with sky and earth and sea as well, are as nothing compared with the totality of the universe.

---

concentrates on Etna. Its last serious eruption before the time he was writing was in 122 B.C., when Catana was destroyed, and it is presumably to this disaster that he alludes in 641–646.

45. **660:** Erysipelas (or cellulitis, of which erysipelas is one form), a bacterial skin infection that makes the skin become red, hot, and swollen. It used to be popularly known as St. Anthony's Fire or the Rose.

680   To return to my subject, I will now explain how that flaming blast is
suddenly provoked and bursts out from the huge furnaces of Etna.

First, the whole mountain is hollow underneath, being supported for
the most part by cavernous basalt. And all its caves contain wind and air.
Air, I should explain, becomes wind when it is agitated. Now, when this
wind has grown exceedingly hot and in its fury has heated all the surrounding rocks and earth with which it comes in contact and has forced
from them fire fierce with frantic flames, it mounts up and ejects itself
690   high into the air, passing straight through the volcano's jaws. And so it
carries its blaze afar, afar scatters hot cinders, rolls on smoke sooty with
dense darkness, and at the same time flings out rocks of stupendous
weight. Therefore you may be sure that these effects are produced by a
vehement wind.

Moreover, the sea for a considerable distance breaks its waves and
sucks back its surf at the foot of the mountain. From the sea subterranean
caverns extend all the way up to the jaws of the lofty volcano. Through
these caverns, one must admit, [a mixture of wind and water] passes in
and is compelled [to rise][46] and penetrate deep within the mountain from
700   the open sea, and then to burst out, shooting up flames, ejecting rocks,
and raising clouds of sand. For at the summit of the volcano are what the
Sicilians themselves term craters,[47] but what we call jaws or mouths.

There are some phenomena for which it is not sufficient to state one
cause: you must mention several causes, though only one of these will be
the true cause.[48] Let me illustrate this point. If you saw a lifeless human
body lying at some distance, you would naturally enumerate all the
possible causes of death, to ensure that you mentioned the one true cause.
For you could not be certain that the victim had perished by the sword, or
710   by cold, or by disease, or maybe by poison. But we do know that it is
something of this kind that has occasioned the death. And the same
applies to numerous phenomena.

The Nile, the river of all Egypt, is unique in the world in that it rises
and inundates the plains as summer advances. The reason why it reg-

---

46. **697:** At least one line is lost after 697.

47. **701:** The Greek word *kratēr* literally means "mixing bowl" (usually for wine
and water). Lucr. implies that the word is an apt one, not only because the mouth
of the volcano is shaped like a mixing bowl, but also because fire, rocks, and sand
are mixed together in it.

48. **703–711:** Cf. 5.526–533 and see pp. xxiv–xxv.

ularly irrigates Egypt at the height of the hot season may be that in summer northerly winds, which at that time of the year are known as etesian[49] winds, are dead against the mouths of the river; by blowing against the current they check its flow, force the waters upstream, fill the 720 channel, and oblige the river to stand still. It is undoubtedly true that these winds do blow full against the current, because they come from the icy constellations of the North Pole. The Nile, on the other hand, flows from the south, from the torrid zone, rising deep within the midday region among the tribes of people blackened by the scorching sun.

It is possible too that a vast mass of sand, swept inshore by the wind-embroiled sea, accumulates at the mouths of the Nile in such a way as to obstruct its waves, and that consequently the outlet of the river becomes less free and the downward flow of its waters less impetuous.

A further possibility is that rains are particularly heavy at that season 730 near the river's source because[50] then the blasts of the etesian winds collect all the clouds into those parts. You may be sure that, when the clouds have been driven toward the midday region and have congregated there, they are eventually thrust together on the mountain heights, where they are concentrated and forcibly compressed.

Yet another possibility is that the river swells deep among the lofty Ethiopian mountains, when the all-illuminating sun's dissolving rays make the shining-white snows depart to the plains.

Now then, I will explain to you the nature of all the places and lakes that are called Avernian.

First of all, their name is derived from the fact that they are inimical to 740 all birds.[51] As soon as any bird has arrived in flight directly above such a place, it forgets its pinioned oars, drops its feathered sails, and with neck limp and drooping falls plumb down to the ground, if the nature of the place allows it, or into the water, if an Avernian lake happens to be outspread beneath. Such a place is to be found near Cumae, where the hills are charged with pungent sulfur that they exhale from abundant hot springs.

---

49. **716:** See note on 5.742.

50. **730:** I translate Marullus' *quod* for *quo.*

51. **738–741:** Avernus is a lake near Cumae (see 747), west of Naples. Lucr. identifies its name with the Greek *aornos,* "birdless," and applies the adjective "Avernian" to all places whose noxious exhalations render them birdless. On a visit to lake Avernus, I did not see any birds flying over it, but I observed that the place is not inimical to water-skiers.

There is also a spot within the walls of Athens, on the very summit of
750 the Acropolis, close to the temple of Tritonian Pallas[52] the life-giver, to
which raucous crows never direct their flight, not even when the altars
are smoking with offerings. It is not true that, as the poets of Greece sang,
they are warily avoiding Pallas' violent wrath which they provoked by
their vigilance;[53] rather the nature of the spot produces this effect of its
own accord.

In Syria too, so it is reported, one can see a place which, the moment
quadrupeds have entered it, by its own natural power causes them to fall
heavily, as though they were suddenly slaughtered as a sacrifice to the
infernal deities.

760 All these phenomena are produced by the operation of nature, and the
causes that give rise to them are apparent. So we must not believe that
gates of Orcus can be situated in these regions; and we cannot possibly
suppose that from these spots the infernal deities draw down souls to the
shores of Acheron,[54] in the same way that fleet-footed stags are often
thought to lure creeping serpents from their lairs by the breath of their
nostrils.[55] Observe how far these tales are removed from the truth; for I
will now endeavor to give the true explanation.

770 My first point is one that I have often made before:[56] the earth contains
elements of all kinds of things—many that are nutritious and beneficial to life, and many that are capable of causing disease and hast-
ening the approach of death. And as I have already shown, certain
substances are better suited than others to certain creatures for the purposes of life, on account of their different natures, their different structures, and the different shapes of their component atoms. Many noxious
elements pass through the ears; many that are offensive and rough in
contact penetrate the nostrils; and there are more than a few that should

---

52. **750:** Pallas is Athena, and her temple is the Parthenon. The meaning of the
epithet "Tritonian" or "Trito-born" is disputed.

53. **753–754:** Lucr. alludes to the story that Athena entrusted to the three daughters of Cecrops (legendary king of Athens) a chest containing the infant
Erichthonius, and at the same time commanded them not to open it. The girls
disobeyed her orders, and a spying crow reported them to the goddess, who
punished the bird for "sneaking" by banishing crows from the Acropolis forever.

54. **762–764:** Lake Avernus, because of its exhalations, its depth, and its gloomy
situation with dark woods all round, was thought to be an entrance to the
underworld.

55. **765–766:** This tale about stags and serpents is found in several later writers
(see note in the Loeb for references).

56. **769:** See 1.809–822, 2.398–477, 4.633–672.

be avoided by the touch or shunned by the sight or that are bitter to the   780
taste.

Again, you may see how many things are intensely offensive to the
human senses, in that they are loathsome and injurious.

First, certain trees[57] have a shade so exceedingly noxious that they
frequently give headaches to those who have stretched themselves on the
grass beneath them. Moreover, on the mighty mountain slopes of Helicon there grows a tree[58] whose flower is usually fatal to human beings
who inhale its foul scent. Evidently the reason why all these things grow
from the ground is that the earth contains countless seeds of countless   790
things mingled in countless ways and sorts them out before distributing
them.

Again, when the acrid smell of a recently extinguished night-light
strikes the nostrils of one who is liable to fall to the ground foaming at the
mouth in epileptic fits, it sends the person to sleep then and there. And a
woman will fall back, overcome with sleep, and let her elegant work slip
from her delicate hands, if she smells the strong scent of castor[59] during
menstruation. And there are many other substances that affect all the
limbs of the body with faintness and languor and shake the spirit within
its abode.

Then again, if you stay long in a hot bath when you are too full after a   800
banquet, it is often only too easy to collapse in the middle of the tub of
boiling water. It is only too easy also for the oppressively powerful fumes
of charcoal to penetrate the brain, unless somehow we shut them out
beforehand.[60] And when a fiery fever has taken possession of someone's
limbs, the odor of wine strikes with the force of a murderous blow.

Have you not observed too that within the earth itself sulfur is produced and bitumen forms foul-smelling concretions? Again, when men
are exploiting veins of silver and gold, exploring with their picks the
hidden depths of the earth, what fumes Scaptensula[61] exhales under-   810
ground! What noxious exhalations issue from gold mines! What faces,
what complexions they give the workers! Have you not seen or heard

---

57. **783:** Lucr. is probably thinking of juniper (see Virgil *Eclogues* 10.76) and of
box and walnut (Pliny *Natural History* 16.70, 17.89).

58. **786:** It is not known what tree is meant.

59. **794:** A reddish-brown substance obtained from the groin of the beaver and
used in perfumery and medicine.

60. **799–803:** In 800 I have adopted Brieger's *ex epulis* for *eff(l)ueris* of the
manuscripts, and in 803 I read *nisi qua* (E. J. Kenney, for *nisi aqua) praecludimus
ante*. For full discussion, see M. F. Smith, *Museum Helveticum* 58 (2001) 65–69.

61. **810:** A town in Thrace famous for its mines.

how soon the miners usually die, and how vital force fails those who are confined in such employment by the strong constraint of necessity?[62] All these vapors, then, are emitted by the earth which exhales them into the open air, into the clear spaces of the sky.

In the same way the Avernian spots must send up fumes fatal to birds.
820 These fumes rise from the earth into the air and infect a certain part of the atmosphere. As soon as a bird has flown into this part, it is arrested and trapped by the invisible poison and plunges plumb down in the direction from which the exhalation rises. And when it has fallen there, the same exhalation removes the remnants of life from the whole of its body. For at first it merely induces a sort of giddiness; but afterward, when the bird has plunged into the very source of the poison, it must spew out life itself, because it is surrounded by a vast amount of noxious vapor.
830   It may sometimes happen too that the Avernian exhalations are so powerful that they dispel the air that intervenes between the birds and the earth, thus creating a virtual vacuum. The moment the birds have arrived in flight directly above such a place, the beating of their wings falters and is rendered futile, and all the efforts of both their pinions are ineffectual. And then, when they are no longer able to buoy themselves up or rest upon their wings, nature of course forces them to fall to the earth by their own weight; and as they drop through a virtual vacuum, they exhale their spirits through every pore of the body.

840   The[63] reason why the water in wells becomes colder in summer is that the earth is then rarefied by the heat and releases into the air all the heat particles it happens to have. So, the more the earth is drained of heat, the colder becomes the moisture that is concealed in the ground. On the other hand, when all the earth condenses and contracts and congeals with the cold, then of course, as it contracts, it squeezes out into the wells whatever heat it holds.

Near the shrine of Ammon[64] there is reported to be a spring that is cold
850 by day and hot by night. People regard this spring with extraordinary

---

62. **815:** The miners were slaves.

63. **840:** Most modern editors assume a lacuna before 840, usually supposing that a whole leaf of the archetype has been lost. But it is by no means certain that this assumption is correct.

64. **848:** An Egyptian god (Amun) identified with Zeus by the Greeks, with Jupiter by the Romans. The shrine mentioned by Lucr., at the oasis of Siwa in the Libyan desert, was a famous oracle center. The earliest description of the amazing spring near the shrine is that of Herodotus 4.181.3–4.

wonder, and some suppose that it is made to boil by the fierce heat of the sun beneath the earth, when night has spread its pall of dreadful darkness over the lands. But this supposition is far removed from the true explanation. For if the sun, acting on the uncovered body of the water, has failed to warm even the surface, despite the intense heat that its light possesses as it shines from above, how could it make the whole spring boil, saturating it with heat, when the earth's thick mass is interposed? After all, it can scarcely make the heat of its rays penetrate the walls of a house. 860

What is the explanation, then? Doubtless it is that the earth around the spring is more porous than anywhere else, and that there are numerous particles of fire near the water. And so as soon as night inundates the earth with its dewy waves, the ground grows cold deep down and contracts. Thus, as though it were compressed by the hand, it squeezes out into the spring all the particles of fire it holds, and these make the water hot to touch and cause it to steam. Then when the rays of the rising sun have loosened the soil and rarefied it by mingling their heat with it, the 870 igneous elements return again to their original positions and all the heat of the water retires into the earth. Consequently the spring becomes cold in the daytime.

Furthermore, the water is struck by the sun's rays and, as daylight advances, is rarefied by the quivering heat. The result is that it releases all the igneous particles it holds, just as water often releases the frost that it contains, melting the ice and loosening the bonds that bind it.

There is also a cold spring[65] of such a nature that tow, when held over 880 it, will often catch fire at once and emit flames; similarly a torch can be lit and will shine among the waters wherever it floats under the impulse of the breezes. Undoubtedly the explanation of the phenomenon is that the water contains very many elements of heat; and other igneous particles emanating from deep down in the earth itself must rise up through the whole spring and at the same time must be exhaled and pass off into the air; and yet these particles are not so numerous as to be able to make the spring hot. Moreover, the force of impulsion compels the igneous elements to burst up suddenly through the water unattached and then to unite above the surface.

Similarly there is a spring in the sea at Aradus,[66] which gushes out 890 fresh water and thrusts aside the briny waves that surround it; and there

---

65. **879:** Lucr. refers to the spring at Dodona in Epirus. Dodona was famous for its ancient oracle of Zeus (Jupiter).

66. **890:** An island, with a city of the same name, just off the coast of what was Phoenicia and is now southwest Syria.

are many other places where the sea affords a timely relief to thirsty sailors by spewing up fresh water amid the brine. In the same way then the particles of fire are able to burst up through that other spring and gush out; and when they meet together on the tow or adhere to the substance of the torch, they easily blaze up at once, because the tow and floating torches also contain numerous elements of fire.

900 Have you not observed too that when you move a recently extinguished wick close to a night-light, it ignites before it touches the flame, and that a torch does the same? And there are many other things that are set ablaze at a distance by contact with the mere heat, before the fire is close enough to steep them. So we must suppose that the same happens in the case of that spring.

Turning to another subject, I will proceed to explain by what law of nature it comes about that iron can be attracted by that stone which the Greeks call the magnet after the name of its place of origin, the territory

910 of Magnesia.[67] This stone is regarded by people with astonishment; for it often forms a chain of rings suspended from itself. You may sometimes see five or more hanging in a string, dangling in the gentle breeze; one ring hangs from another, clinging to it underneath; and each feels from its neighbor the influence and attraction of the stone: so thoroughly does its power permeate them all.[68]

In matters of this kind one must establish many principles before one can give an explanation of the phenomenon itself: the approach must be

920 made by an exceedingly circuitous road. So I beg you to give me all the more attention of ears and mind.

In the first place, all objects that are visible to us must necessarily discharge and scatter a continual stream of particles that impinge on the eyes and provoke vision. Moreover, from certain things odors flow in a perpetual stream; cold emanates from rivers, heat from the sun, and spray from the waves of the sea—spray that erodes the walls skirting the shore. Various sounds are continually floating through the air. Again, when we

930 walk near the sea, a briny taste often makes its way into our mouth; and

---

67. **909:** Magnesia (ad Sipylum) in Lydia, western Asia Minor, not Magnesia (ad Maeandrum) in Ionia, which is about fifty miles south of its namesake. The magnet naturally attracted (!) the interest of Greek philosophers from the beginning. Thales, early in the sixth century B.C., believed that it contains a "soul" and is alive. Empedocles and Democritus anticipated Epicurus in using a theory of emanations to explain the phenomenon.

68. **910–916:** The description recalls, as the sixteenth-century commentators Pius and Lambinus saw, that of Plato *Ion* 533d–e.

when we watch wormwood being diluted and mixed, its bitterness affects our palate. So true is it that from all objects emanations flow away and are discharged in all directions on every side. These effluences stream away without any delay or interruption, since we constantly experience sensation and we may at any time see, smell, and hear anything.[69]

Next let me remind you of a point that has already been clearly proved in the first book of my poem,[70] namely of how porous a consistency all objects are. Although knowledge of this principle is pertinent to many problems, in regard to the matter which I am endeavoring to discuss it is 940 particularly necessary to establish that there is no perceptible object that is not a mixture of matter and void. In the first place, it is a fact that the rocky roofs of caverns sweat moisture, which they distill in oozing drops. Similarly perspiration is exuded from every part of our bodies; the beard grows, and hairs invest all our members and limbs; food is channeled into every vein and strengthens and sustains even the extremities of the body, including the nails. Moreover, we feel cold and heat permeate bronze; and we feel them permeate gold and silver as well, when we hold 950 brimming beakers. Again, sounds wing their way through the stone walls of houses; smell penetrates them too, and cold, and the heat of fire that even has the power to pierce iron for all its strength. Furthermore, the corselet of the sky that encompasses us all round [is penetrable to the particles that compose clouds and storm rack],[71] and also to the infection of disease when it comes in from outside our world. And it is natural for the tempests that arise from the earth and from the sky to retire and disappear into the sky and the earth respectively. For there is nothing that is not of a porous consistency.

There is the further point that not all the particles discharged by 960 objects produce the same effect on the senses, and not all are adapted in the same way to all substances. Thus, whereas the sun bakes and dries up earth, it dissolves ice and causes the snows high-heaped on the high mountains to melt beneath its rays. Wax too liquefies when exposed to the sun's heat. Again, fire fuses bronze and melts gold, but shrivels and shrinks hides and flesh. Moreover, whereas water hardens iron taken straight from the fire, it softens flesh and hides that have been hardened by heat. The wild olive affords as much delight to bearded nanny goats as 970 if it actually distilled ambrosia and were steeped in nectar; and yet to

---

69. **923–935:** Repeated, with one or two minor alterations, from 4.217–229.

70. **937:** 1.329–369.

71. **954:** A lacuna has to be assumed after this line. Probably only one line is lost, and I have translated my suggestion *corpora quae faciunt nubis nimbosque penetrant* (cf. 484, and for *penētrant* cf. 4.613).

human beings its foliage tastes more bitter than any other green growth. Again, pigs are repelled by marjoram and fear perfume of every kind; for what sometimes seems to put new life into us is rank poison to bristly swine. On the other hand, the same mire that is the foulest of filth to us is manifestly so attractive to pigs that they wallow all over in it with insatiable enjoyment.

980   Before I proceed to speak specifically of the magnet, it seems necessary to make one further point. The multitudinous pores by which different objects are penetrated must be distinguished by differing natures: each must have its own characteristics and its own passages. Thus living creatures have different senses, each of which perceives its own appropriate object. We observe that sound penetrates into one sense

990 organ, taste into another, and smell into yet another. Moreover, one thing is seen to pierce through stone, another through wood, another to pass through gold, and yet another to penetrate silver or glass. We see images stream one way, heat pass another, and some things penetrate more quickly than others through the same passages. Evidently these differences of effect are caused by the innumerable variations, to which I have drawn attention just above, in the nature of the passages, owing to differences in the nature and structure of objects.

Well, now that all these preliminaries have been properly established and laid down, and all the ground has been prepared and made ready for

1000 us, it will be easy on the basis of these principles to explain the magnet and disclose in full the cause of the attraction of strong iron.

In the first place, multitudinous particles must emanate from this stone, and the impact of these emanations must disperse all the air that separates the stone from the iron. As soon as this space is emptied and a considerable vacuum is created in between, the particles emitted by the iron dart forward and fall into it in a body. The result is that the ring itself follows and moves forward with its whole mass; for there is no substance

1010 whose constituent elements are more firmly compacted and whose consistency is closer than the cold, rough substance of solid iron. This makes it less surprising if, [as I have stated just above,][72] it is impossible for the numerous particles emanating from the iron to pass into the vacuum without the entire ring following. This the ring does, and continues to follow until it reaches the stone itself and adheres to it by invisible fastenings. The same process may occur in any direction: wherever a vacuum is made, whether at the side of the iron or above it, the nearest

1020 particles at once move into the empty space; and they do this under the

---

72. **1012:** Reading, in the second part of the line, *quod paulo diximus ante,* as suggested by Lambinus.

impulse of impacts from the opposite side:[73] they cannot spontaneously rise upward into the air.

Moreover, there is an additional cause that makes the operation easier by assisting the movement of the ring: as soon as the air in front of the ring has been rarefied and the space has been made more empty and void, the immediate consequence is that all the air that lies behind the ring gives a forward impulse to it from the rear. For things are continually being buffeted by the air that surrounds them; but in a case like this the air is able to drive the iron forward because on one side there is an empty space ready to receive it. And this air of which I am speaking, subtly insinuating itself through the numerous interstices of the iron into its smallest parts, thrusts and drives it on, as the wind propels a ship under sail.[74] Furthermore, all compound bodies must contain air in their substance, since they are of a porous consistency and air surrounds and is contiguous to all things. This air, then, which is hidden deep within the iron, is continually tossing about in restless motion and thus undoubtedly buffets the ring and imparts motion to it internally. And so of course the ring moves on in the same direction in which it has already darted forward in its effort to enter the empty space.

It sometimes happens too that iron recedes from this stone, which keeps on repelling and attracting it by turns. I have actually seen Samothracian iron rings dance[75] and iron filings leap about frenziedly inside bronze bowls beneath which magnets had been placed: so strong seemed the iron's desire to escape from the stone. The reason why the interposition of the bronze causes all this discord is undoubtedly that the emanation of bronze arrives first and preoccupies the iron's open pores, so that, when the magnetic current arrives later, it finds all the interstices in the iron full and has no channel to glide through as before. Consequently it is obliged to beat and buffet the fabric of the iron with its waves; and that is why it repels from itself and, acting through the bronze, drives away what without the interposed bronze it invariably attracts.

In this connection, there is no need to be astonished that the emana-

1030

1040

1050

---

73. **1020:** That is to say, from the side away from the vacuum.

74. **1033:** Cf. 4.897.

75. **1044:** Samothracian rings were made of iron with an overlay of gold and were used as amulets. (The ones that Lucr. saw had perhaps not yet been gold-plated.) See Pliny *Natural History* 33.23, where it is made clear that such rings, though taking their name from the island of Samothrace in the northeast Aegean, did not have to be made there. Therefore our passage does not indicate, as some have argued, that Lucr. had visited Samothrace.

tions from this stone do not possess the same power to impel other substances. Some substances remain stationary by reason of their 1060 weight—gold, for example; others cannot be moved at all, because their consistency is so porous that the emanations dart through them unresisted: this class obviously includes wood. Iron, however, has an intermediate nature and so, when it has admitted certain tiny particles of bronze, the emanations of the magnet are able to impart motion to it.

The case of iron and the magnet is by no means unparalleled. I could mention plenty of similar instances of substances that have an exclusive affinity for one another. In the first place, you see that mortar alone can 1070 cement stones. Only bull-glue[76] unites timbers, joining them together so firmly that the grain of the boards often gapes open in cracks sooner than the bonds of bull-glue relax their grip. The juice of the grape consents to mingle with spring water, while ponderous pitch and light olive oil refuse. The purple dye yielded by the murex[77] mingles so closely with wool that it can never be separated from it—no, not even if one should strive to restore the wool's whiteness with Neptune's billowy waters, not even if all the entire ocean's waves should wish to wash out the color. Again, is there not only one substance[78] capable of coupling gold to 1080 gold, and is not bronze soldered to bronze only by tin? How many other examples might one find! But why mention more? You have no need whatever of such a detailed demonstration, and I should not spend so much time and trouble on this matter. It is better to embrace all these cases in a brief summary. Those substances whose textures mutually correspond in such a way that the cavities of the one answer to the projections of the other form the closest combinations. It is possible too that certain substances may be interlocked and held in union by sort of hooks and eyes; and this seems more likely to be the case with iron and the magnet.

1090   And now I will disclose the cause of diseases and explain what enables a violent storm of pestilence suddenly to gather and breathe a deadly and destructive blast on the human race and flocks and herds.

In the first place, there are, as I have shown above,[79] elements of numerous substances that are beneficial to our life; on the other hand,

---

76. **1069:** Pliny says that the best glue is made from bulls' ears and genitals (*Natural History* 28.236).

77. **1074:** Cf. 2.501 and see note there.

78. **1078:** The reference is to *chrysocolla* (a Greek word meaning "gold solder"), generally identified with borax.

79. **1094:** 769–780.

there must be many flying about that produce disease and death.[80] When
these have accidentally and fortuitously gathered together and disturbed
the atmosphere, the air becomes diseased. And all these pestilential
forces, all these plagues, either originate outside our world and come
down through the sky, like clouds and mists, or else, as often happens,   1100
rise in a body from the earth itself, when the ground, sodden by immoderate rains and beaten upon by the excessive heat of the sun's rays, has
undergone putrefaction.

You must be aware, moreover, that those who travel to places far from
their homeland and home are affected by the change in the climate and
the water, because conditions vary widely. How different, we must suppose, is the climate of Britain from that of Egypt, where the axis of the
world slants askew! How different is the climate of Pontus from that
which extends from Gades[81] right on to the tribes of people blackened by
the scorching sun! Just as there are obvious differences between these   1110
four climates at the four winds and quarters of the sky,[82] so there are
manifestly wide differences in the color and appearance of the inhabitants. It is evident too that particular diseases attack particular races.
There is elephantiasis, which is found on the banks of the river Nile in
mid-Egypt and nowhere else. In Attica the feet are attacked, in Achaean
territory the eyes.[83] Thus various regions are injurious to various parts of
the body; and these effects are due to variations in the air.

Consequently when an atmosphere that happens to be unsuited to us
starts to move and the noxious air begins to drift, it glides along gradu-   1120
ally, like mist or cloud, disturbing everything, wherever it goes, and
compelling change. And when it eventually reaches our tract of sky, it
infects it, making it like itself and so rendering it noxious to us.

All of a sudden this unfamiliar plague and pestilence either drops
down upon the waters or even settles on the crops or other foods of
humans and animals; or else it remains hovering in the atmosphere itself,
so that, when we inhale the infected air, we inevitably absorb the germs   1130
into our bodies at the same time. Similarly a murrain often falls on cattle
and a distemper on the lazy flocks of bleating sheep.

The effect is the same whether we go into a climate that is uncongenial
to us, changing the sky that mantles us, or whether nature takes the

---

80. **1095–1096:** See note on 30.

81. **1108:** In 5.507 Pontus is the Black Sea. Here it is the region of the Black Sea.
Gades is Cadiz.

82. **1110–1111:** Britain, Egypt, Pontus, and Gades represent west, east, north,
and south respectively.

83. **1116:** The reference may be to gout in Attica and to conjunctivitis in Achaea.

initiative and brings us an infected atmosphere or something else that we are not accustomed to experience, whose sudden coming may prove harmful to us.

Such was the epidemic, such was the deadly miasma that once fell on
1140 the land of Cecrops,[84] making the countryside a scene of death, emptying the streets, and draining the city of citizens. For it originated in the heart of Egypt and, after a long journey through the air and over the floating plains, eventually brooded over the whole people of Pandion.[85] Then they were delivered by thousands to disease and death.

The first symptoms were a burning heat in the head and a reddening of both eyes with a suffused glare. The interior of the throat turned livid and exuded a bloody sweat; the vocal passage became clogged and choked
1150 with ulcers; and the tongue, the mind's interpreter, enfeebled by the disease, heavy to move and rough to touch, oozed out blood. After that, when the morbid influence, passing down through the throat, had filled the breast and flooded right into the patient's mournful mind, then indeed all the vital fastenings were undone. The breath issued from the mouth with a foul stench similar to that given off by carcasses that have been thrown out and left to rot. Then the mind lost all its vigor, and the whole body grew languid, being already on the very threshold of death. These unbearable sufferings were invariably accompanied by an agonizing
1160 anguish and complaining mingled with moaning. Moreover, a convulsive retching, often continuing all day and all night, persistently racked the sinews and limbs, wasting the victims away and making the weary wearier still.

In no case did the surface of the body give the appearance of being inflamed with excessive heat; rather it felt tepid to the touch, though at the same time it was all red with ulcerous scars, as is the case when the

---

84. **1138–1286:** The disastrous plague of Athens (of which Cecrops was a legendary king) occurred in 430 B.C., the second year of the Peloponnesian War. It is described by Thucydides (2.47–52), whom Lucr. follows closely for the most part. His modifications of the Greek historian's account are mainly due to his tendency to see the plague-stricken Athenians as having failed not only physically, but also morally, in the face of the disaster, and furthermore to regard the plague as symbolic of the moral sickness that afflicted and afflicts those ignorant of Epicurus' doctrines. See pp. xxxiii–xxxiv, where I stress that the grim account of the plague must be considered not in isolation, but in close connection with the optimistic preface to Book 6. See also note on 30. Lucr.'s description influenced several Latin writers, including Virgil, Ovid, and Lucan.

85. **1143:** Legendary king of Athens, father of Procne and Philomela.

holy fire[86] spreads over the limbs. But the internal parts of the body were burning to the bones, and flames were raging within the stomach as within a furnace. There was no covering so light and thin that it could be 1170 used to bring relief to the bodies of the sick: all they wanted was a cooling breeze. Some would fling their limbs aflame with fever into ice-cold streams, hurling their bodies naked into the waters. Many tumbled headlong down into deep wells, meeting the water open-mouthed. Their bodies were parched through and through with an insatiable thirst that made vast drafts of water seem no more than a few drops.

They found no respite from their suffering; their bodies lay utterly exhausted. The medical profession, frightened into silence, could only mumble, as the sick again and again rolled their staring, sleepless eyes, 1180 ablaze with fever.

Then numerous symptoms of death appeared as well:[87] the mind distracted with despair and dread; the clouded brow; the fierce and frenzied countenance; the ears besieged and bothered with buzzings; the respiration rapid, or ponderous and slow; the neck bedewed with glistening beads of sweat; the saliva thin and scanty, salty and flecked with yellow, expectorated with difficulty by a raucous cough. All the time the 1190 tendons of the hands would twitch, the limbs would quiver, and a coldness would gradually creep upward from the feet. Moreover, as life's final hour approached, the nostrils became constricted, the tip of the nose sharper, the eyes deep-sunk, the temples hollow, the skin cold and hard, the mouth unvaryingly agape, the forehead constantly tense. Soon afterward the limbs lay stretched in the stiffness of death. And it was usually at the eighth rising of the dazzling sun, or else at the ninth appearance of the lamp of day, that they yielded up their lives.

And even if, as was possible, sufferers had so far escaped death's doom, they were destined to perish later, wasted away by ghastly ulcers 1200 and black discharges from the bowels; or else a flux of purulent blood, often accompanied by a headache, issued from the choked nostrils, and with it streamed all their strength and substance.

Moreover, even if the victims survived this virulent discharge of foul blood, the disease would pass into their sinews and joints, and right into their genitals. And some were so intensely afraid of crossing the threshold of death that they cut off their sexual organs and so prolonged their existence. Some lingered in life by lopping off their hands and feet, and 1210 others gouged out their eyes: so desperate a dread of death had taken hold

---

86. **1167:** See note on 660.

87. **1182–1196:** This list of symptoms of approaching death is based not on Thucydides, but on Hippocratic writings.

of them. And there were some too who were seized with such a complete loss of memory that they did not even know who they were themselves.

Although numerous corpses lay unburied on the ground in heap upon heap, the birds and wild beasts either fled far away from them to escape the foul stench or, after having tasted the flesh, drooped and quickly died.

1220   Indeed during those days it was very rare for a bird to appear at all or for the grim beasts of prey to leave the woods. Most succumbed to the plague and died. The chief sufferers were the faithful dogs: they lay stretched in every street and reluctantly relinquished the life that the violence of the plague wrenched from their limbs.

Funerals, unattended by any mourners, were hurried through with emulous haste.[88] There was no sure method of treatment that was universally effective: what had enabled one person to continue to inhale the vital air and to survey the precincts of heaven proved poison to others and caused their death.

1230   The most deplorable and distressing feature of the disaster was that, when people realized that they were ensnared by the plague, they behaved as though they were doomed to die: all their courage failed; they lay down despondent; and thinking only of death, they surrendered their life then and there.

At no time did the contagion of the rapacious pestilence cease to claim one victim after another, as though it were spreading among fleecy flocks or horned herds. And it was this circumstance more than any other that piled up death upon death. For all who shrank from visiting their stricken

1240   relatives were punished shortly afterward for their inordinate greed of life and dread of death with a squalid and wretched end, perishing through lack of attention, alone and destitute of help; while those who stayed to nurse the sick succumbed to contagion and to the labors imposed on them by their sense of shame and the patients' pleading accents mingled with accents of reproach. So all the worthiest people met death in this way.

. . . and[89] one on top of another, as they struggled to bury the multitude of their dead. When they returned home, worn out with weeping and

---

88. **1225:** Like 1247–1251 (see note there), this line seems to be misplaced.

89. **1247–1251:** If these lines are in their correct position, a lacuna must be assumed before them. Some scholars follow Bockemüller in transferring them after 1286, i.e., in making them the closing lines of the poem. Peta Fowler argues for this transposition in D. H. Roberts et al. (eds.), *Classical Closure* (Princeton University Press: Princeton, NJ, 1997) 112–138. It is tempting to accept this ingenious suggestion, but I resist the temptation, because it is possible that the lines are a misplaced alternative version (of 1278–1281?), which Lucr. may or

wailing, the majority of them were so grief-stricken that they took to
their beds. It was impossible to find anyone who was not affected at that   1250
terrible time by disease or death or distress.

By this time every shepherd and herdsman and every sturdy guider of
the curved plow were succumbing to the infection. Their bodies lay
huddled together in hovels, delivered to death by poverty and plague.
Sometimes you might see the lifeless bodies of parents lying upon their
lifeless children, and sometimes too children expiring upon the corpses
of their mothers and fathers.

To no small extent this pestilence poured into the city from the surrounding countryside, brought in by the crowds of plague-stricken peas-   1260
ants who flocked together from all sides. They filled every space and
building; and their being stuffed together in the stifling heat made them
an easier prey to death, which piled them up in heaps. Many, who had
been prostrated by thirst and had crawled along the streets, lay stretched
out beside the fountains, choked to death by excessive drafts of the
delicious water. Many too might be seen everywhere in public squares
and streets, their languid limbs half-dead, caked with filth, covered with
rags, perishing from physical squalor, nothing but skin and bones, al-   1270
ready almost buried in dirt and ghastly ulcers.

All the sacred shrines of the gods had been filled by death with lifeless
bodies, and all the temples of the celestials, which the sacristans had
crammed with guests, were continually littered with corpses. By this
time neither the worship of the gods nor their divinity counted for much:
they were overwhelmed by the pressure of the present calamity. The
time-honored rites of sepulture, which this people had always practiced
in the past, were no longer observed in the city. The entire population   1280
was in perturbation and panic, and invariably mourners laid out and
buried their dead as time and circumstances allowed. And many dreadful
expedients were prompted by poverty and the sudden emergency. With
loud clamoring people would place their own relatives on pyres piled
high for others and apply torches to them, often engaging in bloody
brawls rather than abandon the bodies.

---

may not have intended to include in his finished work. In this connection, it is
relevant to note that 1225 too seems to be misplaced.

INDEX

accidents (unessential qualities),
1.449–482

Achaea, 6.1116

Acheron, 1.120; 3.25, 37, 86, 628,
978–1023; 4.37, 170; 6.251,
763

acorns, eaten by primitive humans,
5.939, 965, 1416

Acragas, 1.716

Aegium, 6.585

Aeneas, 1.1

Aeolia, 1.721

Agamemnon, 1.89–99

agriculture, 1.208–214; 2.610–613,
1157–1174; 5.14–16, 206–
217, 1110, 1248, 1289, 1361–
1378, 1441, 1448; 6.1–2

unknown to primitive humans,
5.933–934

air, 2.107, 230–234; 4.132, 892–
897; 5.472, 498–503, 511–
516, 522–523, 534–563, 696–
700; 6.684–685, 1022–1041,
1097, 1120

an element of the soul, 3.121–
129, 231–322

mortality of, 5.235–246, 273–
280

not a primary substance, 1.705–
802

Alexander, see Paris

Alinda, 4.1130

all-heal, 4.124

alphabet, see letters

ambition, vanity of, 2.11–13; 3.59–
78, 995–1002; 5.1120–1135,
1233–1235; 6.12–14

Ammon, spring near shrine of,
6.848–878

Anaxagoras, refutation of, 1.830–
920; 2.865–930, 973–990

Ancus Marcius, 3.1025

animals, differences in character of,
3.294–306, 741–752; 5.862–
870

extinct, 5.837–877

origin of, 2.1150–1156; 5.790–
836

See also bees, birds, boars, bulls,
cattle, deer, dogs, elephants,
fish, foxes, goats, horses, pan-
thers, pigs, sheep, snakes, wild
animals, worms and maggots

antipodes, false belief in, 1.1058–
1067

Apollo, see Phoebus

Aradus, 6.890

arboriculture, 5.1361–1378

unknown to primitive humans,
5.934–936

arbute berries, food of primitive humans, 5.940–942, 965

Arcadian boar, 5.25

arts, development of, 5.332–337,
1448–1457

astronomical phenomena, 5.509–
770

ataraxia, see mind, tranquillity of

Athena, see Pallas

Athens, 6.2, 749

plague of, 6.1138–1286

Atlantic, 5.35

atmospheric phenomena, 6.96–
534

atoms, existence of, 1.265–328

infinite number of, 1.951–
1051

insentience of, 2.865–990

The Index is based, with the kind approval of Harvard University Press, on my
Index in the Loeb edition.

Martin Ferguson Smith, Professor Emeritus of Classics, University of Durham, England, has lived since 1995 on the remote island of Foula in Shetland. Among his scholarly achievements are the Loeb Classical Library edition of Lucretius' *De Rerum Natura* (Smith's Latin text, notes, and introduction, with his revision of the Rouse translation), the discovery and rediscovery of many Epicurean texts at Oinoanda in Turkey, and their publication in two books and numerous articles.

GETTING THROUGH GRIEF:
Caregiving by Congregations

93 94 95 96 97 98 99 00 01 02   —   10 9 8 7 6 5 4 3 2 1

This book is printed on acid-free recycled paper.

Library of Congress Cataloging-in-Publication Data

Sunderland, Ronald, 1929–
    Getting through grief/Ron Sunderland.
        p.   cm.
    Includes bibliographical references.
    ISBN 0-687-15882-6 (alk. paper)
    1. Church work with the bereaved. 2. Pastoral psychology. 3. Lay
ministry. 4. Grief—Religious aspects—Christianity. I. Title.
BV4330.S96   1993
259'.6—dc20   92-39284

All Scripture quotations are from the New Revised Standard Version Bible, Copyright
1989 by the Division of Christian Education of the National Council of the Churches of
Christ in the USA. Used by permission.

MANUFACTURED IN THE UNITED STATES OF AMERICA

Getting Through Grief

*Caregiving
by Congregations*

Ronald H. Sunderland

ABINGDON PRESS
Nashville